THE TRIAL LAWYERS

THE TRIAL LAWYERS

THE NATION'S TOP LITIGATORS TELL HOW THEY WIN

EMILY COURIC

ST. MARTIN'S PRESS NEW YORK

 For information, address St. Martin's Press, 175 Fifth Avenue, New York, N.Y. 10010.

Design by Judith Stagnitto

Library of Congress Cataloging-in-Publication Data

Couric, Emily.
The trial lawyers : the nation's top litigators tell how they win / Emily Couric.
p. cm.
ISBN 0-312-051727
1. Trial practice—United States. 2. Lawyers—United States.
I. Title.
KF8915.C63 1988
447.73'7—dc19
[347.3077]

10 9 8 7 6

CONTENTS

ACKNOWLEDGMENTS

This book grew from hours of interviews with ten lawyers. They were kind enough to give their time freely and to explain with care and patience exactly how they try and win their cases. I am very grateful for their generosity.

Many other people in these lawyers' offices also assisted with my research and inquiries. Those who were especially helpful include: Sidney N. Herman and Barbara E. Zarnecki of Kirkland & Ellis in Chicago; Susan E. Stearns of Corboy & Demetrio in Chicago; Sylvia Musser of Harney, Wolfe, Shaller & Carr in Los Angeles; Judy Fogarty and Jan Woodward Fox of Haynes & Fullenweider in Houston; Leslie G. Fagen of Paul, Weiss, Rifkind, Wharton & Garrison in New York; Thomas H. Dundon and Joanne Miller of Neal & Harwell in Nashville; Karen Homer of Wyman, Bautzer, Kuchel & Silbert in Los Angeles; and Julie

Allen of Williams & Connolly in Washington, D.C. Many thanks to them, too.

I am also indebted to my literary agent, Trish Todd, who enthusiastically embraced this project and introduced it to the publishing world. Similarly, my St. Martin's Press editor, Michael Sagalyn, spurred me on with his probing questions and insightful comments. This was clearly a team effort.

I especially appreciate *National Law Journal* editor T. Sumner Robinson's unflagging support and advice. It was he who first suggested that I write about winning trial lawyers' courtroom techniques.

Finally, I must thank my sons, Raymond Wadlow and Jeffrey Wadlow, for their sustained interest, enthusiasm, and patience over the many months I worked on this book. And of course, I am most deeply indebted to my husband, George Beller, who, throughout any of my endeavors, is a constant.

—Emily Couric

A Note to the Reader:

Edward Bennett Williams died on August 13, 1988, as this book was going to press. He had fought an eleven-year battle against cancer with the same determination and will to win that helped him defeat so many of his courtroom adversaries. It was reported that up until the month before his death, Williams worked more hours than any other lawyer in his firm.

FOREWORD

They might best be called the shock troops of the legal profession, the ones called in when all else has failed. After the niceties of early legal wrangling, it is up to the trial lawyers to right wrongs, prosecute or defend the accused, and see that—for at least one side—truth wins out in the courtroom's bright glare.

Of course, real-life courtroom lawyers know that real-life cases seldom are won solely on the basis of flowery oratory. Instead, it's a matter of mastering an extraordinarily complex set of facts and presenting them to jurors in a way that convinces them there is only one possible right version: their client's. And witnesses who confess on the stand, freeing an unjustly accused person, are even rarer; litigation rules now leave few opportunities for dramatic flourishes of that sort.

But the successful trial lawyer remains a breed apart from others in the bar. He or she (and women are slowly being added to top litigators' ranks) is supremely confident of a wide range of skills, not likely to be content with a backseat role in some professional association. They're crack investigators who leave no stone unturned in preparing their client's case. They're willing to fervently take on almost all challenges, often when the client is sure there is no hope left, that he or she has been written off by everyone as a loser.

It is in the courtroom itself where all this pays off. The trite comparison of courtrooms to boxing rings is not all wrong: Most of the time, there is a clear winner; it might not be a knockout, but a TKO often means victory for one side. And for the spectators at a good trial, there is enough counter-punching to whet any appetite for mayhem. Solid blows are landed, and even the glancing shots might slow down the opponent enough to weaken the whole fabric of the case.

For me, the fascination with trial lawyers probably began in the county seat of Walker County, Alabama, in the early 1960s after a bootlegger broke the unwritten rule of the backwoods and shot a federal agent. The ensuing trial, which I covered for the local paper, was part revival and part classroom, and wholly alluring. And that fascination never left, whether I was watching the worst of court-appointed attorneys defending the dregs of the criminal justice system, or watching the nation's best courtroom tacticians defend numerous top Presidential aides—not to mention a Vice President and a President of the United States—in the 1970s as a reporter covering legal affairs for *The Washington Post.*

There has been much talk of "reform" in the jury system. Cases are too complex, the argument goes; jurors are too easily swayed; it boils down to a popularity contest among lawyers. Needless to say, the successful trial lawyers aren't the ones leading that movement. For they know, as would anyone who has prowled the nation's courtrooms—or even watched "Perry Mason" win yet again—that there's a reason the system has remained intact in principle for centuries: It works.

T. Sumner Robinson
Editor-in-Chief
The National Law Journal
New York City, March 1988

INTRODUCTION

Americans like to compete, and some of the best battles in this country take place in the courtroom. We watch raptly as skilled, knowledgeable, and experienced attorneys fight to prove that they're on the side of justice, and that they should be the victors.

The contest holds another interest for us, too. We love the human drama behind a trial—the unfolding of a story through the words of witnesses and experts. Again, the lawyers are most important in this retelling. They direct the characters, weave the plot, and reveal the passion, tragedy, or greed behind their cases. In court, lawyers mesmerize their listeners, much like preachers whose job it is to make believers of all who listen. They meticulously choose their words and carefully craft their sentences. Their delivery may be relaxed and easygoing, or sharp and flashy. It is always compelling. And when these advocates finish speaking, when the trial is over, the lives of their clients may—or may not—be finished, too. Either way, they are forever changed.

This book tells the story of ten famous trials, and how ten well-known lawyers won them. These nine men and one woman represent the upper echelon of their profession. They come from every specialty within the trial bar, and from every part of the country. Among them are corporate lawyers, personal injury and medical malpractice specialists, criminal defense lawyers, a civil rights advocate, and a prosecutor. They control the fate of business leaders and Hollywood celebrities; they advocate the rights of the average man; they represent alleged thieves, arms merchants, murderers, and drug pushers.

The chapters describe the litigators' rise to success—how they began a career, their sources of inspiration, the hurdles they overcame. They reveal the techniques and strategies they use to insure victory. You'll learn the secrets that never made the papers during sensational trials. The lawyers divulge inside information and supply tips and wisdom gained through years of experience. You'll watch them apply their know-how to a trial that epitomizes their success.

The Trial Lawyers takes you into the exclusive world of high-powered law, where fees mount quickly into the hundreds of thousands if not millions of dollars, and trial preparation takes on the flavor of war. You'll learn how the nation's best choose from hundreds of cases the ones they'll accept and sweat blood to win; how they feel about representing criminals; how they develop a working rapport with clients during months or years of close contact; and how they size up the opposition.

It's a demanding, often grueling life. Survival depends on working harder than the competition. That means being the best in pretrial discovery, knowing what to delegate to younger lawyers and what to handle yourself, plotting effective pretrial motions to give a client an advantage later on, and coaching witnesses to deliver impeccable testimony in court. How do the best trial lawyers develop strategy for a case? How do they select a jury? What do they put into opening statements and on closing arguments? How do they prepare and execute the perfect cross-examination? *The Trial Lawyers* answers these questions while providing a sensational, behind-the-scenes look at ten of the titanic legal battles of our time.

The Trial Laywers

Fred H. Bartlit, Jr., Kirkland & Ellis, Chicago. Bartlit knocked out National Business Lists, Inc., when that company sued his client, the Dun & Bradstreet Corporation. NBL claimed that D&B had a monopoly in business data bases. Bartlit stunned courtwatchers by proving instead that NBL had been "stealing" from D&B and was guilty of copyright infringement. The verdict for D&B: $8 million.

Julius L. Chambers, NAACP Legal Defense and Educational Fund, Inc., New York. Chambers is a lifelong fighter for civil rights. Cases he handled from his Charlotte, North Carolina, law firm produced key U.S. Supreme Court rulings on employment and education discrimination. Here Chambers reflects on one of the landmark desegregation cases of the century, *Swann v. Charlotte-Mecklenburg Board of Education,* where for the first time the Court endorsed busing to desegregate schools.

Philip H. Corboy, Corboy & Demetrio, P.C., Chicago. Fifteen-year-old Danny Schaffner was brain damaged when he fell off his bike riding over a Highland Park, Illinois, railroad crossing. Schaffner's parents contacted Corboy. They sued both Schwinn Bicycle Company and the railroad, the Chicago and North Western Transportation Company; the jury found the railroad fully liable and awarded Danny more than $8 million. Corboy is a flamboyant personal injury lawyer, the attorney of choice among other Chicago lawyers, judges, and politicians.

Linda Fairstein, Chief, Sex Crimes Prosecution Unit, District Attorney's Office, New York. Fairstein recently prosecuted Robert Chambers on charges of murdering Jennifer Levin during rough sex; Chambers eventually pleaded guilty to first-degree manslaughter. Earlier, Fairstein successfully prosecuted Marvin Teicher, a suave dentist who sexually abused female patients while they were sedated. Fairstein used a court-ordered undercover camera to catch Teicher in action, disproving Teicher's claim that his caresses relieved respiratory distress.

David M. Harney, Harney, Wolfe, Shaller & Carr, Los Angeles. A sharp-tongued Irish American, this products liability and medical malpractice lawyer takes on clients such as Harry Jordan, a sixty-two-year-old insurance man who had his healthy left kidney removed instead of his cancerous right one. In a poll taken by the physicians' trade journal *Medical Economics,* defense attorneys voted Harney the "best plaintiff's lawyer in the land."

Richard "Racehorse" Haynes, Haynes & Fullenweider, Houston. Nicknamed "Racehorse" by a school football coach, Haynes defends clients in a "Smith & Wesson divorce," where "someone pulls the trigger, and then the marriage is over." He represented Fort Worth, Texas, businessman T. Cullen Davis, acquitted of attempting to murder his wife and of murdering his stepdaughter and wife's boyfriend; and socially prominent Houstonian Dr. John Hill, accused of murdering his wife, but himself murdered before trial. Despite public hostility toward arms dealing, Haynes successfully defended Ian Smalley, charged with selling tanks to Iran and antitank missiles to Iraq.

Arthur L. Liman, Paul, Weiss, Rifkind, Wharton & Garrison, New York. The lawyer who questioned Oliver North for the U.S. Senate committee investigating the Iran-contra affair, Liman tells here how he vindicated the New York Transit Authority when he sued and won $72 million from Rockwell International Corporation after it put defective undercarriages in the city's new subway cars. Liman also represented fugitive financier Robert Vesco, businessman John Zaccaro, investment banker Dennis Levine, and corporate raider Carl Icahn.

James F. Neal, Neal & Harwell, Nashville. One of Neal's most challenging cases was that of Elvis Presley's physician, Dr. George "Nick" Nichopoulos, who was accused of supplying the late singer with drugs leading to his death. Dr. Nick was acquitted. A former Watergate prosecutor, Neal also successfully defended director John Landis, producer of the ill-fated movie *Twilight Zone,* in whose filming actor Victor Morrow and two children were killed; and former three-term Louisiana governor Edwin W. Edwards, on charges of racketeering and fraud.

Howard L. Weitzman, Wyman, Bautzer, Kuchel & Silbert, Los Angeles. Weitzman caught the public by surprise when his client, automaker John Z. DeLorean, was acquitted on charges of cocaine trafficking. Most everyone had seen the "60 Minutes" tape of DeLorean in a hotel room toasting with champagne a suitcase of cocaine. Then Weitzman made a repeat performance, successfully defending DeLorean in a second trial for alleged fraudulent financial dealings. Other clients include actors Marlon Brando and Sean Penn, rock singer Ozzy Osbourne, and palimony lawyer Marvin M. Mitchelson.

Edward Bennett Williams, Williams & Connolly, Washington, D.C. Williams, whose name is synonymous with trial expertise, has built one of the best litigating firms in the country, with clients including U.S. Senator Joseph R. McCarthy, former Teamsters chief Jimmy Hoffa, and Richard Nixon's treasury secretary John B. Connally. When Connally was tried on charges of accepting an illegal gratuity in the infamous milk fund case, Williams proved that his client's accuser was lying to protect himself from criminal exposure.

In the ten case stories described here, these lawyers say they were on the right side of the law. They say they deserved to win.

Yet more importantly, they also say that justice is not a easy victory. It is, rather, a competition, one that demands the best minds, the most finely tuned skills, and the know-how that comes from the experience of many earlier battles.

THE TRIAL LAWYERS

FRED H. BARTLIT, JR.

Kirkland & Ellis, Chicago

Jon M. Ricci

As a successful trial lawyer, Fred H. Bartlit, Jr., overcomes two obstacles. The first is his appearance. Bartlit is movie-star handsome. Six feet two inches tall and 216 pounds, he strides into a courtroom impeccably dressed in an Italian double-breasted suit. He's straight-arrow tall, with shoulders held back and square jaw forward, waves of graying brown hair combed securely in place. Many jurors dislike Bartlit precisely because of his looks, including, he says, "successful men about my own age and young attractive women in their twenties." The latter, he surmises, don't trust him. "Historically, I've done better in long trials than in short ones," observes the fifty-six-year-old Bartlit, who likes time to build up that trust.

Second, Bartlit represents corporate America, companies

such as the General Motors Corporation, Monsanto Company, and Standard Oil Company—Goliaths with money and power far beyond the comprehension of typical jurors, people more likely to think of themselves as Davids. "I always represent somebody who is claimed to have done something horribly wrong," explains Bartlit. It's tough for him to work the jurors' emotions around to his side; public sympathies naturally lie with the underdog. "There's a saying," says Bartlit, " 'Don't make the jury cry for Standard Oil.' They'll hate you for it." Rather, corporate attorneys must counter plaintiffs' often emotional bombasts with the opposite tack. Corporate trial lawyers must stay cool and calm, arguing with facts and appealing to reason, appearing straightforward and honest. "When you're a defense lawyer," says Bartlit, "you have to have a style that fits" that role.

That doesn't mean being a patsy. Bartlit likes to do battle; in fact, he doesn't want any part of cases he thinks might settle before trial. "Doing well in big cases requires a lot of hard work and long hours. It's difficult to get yourself in the mental state if you basically think the case is going away," he says. "Who would climb up those cliffs on Normandy beach if they knew the war was going to be over anyway?"

The intensity with which Bartlit prepares for trial—while ignoring potential settlement—has engendered sharp criticism from other lawyers. "Some people criticize me for trying too many cases—that I try cases I ought to settle," says Bartlit, whose annual income approaches $1 million. "But the decision to try a case is the client's." Still, if a client or the client's opponent wants to settle, Bartlit suggests that another lawyer in the firm handle those discussions. "I don't think a good trial lawyer can be a good negotiator," he explains. "I think cases should be settled—but I'm not a settler."

Bartlit's trial focus has psychological advantages over opposing lawyers. "If they see Fred, they know they have to look at a jury," says Sidney N. Herman, a younger Kirkland & Ellis partner. For most attorneys, putting faith in a jury—a group of unknown and unpredictable persons—is a lot scarier than talking out a settlement resolution with the other side.

Yet for Bartlit, courtroom warring doesn't conjure up the traditional behemoth law firm sounding the trumpets for its armies of attorneys to charge forth. Bartlit envisions himself, rather, as the general in a finely tuned and rigidly contained military maneuver. Appropriately, he's a West Point graduate, and he served as a Ranger before entering the University of Illinois law school. As a litigator, Bartlit relies on strategy and diligence rather than on sheer numbers of people. "Whatever I do could be done in a five-person law firm if they knew what they were doing," he insists.

When Dun & Bradstreet, Inc. asked Bartlit to defend it in a major antitrust lawsuit, Bartlit knew he'd be in court. Other Kirkland & Ellis lawyers had been working on the case for six years; but in July 1980, two months before the trial, Dun & Bradstreet asked Bartlit to step in.

The plaintiff, National Business Lists, a company that compiled, rented, and sold mailing lists, accused Dun & Bradstreet of obtaining and monopolizing, through the operation of its highly successful credit rating business, information needed for these lists. The story behind the charge involves the history of Dun & Bradstreet itself.

In 1841, Lewis Tappan, a New York merchant, founded the precursor to Dun & Bradstreet—The Mercantile Agency—to evaluate different businesses' creditworthiness and to publish credit reports that he then sold to banks, insurance companies, manufacturers, wholesalers, service companies, and others who found a need for them. Tappan hired correspondents across the country to visit companies in order to evaluate them. They then sent on their findings to Tappan's New York office. The business grew over the years into a respected and lucrative credit reference service. The New York–based information service company now publishes credit ratings, business information reports, and directories on millions of American businesses.

National Business Lists maintained in its lawsuit that D&B "has no competitors which hold themselves out as able to furnish equivalent services." D&B's "only competitors . . . offer only specialized services, concentrating in one or several industries or in one or several restricted geographical locations." D&B "has thus achieved a monopoly position in that line of commerce."

What National Business Lists really objected to, however, was D&B's decision in 1964 to go into the list rental business, thus becoming a direct competitive threat to NBL. NBL maintained that D&B compiled its mailing lists by using the very information it gathered through its credit rating business, that D&B incurred little additional costs in compiling these lists, and that any costs it did incur were offset by income from selling D&B's widely accepted credit reference books.

Further, NBL argued to the court, because of D&B's extensive credit gathering information, it would be able to include in its lists "numerous items of information about business establishments that are not available to [the] plaintiff from other sources. Defendant would have the capacity to compile lists of businesses in a given field by numbers of employees, by sales volume, or by concentration in particular markets," NBL's complaint read. D&B "could also furnish its potential list rental customers with the names and addresses of the chief executive officers of such businesses."

National Business Lists said that, unlike D&B, NBL had no ready access to data necessary for compiling mailing lists, and that the cost of compiling its own and more limited lists from scratch was "prohibitive." When NBL asked to buy D&B's credit rating data, D&B refused.

"Any new entity attempting to enter the business mailing list field would also have to enter the credit rating field," said NBL, which was difficult if not impossible because of D&B's credit rating "monopoly." NBL claimed that its mailing list business suffered a loss of $2.5 million. It asked the court to award it three times that amount—$7.5 million—and to require that

D&B either sell its credit list information to NBL at D&B's incremental cost for organizing the information into mailing list format, or that D&B be required to sell its mailing list business to a separate and independent company, and then to sell its list information to that company on the same basis under which it sold to NBL.

National Business Lists based its lawsuit on a 1979 decision by the U.S. Court of Appeals for the Second Circuit in New York, *Berkey Photo, Inc. v. Eastman Kodak Company,* one of the largest and most significant private antitrust suits up until that time. Berkey, which competed with Kodak in the film industry, had successfully argued in district court that Kodak's monopoly in camera production gave it unfair advantage when manufacturing and marketing film. On appeal, the Second Circuit held that "it is improper, in the absence of a valid business policy, for a firm with monopoly power in one market to gain a competitive advantage in another by refusing to sell a rival the monopolized goods or services he needs to compete effectively in the second market." Similarly, NBL claimed that D&B had monopoly power in the business credit information market that gave it a competitive advantage in the separate, fast-growing business list market.

As Bartlit learned more about the NBL case, he focused on one of his major tenets for winning a lawsuit. Bartlit—who earned the highest grade average in the history of the University of Illinois law school, and who has won more than four-fifths of the thirty-one cases he has brought to verdict in the last seventeen years—is a believer in simplicity. He tries to find the one or two or three arguments that will convince a jury he is right. Most lawyers offer the jury as many arguments as they can possibly think up, producing what often becomes a long and confusing list. Bartlit says so many arguments just cloud the picture.

"The secret," he says, "is to get two or three issues that complement each other and keep supporting those issues" so the result is not "a morass of separate, isolated points." The mind of the judge or jury, he says, "is like an empty cup that you're filling with coffee. New issues may flow over the side and you may tip the cup over and lose everything."

The Dun & Bradstreet case, says Bartlit, "was immensely complicated in terms of possible theory, and there would have been a normal temptation to start arguing this case in terms of economic issues." The antitrust arguments focused primarily on definitions of the competitive markets for credit information and for business lists, and on whether data gathered in the former market was used unfairly in the latter. Many thought NBL's antitrust charge would hold up. But Bartlit found a simple way around being backed into that defensive corner. He chose to take the offense. While being briefed by the other Kirkland & Ellis lawyers, Bartlit learned that for twenty-five years, National Business Lists actually had been copying the information it needed for its mailing lists out of D&B's credit reference books. D&B knew NBL had been copying, although NBL had never asked permission to do so; but neither had D&B asked NBL before the lawsuit to stop.

"Do you mean to tell me these guys ran their business on information they stole from us?" Bartlit asked incredulously. He zeroed in on D&B's countersuit against National Business Lists for copyright infringement, making it the crux of his case. NBL "had been stealing from us for years—and now they're complaining that they can't steal more," Bartlit emphasized.

"That," he said, standing in his modern glass-and-marble office on the Standard Oil building's fifty-fifth floor overlooking Chicago and Lake Michigan, "is a theory we can sell."

Having decided on his approach to the case, Bartlit swung open the gray linen-covered panels on his office wall that hid the executive whiteboard where he kept listed in grease pencil all the projects on which he was working. He immediately channeled his less pressing cases to other lawyers in the firm and began devoting sixty percent of his time to D&B.

But before digging into actual trial preparation, Bartlit had to find out if his theory of the case—the countercharge of copyright infringement—was really going to work.

Testing out a theory for a case, Bartlit feels, is akin to advertisers trying out a promotional campaign for a new product before embarking on a major media blitz. Test-marketing an advertising campaign—or a trial theory for a lawsuit—makes sure the program is effective before spending a lot of money advancing it. "I guarantee when General Motors decides they're going to have a new advertising program, before they spend the millions of dollars in the advertising program, they test-market that program on actual people," says Bartlit. "They want to make sure their program is good; they want to make sure it's effective. [Traditionally,] lawyers have never done this.

"Lawyers think they intuitively understand the theory of the case that will sell best," continues Bartlit. What's more, they think that they only need to answer the plaintiff's argument to disprove what the plaintiff says. "They go into court and spend all their time fighting the other side."

Instead, he says, defendants must decide early on what will be their own theory of the case, the reasoning they are going to advance themselves, on behalf of their client. That theory must be "internally consistent," says Bartlit. "A lawyer can't say, 'My product is a safe product, but if it's not safe, I warned that it was dangerous.' A jury will be bothered by that theory.

"Every time I've had a simple theory, I had a good result," says Bartlit. "If you argue ten points, even if each is a good point, when they get back in the jury room, they won't remember any." Company lawyers, he says, often try to get their outside counsel to address every theory presented by a plaintiff. They're perfectionists in wanting to cover every point. "We can not pick up every rusty nail, every red herring the plaintiff leaves, or our defense will be so diluted we'll lose our point," counters Bartlit, whose development of the evidence in a case keeps a jury focused on his line of argument. "It's the big issues that get them," he says of his strategy.

Based on this philosophy, and on experience, Bartlit felt that in the Dun & Bradstreet case he could convince the average "man on the street" with the simple and straightforward theory that not only was D&B innocent of antitrust violation, but National Business Lists was guilty of copyright infringement. To prove this hunch, Bartlit could have done what other lawyers who subscribe to the philosophy of pretesting do: spend between $100,000 and $150,000 by hiring jury consultants. The consultants conduct extensive surveys to determine the characteristics and attitudes within a community, and then assemble for the lawyer a practice jury with individuals who reflect those same community characteristics and attitudes.

Bartlit claims he can get the same results for a lot less money. "My techniques cost nothing, can be done in any law firm, and are eighty-five percent as accurate as elaborate studies," he asserts. He prepares two thirty-minute argumentative opening statements for the case, one for the plaintiff, based on information already filed with the court, and one with his own defense theory. He asks another Kirkland & Ellis lawyer to deliver the plaintiff's statement; Bartlit himself delivers the defendant's. Both are presented in a courtroom setting, or at least in a room set up to reflect a courtroom atmosphere, and both are videotaped (with equipment costing around $15,000). Because he videotapes the plaintiff's and defendant's presentations, Bartlit can play them for multiple practice juries to get a large sampling of reactions to the two sides' arguments.

But where does he find these practice juries? Bartlit walks down to his building's cafeteria and asks people there if they would work for him for a couple of hours. "I get people who run the cash register, who are washing dishes, who are fry cooks," he explains. He hires eight at a time, paying each twenty to thirty dollars for two hours. During the first hour they watch the tapes of the opening statements, and during the second they deliberate behind a one-way mirror. Bartlit videotapes these practice jurors so he can go back and analyze their comments throughout the entire process. In all, he hires, organizes, and tapes about seven or eight practice juries for each case.

Bartlit does find expensive community attitudinal surveys monetarily worthwhile for trials involving societal issues, such as pollution or sanctuary for aliens. Because these issues elicit strong emotional responses, it is helpful to know how different members of a community from which jurors are drawn generally feel about them. But if the issues are economic—as in an antitrust case—"there's a much narrower range in attitudes among different economic groups," Bartlit explains.

For his homespun mock juries, Bartlit is surprisingly able to duplicate the authenticity of a trial. Kirkland and Ellis has equipped a model courtroom in its own offices and has on its payroll a full-time video technician. The wood-paneled and beige-carpeted room, complete with a U.S. seal behind the judge's bench, and U.S. and state flags on either side, is a favorite stopping point for visitors at Kirkland & Ellis's offices. Although convenient and helpful, Bartlit argues that this elaborate a setup is not mandatory.

With several mock juries Bartlit says he is able to find common reactions. "You do not learn who is going to win the case," he says, "but it is fascinating as you watch those juries and hear what they have to say about those two openings. They say different things, but gradually some themes emerge. You begin hearing the same points being raised, what they've understood and what is palatable to them and what is not palatable. If it's sticking in their craw, you better get a new theory for your case."

It is important, Bartlit emphasizes, to get a practice jury early in the case, "because if you don't, you hire experts and go way down the path" and spend money to support a theory that doesn't work out. Also, he adds, preparing for a practice jury forces lawyers "to think hard about how they're going to put the case on, and what they will have to say down the road, so they're more likely to pull together the evidence they'll need."

Total cost to the client: a few hours of partner time to prepare and deliver the opening statements, the practice jury costs, and the cost of the technician (or a paralegal) to oversee the practice jurors and to run the videotape equipment. Bartlit takes the tapes home with him, where, in the evenings after work, he studies them—over and over again.

For the Dun & Bradstreet case it so turned out, the cashiers, the dishwashers, and the fry cooks thought that D&B was right. To them, NBL should never have been stealing the information in the first place.

To support a theory, Bartlit says that he likes to select witnesses who are "nice people." What he means is that he wants representing his client on the stand people who are pleasant and likable, and with whom jurors can identify. "Look for witnesses who are nice guys, sometimes comfortably overweight, decent, straightforward, basically modest people," he says. Typically, Bartlit will tell a client he needs ten witnesses for a trial, but that he needs twenty to twenty-five from whom to choose. It's like a beauty contest, he says, albeit not a traditional one.

For the Dun & Bradstreet case Bartlit decided that Robert J. Mitchell, president of Dun's Marketing Service, the unit within D&B that sold its mailing lists, was a perfect witness. Forty years old, brown-haired, and stocky in build, Mitchell had grown up in a rural New Jersey community. Following graduation from college in Florida, where his parents had retired, he married and was drafted into the Army.

"Much of the key substantive material that Robert Mitchell testified on came out [previously] in [NBL president Leo] Gans's cross-examination," says Bartlit. "What I had to do on direct was to humanize Bob even more than his natural tendency. The jury was fascinated by this. The purpose is not to gain any unfair advantage, but simply to humanize the witness so the jury knows the kind of man they are dealing with."

With Mitchell on the stand, Bartlit asked:

Q. Can you summarize a little bit of your military experience? What kind of training did you have, and where did you go?

A. I moved quite a bit actually. I was assigned as a psychiatric social worker, which meant I would do the work in a large general hospital with in-patient service or else I would work in a mental hygiene clinic.

I was sent—after basic training at Ft. Sam Houston, Texas, for about a year—then I was assigned to the 101st Airborne Division in Ft. Campbell, Kentucky, where I worked on in-patient service. Then I was transferred to Frankfurt, Germany. I was assigned first to the Third Armor Division. After that, I worked at the Ninety-seventh General Hospital in Frankfurt, a very large military installation in Frankfurt that handled psychiatric cases.

My last assignment was in Ft. Gordon, Georgia, Augusta, Georgia. I worked there in the mental hygiene clinic at Ft. Gordon, Georgia.

Q. How long were you in the Army?

A. About three years.

Q. Were you married this whole time?

A. Yes, I was.

Q. Did you have any children at that time?

A. We had a child that was born during our first year of our marriage who died in infancy. I had a child that was born to us in Frankfurt, Germany, who died there, also in infancy. She was seven months old. I had a compassionary assignment which got me back to Augusta, Georgia.

Q. That is how you got back?

A. Closer to my home in Florida, that's right.

Q. Do you have children now?

A. Yes, I do.

Q. How many?

A. Two: boy, girl.

Q. Now, what year is it? You are back. You had got transferred back to the United States and you were where—Ft. Gordon, Georgia."

A. Ft. Gordon, Georgia, was in Augusta, Georgia.

Q. Is that where you got mustered out?

A. Yes.

Q. Is that when you got hooked up with D&B?

A. Yes. I was interviewing actually before I left the military actively. I had three-day passes and so forth and lots of leave time that I had accumulated. My wife and I didn't have any desire to go back to Florida. She was a Floridian, but we thought we would like to try something other than Florida. I was interviewing the surrounding Southeast, primarily Atlanta. I have a brother who is in Atlanta, Georgia. I interviewed with several companies in Atlanta while I was still in the military and was offered a position by Dun & Bradstreet upon my release. Shortly after my release, I think within weeks actually, I joined D&B as a credit reporter trainee.

Q. What year was that, Mr. Mitchell?

A. 1964, November of 1964.

Q. Since you got out of the Army and went to work for D&B, have you ever had another job with another company?

A. No, sir, I haven't.

Once Bartlit made it clear to the jury that Mitchell was a person like them, and not a reprehensible corporate executive, he went on to ask Mitchell how D&B acquired its mailing lists. The point, Bartlit emphasized, was that D&B worked hard to bring together the information, sending armies of credit reporters such as Bob Mitchell across the nation.

In contrast to Mitchell, Leo Gans, NBL's top executive, appeared tense and uncomfortable. Juror Mary Foresta, who kept a trial diary, wrote: "It is my impression that Mr. Gans and Mr. Bartlit do not like each other too much, especially Mr. Bartlit by Mr. Gans."

Early in the trial Bartlit seized an opportunity to paint Gans, sixty-five, as the opposite of Bob Mitchell—a self-indulgent high flyer. Gans was hardly, Bartlit showed, the poor, suffering small businessman he claimed to be, someone who couldn't make a living because a big corporation—Dun & Bradstreet—wouldn't give him a chance.

Gans's own attorney, Lionel G. Gross of Altheimer & Gray in Chicago, gave Bartlit the chance to make this point. When Gross showed the jury, through his questioning, that Gans had a meager childhood of limited means, Bartlit objected, claiming that was irrelevant. The judge overruled him. So, when it was Bartlit's turn to cross-examine Gans, he decided to continue along the same theme of the NBL president's material wealth. Gans, it turned out, made a pretty nice living through NBL.

Q. You testified at the beginning of your direct examination that in the wintertime, you spend up to five months a year in Palm Springs. Do you recall that?

A. Up to six months a year.

Q. Six months a year. What months are those?

A. November, sometime in November through March or April. . . .

Q. Do people come from the Chicago office to work with you there?

A. Yes.

Q. How many come down at a time?

A. At times there have been—well, we have held board of directors meetings there. So, that would bring in about eight or ten people.

Off and on during Bartlit's cross-examination, Gross objected to questions about possessions supplied Gans by his company. Anxious not to appear overly aggressive, thus turning the jury's sympathies in favor of Gans, Bartlit held back temporarily.

"At an off-the-record conference in chambers between the beginning of the cross and the end of the cross, I pointed out to the Court that the plaintiff had opened the door to this sort of material by arguing and testifying that Gans had been a poor boy back in the late 1930s and early 1940s. I argued this opened the door to my showing that he is no longer a poor boy."

Later in his cross-examination Bartlit led Gans to admit that NBL owned a half interest in his apartment in Chicago's posh Gold Coast district, and that the company had paid $10,000 for furnishings. Bartlit showed the jury all this, in contrast to National Business Lists' argument that it didn't have the money to hire the large numbers of salesmen employed by D&B.

Q. Mr. Gans, did the company pay for a Mercedes-Benz for your use in Palm Springs?

A. Yes.

Q. Did the company pay for another Mercedes-Benz car for your use in Chicago?

A. Yes.

Q. Did the company pay the initiation and dues for you at the Palm Springs Racquette Club?

A. Yes.

Q. Did the company give you amounts—did the company write off loans to you and then turn around and loan you one hundred and twenty-six thousand dollars at six percent in 1973 that you haven't paid back yet?

Gross objected again. "I really can't see any relevancy of that," he complained to the judge. "We are simply back to proving that Mr. Gans is a bad guy."

Fred Bartlit "is marvelous at wearing the white hat," says Arnold Buffum Lovell, senior vice president and general counsel for Dun & Bradstreet, Inc.

When interviewing jurors after the trial, Bartlit found out how well the "good guy–bad guy" approach had worked. Juror Susan Lavaty said that when Gans had first testified, she thought he was hardworking, came from a meager background, had made everything for himself, and was proud of his success. But then, she told Bartlit, he turned the case around—and won it—on cross-examination.

"Gans was snotty on cross-examination. . . . I didn't like the man. . . . Most of us didn't like him after we heard the cross. He was too argumentative," said Lavaty, a college graduate about thirty years old.

She emphasized that all of D&B's witnesses had been in the Army, were nice people, and had worked for D&B all their lives. She thought that NBL's witnesses had expensive suits and were making a lot of money. "Where did you get your witnesses?" the judge asked Bartlit. "Central Casting?"

Even when Bartlit has what he considers a "nice" witness, he, like other trial lawyers, prepares that individual for depositions and trial. But Bartlit's witness preparation is somewhat unique. "Fred has the most effective witness preparation technique I've ever seen," says Lovell, who had sixteen years of trial experience himself before going to D&B. First, Bartlit goes over the facts of the case to find out what basic information the witness knows. Then, instead of working through a list of potential questions the opposing lawyer might ask and interrupting to provide a correct answer whenever the witness responds unsatisfactorily, Bartlit proceeds straight through.

"If the witness gives a silly answer," explains Lovell, "Fred exploits it and tries to trip him up. He goes at it and tries to tear up the witness. If he can, he reduces him to a ball of jelly." In the meantime, one of Bartlit's associates is taking a steady stream of notes, and after the practice cross-examination, Bartlit goes over it, point by point.

"The way most lawyers do it," says Lovell, because of all the interruptions "the witness never really gets a feel for what's going to happen in the deposition room or the courtroom. If he has to undergo the experience of being roasted by a skilled cross-examiner, it's better it's his own lawyer. I've seen a lot of witnesses come out [of a deposition or a trial] and heave a sigh of relief and say, 'Gee, that lawyer wasn't nearly as bad as Fred.' "

Bartlit limits his corrections because witness spontaneity is important. "As long as a witness's answers are acceptable, I leave him alone totally," says Bartlit. "The spontaneous acceptable answers will be repeated. The worst thing is fine-tuning word choices." A case is decided based on big points and impressions, not on details, he explains.

For the more difficult questions Bartlit uses a whiteboard, Magic Markers, and a pointer to help his witness practice. "If we get a problem, we talk about it, get it in his words, and I write it in red. Usually there are not more than four or five points where a witness is having trouble," he explains. "We go through the questioning again, and where the witness is in trouble, I will point [on the whiteboard] to what we worked out. As we get close to the dangerous subject, I start pointing." It's important, says Bartlit, not to prepare in one day. "If you have the luxury of five two-hour periods, that's better than one ten-hour period."

When choosing experts, Bartlit is equally concerned about appearances. "Unfortunately, the most important thing in selecting an expert today is the expert's demeanor—and not credentials," he says. Humility is key. NBL's expert economist was "a Nobel Prize winner, one of the most brilliant people in America," recalls Bartlit. D&B's expert was a quiet and demure economics teacher from a mid-level business school. "The jury hated the Nobel Prize winner; they loved my guy," says Bartlit. "Now, why is that? Academicians who have been platform lecturers all their lives feel extremely smart," he answers. "They also have never been challenged, and as a result, they come across as pompous."

Better yet, Bartlit says, is choosing experts from the client's own staff—people who support their cause vehemently because they work for, and identify with, the company. These individuals are more believable than an outsider who comes into court only because he's paid $300 an hour.

Whomever he chooses, Bartlit again relies on a "beauty contest." "I find the five best people in the country, bring them to Chicago, and talk to them over a period of days. We decide who looks best," explains Bartlit. He videotapes the experts while they practice direct and cross-examination, and he shows those tapes to two groups of six people (office paralegals and other staff). "What do your remember? Whom do you believe?" Bartlit asks the office staff after they watch the videotapes of the different experts he might use for his case. It is inexpensive to videotape and try out a number of expert witnesses, says Bartlit of his selection technique. In only two hours a good trial lawyer can prepare a proposed expert for a practice run, he explains.

To keep his experts human, and to make them immediately interesting to the jury, Bartlit questions them on the stand in a nonconventional way. Rather than beginning by asking the expert to state his or her occupation, background, and credentials, as most lawyers do, Bartlit jumps right into the subject of the trial. Only later does he ask the expert to tell the jury about credentials, and then only as they relate to the expert's knowledge necessary for the trial proceeding. Bartlit asks for essentials—not the long list of degrees and awards and successes an expert has accumulated. "People don't like to hear other people say how smart they are," says Bartlit. But just to make sure that the jury knows the capability of his expert, while that expert is on the stand, Bartlit projects his curriculum vitae with an overhead projector onto a screen.

During various facets of trial preparation, each person on Bartlit's three-lawyer team has his or her own role. As leader, Bartlit takes all the important depositions himself, including the other side's experts, the plaintiff himself, and key witnesses for the other side. The number two lawyer—a younger partner or an associate with considerable trial experience—takes all the other depositions, writes the first draft of the defense brief, and handles day-to-day contact with the client. The third lawyer on the team—an associate—tracks down witnesses and works with the legal assistants, among other tasks.

Today, Bartlit charges $235 an hour for his time. His number two lawyer generally bills at $160, and the associate at $90 to $100. Sometimes Kirkland & Ellis will offer clients of a team like this one a blended rate of about $130 an hour. Back in 1980, Dun & Bradstreet's bill for the NBL trial, including legal assistant time, out-of-pocket expenses, and expert fees, totaled more than half a million dollars.

If the lead lawyer in a case doesn't take the important depositions, that person won't really be prepared for trial, insists Bartlit, who has around two dozen lawyers working for him on various cases at any one time. He is not unmindful that his own intimate involvement in trial preparation could be viewed by clients as an expensive strategy. But Bartlit counters that concern: "A young lawyer will spend three days preparing to cover everything—and then three days taking the deposition" because that lawyer doesn't want to miss anything. Bartlit says that with his experience he can do the job in much less time, providing a cost-effective use of client resources.

The trial-team leader's active participation in case preparation has its psychological advantages, too. "There is a great tendency in pretrial appearances with the judge to have the mid-level person" represent the client. "This is okay up to a point," says Bartlit. But "if the [top] trial lawyer never shows up, you're losing credibility with the other side—and with the judge." Nor does a legal team make a good impression in court, during the actual trial, if the younger lawyer is always having to explain to the senior lawyer information acquired earlier in pretrial preparation.

Bartlit's heavy involvement in every case he handles creates an impressive monthly billing sheet. In 1980, the year Bartlit argued the Dun & Bradstreet case, he set his billing record, one that is still unbroken. The total that year was 3,200 hours, due in large part to three two-month jury trials, one three-month jury trial (D&B), and a bench trial. That's more than 60 hours a week directly on client matters. On the average, Bartlit bills about 2,200 hours a year, with another 500 hours devoted to firm management.

Despite his heavy workload, Bartlit leads what he considers to be a balanced life. "I tend to take long weekends," says Bartlit of his annual schedule, which doesn't include the lengthy glamorous vacations to which many successful attorneys treat themselves. "The last time I took seven days off in a row was probably 1978 or '79," he notes. Instead, Bartlit is more of a catch-as-catch-can vacationer. "I like the ability and the independence of—if I can get off—just taking a break." Many of Bartlit's breaks consist of skiing or playing golf in Colorado, near his Vail vacation house. "I do take time off. I'm not a workaholic. I'm not a nut," he insists.

Time off wasn't on Bartlit's mind in September 1980. Having chosen and fully prepared his witnesses and experts for the Dun & Bradstreet trial, and having taken all the key depositions of NBL's witnesses and experts himself, he began after two months' preparation to gird himself for the fight. "These big cases are like D day, Normandy beach," Bartlit says, again emphasizing his war theme. "They really have to be planned. There are too many ways to make mistakes if you're not absolutely organized."

Just to make sure everyone on his team knows what to do, Bartlit hands out his standard eight-page trial procedure memorandum. "I give the procedure to the whole staff when we're coming up for trial," he says. "I was spending all my time [before] telling people what to do, so the next time I had a case I wrote it all out.

"It's a war, and in a war there are overall strategy and day-by-day tactics," he expounds. "Preparation is almost everything. People have got to know what they are going to do. A perfectly prepared mediocre lawyer in a close case will normally defeat a poorly prepared brilliant lawyer."

Bartlit's procedure, he explains, lays out everything he expects from his team, down to the most nitty-gritty demands, such as a list of supplies and equipment in the courtroom. That list includes thirty-one items, such as an overhead projector and rolling cart, a six-foot-by-six-foot screen, a Polaroid camera with film and flash, a portable calculator with tape, a large portable whiteboard with three boxes of large felt-tip markers, several extension cords, legal pads, steno pads, extra folders and envelopes, Scotch tape, and a roll of coins for the court copying machine.

The trial-day schedule requires that the junior lawyers place on Bartlit's desk each day of trial, prior to six A.M., the material he needs for that day's witnesses—including "selected documents, highlighted, in separate folders" and "deposition nuggets, single-spaced, separated by two spaces." Bartlit prepares for his day during the four hours between five and nine A.M. "I sit there with a steno pad and outline the cross-examination based on the deposition and the documents," he explains. "It could be an hour or an all-day cross; I could have five crosses in one day. But I always prepare a little beyond the day." He also uses the trial lunch break to prepare further for the afternoon.

Bartlit meets the court reporter before a trial and tips that person every day to make sure he can get a transcript of the morning proceeding that afternoon, and of the afternoon proceeding that evening.

In Dun & Bradstreet, Bartlit argued the entire case himself, never turning the jury over to a younger attorney for even a short time. At the end of each day, after a half-hour meeting with Mitchell and Lovell, Bartlit escaped to his favorite gym for an hour, rejoined his client and other lawyers on the team for dinner, and went to bed at eleven P.M. During the Dun & Bradstreet trial—from late September 1980 to mid-December 1980—Bartlit lost twenty pounds (also due in part to the high number of cases he tried that year).

Bartlit's physique concerns him—in a constant way that some may view as an obsession, and others as an admirable desire for good health. When he's not in trial, he works out two hours a day, often with his new wife, forty-one-year-old Jana, a knock-your-socks-off blonde from a Texas oil family who at 110 pounds can lift up to 225 pounds in weights. Together, the two hired a trainer to attend personally to their workouts at the exclusive East Bank Club in Chicago.

The rest of Bartlit's trial procedure instructions are detailed and exact. One command reads: "Chief paralegal receives telephone call to meet FHB 7:30–8:00 A.M. to receive selected exhibits, make four copies from unmarked original (or copy) [and] one transparency [for use with an overhead projector]. Mark with exhibit number, place in folder boldly marked with exhibit number (across front of folder as well as tab), return to FHB."

At lunchtime a Kirkland & Ellis messenger picks up Bartlit's notes from the morning trial session so they can be typed immediately. Another secretary types the afternoon notes that same evening. Bartlit runs three shifts of secretaries: from 7:45 A.M. to noon, from noon to five P.M. and from five P.M. to midnight. Each has elaborate instructions for typing, labeling, and collating Bartlit's work. The chief legal assistant, the evening paralegal assisting the chief legal assistant, and even the messengers who run back and forth between the courthouse and Bartlit's office, all have written instructions.

In the courtroom Bartlit is aware of his every move, as if both he and his client are personally on trial. "From the day you set foot in the courthouse until the end of trial, the jury notices everything," warns Bartlit, who wears no jewelry in court except his wedding ring. He thinks that a series of juror perceptions throughout the course of the trial—no matter how small those perceptions are—build up to a favorable impression on his behalf. No one thing is going to turn the tide to create that favorable impression; it's the cumulative effect that counts.

Bartlit knows exactly what counts with jurors because after every trial for the past fifteen years, he has had a Kirkland & Ellis paralegal interview (or as he says, "debrief") the jurors in that trial, asking what they liked, and didn't like, about the lawyers.

(In doing so, the paralegals keep their own professional affiliation confidential, says Bartlit, so they don't influence the jurors' comments.) Thus Bartlit's carefully studied style of conduct draws from his own firsthand experience.

If Bartlit travels to try a case, he goes to great pains not to let the jury know that he's an out-of-town lawyer. He feels that jurors are less sympathetic—and even resentful—of an outsider in the courtroom. To prevent exposure Bartlit asks the judge and the opposing lawyer to agree ahead of time that they won't reveal Bartlit's home. Once in a Denver courtroom, however, all of Bartlit's effort to conceal his foreign identity failed. One of his partners in Denver (Kirkland & Ellis has an office there) ran into the jury foreman from that trial in a bar about a week later. The two started discussing the case, and the partner asked the foreman how he liked Fred Bartlit.

"We liked him," replied the foreman, "but the one thing we knew was that he wasn't from Denver."

"How did you know?" asked the incredulous partner, recognizing full well that Bartlit makes arrangements before a trial to keep his hometown private.

"We all noticed that he wore the same pair of shoes every day for two weeks," said the foreman.

Jurors never miss a thing. Foresta even commented in her juror notes on gestures, habits, and grooming of the entire plaintiff's legal team. But Bartlit thinks having teams of lawyers in court creates a bad impression anyway. After the trial, juror Lavaty told Bartlit that it was good he sat at the table alone. According to Bartlit, Lavaty said that even with assistants, Gross always seemed to be groping for his material.

"When I try a case," Bartlit emphasizes, "I like to get out of a cab with [only] the representative of the client. If I don't have a representative of the client who is a decent, nice guy, I'll sit there [at the counsel's table] by myself. The worst thing you can have is somebody epitomizing the client who is some smug bastard. I lost a case once in Des Moines twenty years ago—I thought I had a client who was a nice guy, but the jury said he smirked the whole time. "He wasn't smirking," Bartlit insists, still showing his frustration over that incident. "But he had a funny look on his face."

Bartlit prohibits assistants from following him into court. "We don't have armies of paralegals carrying our bags, we don't have armies of associates," he says. "We walk into court, we sit down at the table. We don't have the table piled high with junk, we don't have carafes of water on the table, drinking out of them when the poor jurors can't drink. We get all that off the table.

"I have all my documents under the table, and I do all the document work myself," he continues. "I have them all organized in files so if somebody says 'plaintiff's exhibit so-and-so,' bam-bam, I've got three copies. If the other side needs a copy, I might say, 'Here, I have an extra copy.' "

Bartlit's keen sense of independent organization did backfire on him one time, in fact, in the very Denver case when he "mistakenly" wore the same pair of shoes every day for two weeks. Bartlit represented Standard Oil, and he did get "a good result" in the case. But when he tried it, he thought that if he had a clean table before him in the courtroom, it would look as if he were really efficient and clean, had a simple case, and was very prepared. On the other hand, he reasoned, the lawyers on the other side—who had mounds of paper before them—would look really frantic. Instead the jurors thought Bartlit was the one who was unprepared. "Afterward, the jurors said to my paralegal, 'For a couple of days we thought Mr. Bartlit was just unprepared because he didn't have anything.' "

So, Bartlit thought, to himself, "If I were a juror, what would make me think a lawyer was prepared?" Today when he goes to trial, he puts on the table before him a notebook (which may have nothing in it), a pad, a pencil, two or three key documents, and perhaps a law book (again, an unneeded prop). When he first developed this scenario, Bartlit didn't write anything on the pad while the other side was presenting its case because he didn't want to look worried. But then one juror said after a trial that Bartlit didn't look interested in what was being said. Now he takes notes.

"Sometimes the notes are unimportant," he admits, but "I want the jurors to think I'm a zealous person who is interested in this thing, and they should be interested. [I want them to think] that I'm organized and prepared. That's the image I want the table to create.

"I don't want to fool the jury," says Bartlit of his carefully controlled courtroom demeanor. "I might say at the opening, 'I'm not the only lawyer working on this case. Don't worry. We've got people doing back-ups and studying things so I make sure I'm totally prepared.' They know I represent [a big corporation] and that I'm not a one-man deal. But I want them to see that I know the case cold and I'm doing it myself," he concludes, adding that he prepares most of his exhibits himself, in his own handwriting.

Alone at the counsel's table, Bartlit is a study in dignity. He allows no sign of emotion, unless something spontaneously funny happens in the courtroom. He doesn't like whispering with his client, or passing notes. While seated, he listens attentively to what is going on but doesn't show any expression or reactions in response. "I've heard jurors say in debriefings that they can't stand all the lawyers' reactions to the evidence," says Bartlit.

When reading depositions aloud in court, Bartlit uses the opportunity to show the jury that he and his client are simply two people working together to present their case (thus diminishing the image of a major corporation and a high-powered law firm ganging up). When a witness cannot appear in court directly, Bartlit asks the judge if he and his client can assume the roles of attorney and witness in reading the deposition. But here, Bartlit pulls a switch. He plays the part of the witness and requests that his client play the part of the lawyer asking the questions.

"I get on the stand and *I can read those answers,*" stresses Bartlit in his deep, sonorous voice. The rapport of the reading, the sense of two people helping each other to make a point for the jurors, shows them that "we're a team and we're good guys and we like each other," he adds.

Bartlit makes a point to stick by his client throughout the trial, even during lunch. When not preparing for an afternoon session during the Dun & Bradstreet trial, Bartlit and Mitchell would go down to the courthouse cafeteria—where all the jurors were eating their lunches, too. Most lawyers, Bartlit says, would be whisked off to a posh restaurant or club to enjoy "a big spread," but he prefers to maintain his down-to-earth image. "We don't talk to jurors or make eyes at them or anything," says Bartlit. "We go down, we get our trays, and we sit down. The jury sees that we're ordinary people and we're friendly. We talk about things, we may talk about sports or read the newspaper. It's not a big show, we're just being ourselves, but it gives the jurors a chance to see that we're not these remote, high-power, blue-suit lawyers who come and go in our limousines. We're trying to let the jury see who we really are."

Such an attitude may seem hypocritical to some, given that Bartlit is, in fact, a "high-power, blue-suit lawyer." His home is the renovated, 4,000-square-foot thirteenth floor of a fashionable cooperative overlooking Lake Michigan. He dines only in the most expensive restaurants in Chicago. And he attracts eleven million dollars' worth of client business for his firm's lawyers every year, including Kirkland's biggest client, Dallas investor Harold Simmons.

But Bartlit also knows how the other half lives because he hasn't always had it so good. One of two children in a middle-class family, Bartlit grew up in Harvey, Illinois, a southside Chicago suburb. His father was a small-town lawyer, his mother a public school teacher. It's this background, Bartlit says, that enables him to understand how typical jurors think, even though he is now far removed from their lifestyles. Other lawyers from sheltered, privileged backgrounds assume that everyone thinks and feels as they do, explains Bartlit. Or they look down on juries and think that the jurors are stupid. Bartlit knows that neither is true.

Yet Bartlit is a realist when considering the impact a complex case has on jurors. He thought that NBL's antitrust arguments "would be considered complicated by a jury. We felt that if we could make human, common-sense arguments, we might obscure NBL's theory," he recalls.

This approach, however, was more difficult than it seemed at first blush because Bartlit "also had to make a record for appeal on the economic facts contradicting NBL's theory. That is," he explains, "we had to argue that D and B did not have 'monopoly power' in the business credit market because there were many substitutes like 'do-it-yourself' credit checks. This economic and statistical information [supporting these claims] was boring, but we had to make the record while not causing the jury to lose sight of our key issues that NBL was ripping us off, that the company had caused its own problems, and that it was making a lot of money" anyway.

Associate Sidney N. Herman, who assisted in the trial, explains that one way in which Bartlit entered into the record data countering NBL's antitrust allegations was to ask the judge, without the jury present, to admit certain documents into evidence. Thus Bartlit did not bore the jury with the documents, but he protected his right to refer to the information they contained should the case be appealed. Bartlit calls this technique "a shovel-in," explains Herman. During the D&B trial, Bartlit "shoveled in" his necessary documents during two sessions, each lasting several hours, one session at the end of the plaintiff's case, and one at the end of the defendant's. At the same time NBL's attorney also put into the record any documents he chose to treat in a similar manner. This tactic, summarizes Herman, helped Bartlit direct his case simultaneously to multiple audiences: the jury, the judge, and the appellate court.

Bartlit's issued his first salvo of "human, common-sense" arguments during his opening statement. Instead of reacting defensively to Gross's antitrust charges, Bartlit went out for the attack. "Now, what is the believable evidence going to show in this case?" Bartlit asked the jury. "Well, there are three important things. The first important thing is that Mr. Gans, who is sitting over there on the end in the first row, he is the man who runs National Business Lists. He will be the first witness. He started his business from the first day under false pretenses.

"The second important point is that for twenty-five years, twenty-five years, he has run his business with a free ride because these names you have heard about, an awful lot of them were copies from Dun and Bradstreet, just copied. We got the names, not him, and he copied them.

"And the third point is that even after we told him in 1975 to stop copying because it is illegal, he just ignored that and kept right on," Bartlit continued, looking right into the jurors' eyes.

Throughout his forty-minute opening, Bartlit kept hammering on his central theme: that NBL was getting a free ride by copying information D&B works hard to obtain. Bartlit wove in his own small-town beginnings with the story of Dun & Bradstreet:

"Now, Mr. Gross said that he grew up in Sheridan, Wyoming. I grew up in a little town south of here, Harvey, Illinois. There are businesses in that town: Mark's Toggery is a store that sells clothes; Blue Ribbon Cafe is a pizza place that has about the best pizza on the South Side, at least as far as I know.

"It is businesses like that that the Dun and Bradstreet people for one hundred and fifty years have given credit information on.

"Let's say you take Mark's Toggery in Harvey. They are selling men's suits. There is somebody in Hong Kong or some other place, [and] Mark's Toggery wants to buy [their] suits. The fellow who makes the suits has never heard of Mark's Toggery. He doesn't know if they have a history of paying their bills. He doesn't know that they have been in business in Harvey probably for sixty years, and they have paid their bills, and they are good, reliable persons. He can't send somebody from Hong Kong or New York City or North Carolina to find out if he can deliver a shipment of suits to that clothing store and make doggone sure the bill is going to be paid.

"Well, it was to fill that need that Dun and Bradstreet started out in 1841. Somebody got a good idea. They said, why don't we hire these credit reporters or these correspondents, and they can go through these small towns door-to-door and find out about businesses. Walk in and say: You are a new man in town. People are going to want to sell to you on credit. Tell us about your credit experience, and then we can give you a good rating. Then you can borrow money, and your business will grow.

"There is nothing secret or underhanded or anything like that about what Dun and Bradstreet does in helping these businesses get credit. Indeed, it is a historical fact and it is interesting that one of our first credit reporters in the state of Illinois was Abraham Lincoln. He was a young lawyer down in Springfield. He would go around Springfield and send in handwritten reports saying that this hardware store is a good store, and you can sell pots and pans and things on credit, and they will pay their bills. . . .

"Now, what Dun and Bradstreet does when they send out these people door-to-door gathering all this information is this: They pull it together and they put it in these big reference books. You have heard about reference books. This is one here, the 1955 book. This is the book that would have been out the year that Mr. Gans started business.

"The point is that in our business that we have been in for one hundred and fifty years, we have printed these books," reiterated Bartlit. "The books had information in them. The information could be used by somebody to copy and make business lists and sell. That is what happened here. . . . That is what [Mr. Gans] did, because he copied. When he started out, he would buy our books, tear out the pages, and he would have all our names copied. That is how he got started in business."

When Gans bought D&B's credit book, Bartlit explained, he signed a written contract the he would only use the information as credit information for his own purposes. "In writing he promised that he wouldn't copy it, and he wouldn't sell it," stressed Bartlit. "When he signed that contract, which you will see during this trial, he knew he was going to break that promise.

". . . but we don't go to court over just every little thing, and it wasn't until he sued us in this case, it wasn't until he sued us that we stood up and defended ourselves and we sued him back. This is a two-way suit, ladies and gentlemen. We are now asking, and it is because he sued us and started it, we are now asking that he stop this illegal copying that he has built his business on for twenty-five years."

Bartlit talked about Gans's Palm Springs home and his two Mercedes (listing these assets on his whiteboard), and how Gans's bad business judgments were what had hurt the company. But in summarizing, Bartlit again returned to the story of D&B's working hard for its product, and NBL wanting to steal it. "We got this information in the books by knocking on doors, and it was hard work and it took a long time and we paid for it and we own it now," concluded Bartlit. "[Mr. Gans] wants that."

". . . So that what he wants is something for nothing.

". . . at the end of the trial," finished Bartlit, "we are going to ask you for a verdict which says, 'Mr. Gans, you have got to stop that copying.' "

Although the jurors didn't realize it, Bartlit chose his words carefully based on his earlier experience with the mock juries. His closing phrases, such as "he wants from us the results of one hundred and fifty years of hard work," "he wants it overnight," and "he wants it right away; he doesn't want to pay for it," had proven to be the most persuasive in these practice runs.

"The most important thing in a trial is the opening statement," says Bartlit. "A University of Chicago study says seventy-five percent of all cases are won in opening statement." An opening should tell a story, Bartlit emphasizes. "Let the jury reach their own theory through the facts," and that theory will stick.

Bartlit says his biggest challenge is holding jurors' attention. He blames television. "When I grew up, there was no television," says Bartlit. "This was at a time when you turned on the radio and listened. You could build pictures in your head from listening to the radio. The men and women who have grown up on television don't have the ability to listen to words and build a picture. The six o'clock news has ruined people's ability to listen."

Bartlit uses as example Bhopal, the 1984 disaster when more than two thousand Indians died in their sleep as noxious fumes escaped from a nearby Union Carbide plant. The anchorman takes twenty seconds to announce what happened, a photograph of rows of dead bodies flashes on the screen behind him, and after one and one-half to two minutes, the typical person thinks he or she knows everything about Bhopal. Television, with its simplistic graphics and photographs, and its boiled-down news with limited detail, affects forever how lawyers try cases, says Bartlit.

Recognizing this, Bartlit decided to model himself after a television anchorman. When trying a case, he projects visuals on a screen with an overhead projector, writes key words and phrases for his arguments on a whiteboard, and resorts to any tactic that can focus a juror's attention fully and quickly. "All really good lawyers are rethinking the way they do things," says Bartlit. "They're getting away from the rhetoric and learning how to present facts using the techniques and technology of the six o'clock news.

"Nobody in the world has spent more time thinking about how to present ideas in a clear and simple way than I have," says Bartlit. Everything [in television] is shown in strong bursts, using different techniques, while a credible person is looking right at you explaining something he's pointing to." What works for TV, Bartlit reasons, will work for him.

Visuals proved particularly effective during the D&B trial when Bartlit wanted to attack what Gans said on the stand. Along with creating the image of Gans in the case as the "bad guy," Bartlit's second goal was to impeach Gans repeatedly to make the jury question the honesty and accuracy of anything he said in court.

But before his cross-examination, Bartlit explained to the jury his use of visuals. "Ladies and gentlemen, as I mentioned, I put some of my documents on the screen. Unfortunately, it is not real secure, and if you will just make sure you don't hit it too much when you come by, I would appreciate it. I am going to try to get it fixed better.

"Secondly, we have tried this in different parts of the courtroom, and if anybody cannot see or finds that a difficult place, if the craning of your neck bothers you when we look at the documents, just raise your hand and we will try to figure out a better place, but we haven't been able to do better."

"Most documents that are worth asking the witness about, the jury ought to see," says Bartlit. But typically lawyers hand copies of the documents directly to the jurors, who invariably fumble with the papers, sometimes dropping them on the floor and creating a sense of disarray. The overhead projector, on the other hand, gives Bartlit total control.

"Almost nobody in the country outside of Kirkland uses these," says Bartlit of his 3M portable overhead projector and transparencies. Cost is not an inhibitor, he notes. His small, streamlined projector—neither cumbersome nor visually offensive—cost only $450. Instead, Bartlit supposes, lawyers simply haven't thought of the idea; traditionally, projectors aren't used in the courtroom. Bartlit says he hasn't had trouble with his visual approach because he first seeks permission from the judge. He has yet to be refused.

Judge James B. Moran of the Eastern Division of the U.S. District Court for the Northern District of Illinois—who heard the Dun & Bradstreet case—applauds Bartlit's use of an overhead projector and other aids. Moran says he doesn't see these techniques as much as he would expect, but adds that they are most effective in longer, more complex trials that rely on a lot of documents. "I don't know any [judge] who says you can't use them," says Moran.

When Bartlit showed the jury during his cross-examination of Gans that Gans had deliberately breached his contract with D&B, he actually projected the contract itself onto the screen:

Mr. Bartlit: Now, with the Court's permission, I would like to put that document on our screen. I have marked the parts for the jury's convenience that I want to talk about. The exhibit that goes to the jury room will, of course, not be marked, but this is just so on the screen we can pick up the important things.

Let's look at the first page, Mr. Gans, sir. Now, the contract with Dun and Bradstreet up in the upper left-hand corner, do you see that, where it says "Leo Gans, Partner" [underlined in blue], Mr. Gans?

Mr. Gans: I see it. . . .

Mr. Bartlit: Now, let's look at the second page of Exhibit One, and we see at the top that it says "Dun and Bradstreet Subscription." [underlined] Do you see that?

Mr. Gans: Yes.

Mr. Bartlit: Okay. Now, we come down to the center of the page where it says "Authorized signature, Leo Gans." [underlined] Is that written in your handwriting?

Mr. Gans: Yes.

Mr. Bartlit: And do you see where it says "The undersigned subscriber agrees to the terms of agreement" [underlined] on the reverse side of that document? Do you see that?

Mr. Gans: That I do.

Mr. Bartlit: Now, let's look next and let's see what you agree to on the reverse side of the page I have just shown you. Let's turn to the next page of DX-one.

Now, right up there at the top of the page, "Terms of Agreement."

Mr. Gross: Your Honor, could I ask for one more side bar? (A side-bar conference between the lawyers and the judge followed, out of the hearing of the jury.)

Mr. Gross: What I object to, as I look up there, is that the agreement has been altered by at least some blue underlining calling attention to several spots, and I would think that that is just kind of an undue emphasis. I cannot object to the agreement as it was being shown, but this is something being offered in evidence, and like my bit of demonstrative evidence, the underlining is what the lawyer was arguing.

Mr. Bartlit: This is not being offered, Your Honor.

The Court: Right. The one that is being offered in evidence, I assume, will not have any writing on it.

Mr. Bartlit: Yes. . . . (end of side bar)

The Court: Ladies and gentlemen, you recall that I made some remarks earlier about when lawyers prepare something to show to the jury, that often there will be some writing on it that is perhaps more lawyer's argument than anything else. By the same token, when lawyers are showing you exhibits and they really want to call your attention to something which is in the nature of a lawyer's argument, they will do something as here, which is to use some blue to show, direct your attention to what they want to talk about and ask questions about, and in both instances, that is perfectly permissible just as long as you realize that that is what has happened, is that it has been marked up for the purpose of making a point to you and that is really not part of the document.

Mr. Bartlit: Yes, sir, and the documents that go to the jury room won't have these. I am putting them on there because that is the part I want to direct their attention to.

Your Honor, if at any time Mr. Gross wants me to mark any other part of any document or read it at that time, I will do it, obviously.

Now, we were talking about the terms that you

agreed to, and the very first term says: "All information, whether printed, written or oral, submitted in answer to regular or special inquiry or voluntarily furnished to the subscriber"—

Now, you were the subscriber, weren't you, Mr. Gans?

Mr. Gans: Yes.

Mr. Bartlit: (continuing reading)—"by Dun and Bradstreet is for the exclusive use of the subscriber. Such information shall be held in strict confidence and shall never be revealed or made accessible in any manner whatsoever to the persons called upon or to any other."

"Information shall never be revealed to anyone." (Bartlit underlines this heavily.)

Now, you read paragraph one and you signed the contract, isn't that right, sir?

Mr. Gans: That is correct.

Earlier during the cross-examination, Bartlit had asked Gans whether he started his business in 1955 by copying names from D&B reference books. Gans said he had not. Bartlit then read the deposition before trial when Gans had said, "We started out basically and first simply taking every name in the *Dun & Bradstreet Reference Book.*" Later, when Bartlit projected the contract on the screen, the jurors saw that Gans had signed saying he would never copy.

For added effect, Bartlit asks a marshal in the courtroom to assist him. (As with the court reporter, Bartlit introduces himself to the marshals and learns their names before trial.) At the appropriate moment, when Bartlit shows a document with the overhead projector and decides to emphasize some portion that is particularly damning, he asks the marshal to dim the lights. The sharp contrast of the lighted projector screen with the darkened courtroom makes the words almost jump out at the jury.

In all, during the D&B trial, Bartlit projected thirty to forty documents on the screen for the jurors to see.

Bartlit is very precise with his visuals, even in the way he marks them to draw the jury's attention to his points. He uses a set pattern of colors—black for titles, blue for contrasting markings. If something is important, he puts a strong, right-angled box around it, not a circle, because a box looks more authoritative. When writing with markers on his whiteboard, Bartlit always uses a blue marker for words relating to the defendant, and red for words relating to the plaintiff. "In the Army, the good guys are blue, the enemy is red," explains Bartlit. He practices writing on a whiteboard, learning to hold his hand steady and to use the fat, rather than the thin, edge of the marker so the words are dark and heavy. Sometimes Bartlit takes a Polaroid photograph of the board during a break. The photograph becomes an exhibit for the jurors to study in their deliberations.

After working his way through about three dozen witnesses, Bartlit began his final argument. To tell his story of how hard D&B worked, going door-to-door to collect the credit information it published, Bartlit moved the screen for his overhead projector directly in front of the jury.

"Ladies and gentlemen of the jury. Judge Moran. Mr. Gross. Mr. Gans," Bartlit began.

"We started this trial, as I remember, on a very bright, sunny September day, and now it is snowing outside, and on that sunny day, that was my first chance to tell you what I expected that the evidence was going to show in this case. This is my last chance. This is my chance and my duty and my privilege to sum up the evidence on behalf of Dun and Bradstreet and on behalf of Robert Mitchell. . . .

"You may have wondered how in the world can you remember all those important things that happened during the trial. Well, what I am going to do is, I am going to show you every piece of evidence [on which] I rely. I am not going to show you every piece of evidence, because I have gone through the record and gone through it and I have culled out just the things I think are most important. You are not going to have to rely on your memories or your notes or anything else. You are certainly not going to have to rely on my recollection being the truth or being accurate, because you are going to see right up there [on the screen] the evidence in this case and that evidence is going to show that Mr. Gross hasn't made out his burden of proving his case by a preponderance of the evidence, as the law requires that he do."

Several times during his closing argument, Bartlit projected pages from the trial transcript. He noted, for example, that Mr. Gans claimed to have started his business from scratch and had emphasized how difficult that was. "Mr. Gans didn't start from scratch. That is nonsense. He started by copying from Dun and Bradstreet," stressed Bartlit, who proceeded to read out loud from the transcript:

"Your decision was, when you started NBL, you were going to take names right out of the reference book, isn't that true?

"We started out basically and first simply taking every name."

"The ones you wanted, any name you wanted, you copied?"

"That is right."

After nearly three months of trial, the jury was out only a day and a half. According to posttrial interviews, the jurors decided very quickly that NBL had no case against D&B. "Apparently it took only about a half hour of deliberation to decide that part of the case once the [jury] instruction had been received," wrote Bartlit after a posttrial interview with juror Susan Lavaty.

According to Bartlit's notes, Lavaty summarized the main points of the trial as: (1) Gans was doing okay [in his business]; (2) Gans was "shady"; (3) Mitchell explained in his final testimony that, even today, D&B was still willing to provide lists under a brokerage agreement; and (4) D&B knew NBL was copying and NBL should have stopped in 1975 when the counterclaim was filed and they were told to stop.

"As usual," wrote Bartlit in his posttrial memorandum, "the jury was more interested in these three or four main points and in the "bad guy–good guy" material than in the nuances. Ms. Lavaty was unable to explain the theory of Gross's case—that is, the use of monopoly power in one market to leverage into another market." Nor was juror Foresta able to articulate NBL's case against D&B, wrote assisting associate Sidney Herman following his posttrial juror interviews.

Simplicity won the day, Bartlit summarizes. The jury found that National Business Lists had no claim of monopolization again Dun & Bradstreet. But it did find NBL guilty of copyright infringement and assessed NBL $3.85 million in damages. Then it assessed another $3.85 million against NBL based on D&B's additional claim of breach of contract.

In his memorandum denying NBL's request for a new trial of its antitrust claims, Judge Moran wrote on June 11, 1982: "While plaintiff's posttrial memoranda would suggest that D&B's defense was largely an underhanded attack on plaintiff, without any justification, that simply was not so." The liability issues didn't focus solely on the conduct of the defendant, D&B, wrote Moran.

"It was beyond dispute that NBL and D&B are the largest purveyors of compiled business lists. That theory necessarily made relevant NBL's competitive relationship to D&B and within the industry, a subject thoroughly covered in the testimony of plaintiff's witnesses. The purpose of the antitrust laws is to protect competition, not competitors."

Moran did order a retrial on the amount of damages awarded D&B. Ultimately the two companies settled for about $400,000, far less than the jury award, but a significant victory nonetheless given that D&B had seriously been threatened with the dismemberment of its business. A few years later, a third company, Market Data Retrieval, bought out NBL, and Leo Gans retired. In 1986, Dun & Bradstreet acquired Market Data Retrieval.

And earlier this year, Bartlit won still another trial victory for

D&B. Capitol Steel Company, Inc. of Sacramento, California, had claimed that D&B defamed it in a credit report by saying that Capitol Steel was related to another company that had gone bankrupt; Capitol Steel asked the court to order D&B to pay it $12 million in actual and punitive damages. The trial lasted seven weeks, but the jury deliberated for less than two hours before delivering its verdict for D&B.

Bartlit's television-inspired techniques for helping clients such as Dun & Bradstreet have spread through the ranks of Kirkland & Ellis's more than two hundred trial lawyers. Emily Nicklin, one of the firm's rising young partners and a Bartlit protégée, says she has used an overhead projector in every case she's tried. "It really is such an easy and clear way to present a lot of complicated material, and it's cheap," she says. "Any two-hundred-and-fifty-thousand-dollar dispute can afford" this approach.

Nicklin realizes that Bartlit's style is a source of criticism as well as praise. "The same characteristics that make Fred an effective trial lawyer are subject to occasional parody and sniping," admits the young lawyer. Bartlit's "monolithic presence" is the characteristic that probably leads that list. "What makes him able to say 'follow me' and have people follow him can be abrasive to some people," explains Nicklin. It overwhelms others. Some people, she adds, just say to themselves, "Please, God, I'd like to be in the presence of someone other than a Roman gladiator. I'd like to have a beer with someone who doesn't get up in the morning and slay a dozen men."

Bartlit's intense, unilateral focus on his trial skills can grate especially on his competitors in the trial bar. "He's criticized for being so focused on his work—the car phone, the workouts, everything is funneled to make him a larger-than-life gladiator," says Nicklin. "But is being focused a bad characteristic for a trial lawyer?" she asks. "Probably not."

LINDA FAIRSTEIN

Chief, Sex Crimes Prosecution Unit,
District Attorney's Office, New York

David Hornor

"Anything between the knees and the waist goes to me," says Linda Fairstein of criminal matters that hit her desk on the eighth floor of the Manhattan district attorney's office. What Fairstein means is that she oversees all investigations and prosecutions of sex crimes in Manhattan, crimes ranging from violent street attacks to date rapes. Heading the DA's Sex Crimes Prosecution Unit since 1976, with a staff of about ten lawyers, the forty-one-year-old Fairstein shepherds through the legal system between 500 and 800 cases annually. Around 125 of them actually go to trial, with Fairstein herself typically arguing about three a year.

Fairstein's cases are often sensational. They appeal to a universal fascination with sex, including violent, ugly sex. In her most recent trial, Fairstein prosecuted Robert Chambers, who was accused of murdering Jennifer Dawn Levin one night in Central Park during rough sex. The trial involved upper-middle-class white teenagers and their families, people with good jobs and affluent lifestyles who were supposedly immune from this sort of crime. If the killing had taken place in a less desirable neighborhood, says Fairstein, the press and its readers wouldn't have been as interested. But the "preppie killing," as Chambers's case was dubbed, caught and held the attention of people throughout New York and elsewhere. It made headlines from the time Levin's death was first reported in August 1986 until the end of Chambers's 13-week trial in March 1988 when, in a surprise move, he decided to plead guilty to first-degree manslaughter.

Fairstein's Sex Crimes Unit holds an eighty percent conviction record. Fairstein herself has lost only two of the thirty-one cases she's tried in her career. A Vassar College and University of Virginia Law School graduate who joined the DA's office immediately after law school, Fairstein also has prosecuted cases against Max Lindeman and Harold Wells, who sexually assaulted and mutilated a nun in a Harlem convent; Ronald Jamgochian, the "Playboy Bunny Rapist;" Anthony Troiano, the "Greenwich Village Rapist;" and Russell West, the "Midtown Rapist." Fairstein is a tough attorney in a difficult arena. For the purposes of a trial, she will talk about sex acts, sex organs, and strange sexual behavior in a direct, matter-of-fact manner. Working from her cluttered office with regulation metal government furniture, she epitomizes the public servant committed to fighting sex crimes, to lessening the incidence of this dangerous, degrading, and intensely personal violence.

Fairstein has pursued her goal successfully by being thorough, methodical, and deliberate, a lawyer not given to courtroom flamboyance or hysteria even though her cases are highly emotional. She perseveres with intelligence and reason from preparation through final argument. One New York attorney labeled

Fairstein's style the "snowball technique." It is, he says, like "rolling down the hill, picking up speed and picking up mass, and then crushing everything that gets in the way."

"Linda is thorough and careful in her investigations and she prepares her cases extremely well," agrees Fairstein's boss, noted District Attorney Robert M. Morgenthau. "Ninety percent of [being] a good trial lawyer is being prepared." In court, he adds, Fairstein "comes across as being totally honest and sincere and extremely credible," an image enhanced by her low-key, albeit strong, style and her no-nonsense approach to cases. "A lot of jurors make their decision not only on the evidence but on whether the lawyer is believable," says Morgenthau.

In an age of growing numbers of women attorneys, Fairstein also offers a strong role model for other women who seek success. Young female lawyers today are anxious to find examples of older couterparts who have learned how to succeed in a previously all-male world where successful behavior embraced traditional attributes such as aggressiveness, competitiveness, and a desire to prevail over others. The very first women who broke into the law profession often fell into one of two undesirable stereotypes: those who became so aggressive and hard-nosed that they lost their femininity in the quest for professional acceptance; and those who retreated to the then less glamorous, less competitive, and less visible areas of practice such as domestic relations or probate law, which were considered appropriate specialties for women. Fairstein, who married her husband, attorney Justin Feldman, in 1987, fits into neither of these old stereotypes. She is the modern woman lawyer—one who is both feminine and professionally competitive. She cares about her looks; she cares that she wears attractive clothes. But Fairstein also has chosen one of the most combative and demanding areas of law practice—litigation—and she seeks professional competence and success in her field more actively than many men. Fairstein's balancing of femininity and professional toughness is a goal that still frustrates some women lawyers today.

One reason Fairstein is successful is that she has cultivated a trial specialty in a field demanding special skills and defined areas of expertise. For example, Fairstein's skill in working with sex crimes victims is critical to prosecuting her cases. Fairstein, who believes that men can be as effective in victim counseling as can women, questions sexual abuse victims gently and calmly, moving slowly to gain the victim's trust before broaching the most difficult and embarrassing queries. She also helps these women prepare to face the public and their alleged assailants in court by reviewing their testimony with them ahead of time. In her work with sex crimes victims, Fairstein has noted an increased reporting of date rapes, which she estimates comprise half of all the rapes in Manhattan. The percentage of acquaintance rapes is slightly higher, says Fairstein, because this is the larger category that includes date rapes. Fairstein doesn't know if increased reporting means that date rapes are more common today or that women are simply reporting them more often. Still, she adds, acquaintance rapes continue to be the most underreported category of sex crimes.

Despite her counseling skills, Fairstein does not represent the sex crimes victim in court; she represents the state. And it's on the state's behalf that she prosecutes alleged sex abusers. In addition to working closely with the victim, Fairstein also carefully researches the defense attorney opposing her, the judge assigned to her case, and when she knows their names ahead of time, the defense's expert witnesses. She asks her own experts to help her prepare for cross-examination of the defense experts. And she takes copious notes in every aspect of her preparation and throughout a trial. Fairstein delegates little to other lawyers, preferring to handle most trial-related tasks herself.

Some of Fairstein's most difficult cases are those where the accused rapist is an established professional, a doctor or a dentist, for example, whom the community respects. Typically these men are well dressed, articulate, and confident. They're often married. It's hard to investigate this type of man for alleged rape or sexual abuse, says Fairstein. And when he stands accused, juries find themselves plagued by disbelief. "Why would he need to do that?" they wonder. "It's so much more difficult for the victim because juries tend to believe the professional who is educated, articulate, and has no criminal record," says this prosecutor.

Such was the case of Marvin Teicher, a tall, handsome, fifty-three-year-old dentist with an office in lower Manhattan, who sexually abused his patients while they were sedated. Fairstein prosecuted Teicher under a New York law defining sexual abuse as subjecting someone to sexual contact either by force, or because the other person is physically helpless or less than eleven years old and unable to consent to the conduct. The Teicher case hinged on innovative investigative techniques, complicated and esoteric expert medical testimony, and the discrediting of a professional man's character witnesses. It required that Fairstein meet head-on one of the most famous and flamboyant defense attorneys in New York at the time, and that she convince a judge dedicated to protecting defendants' rights that the accused dentist committed the crime he so vehemently denied.

On May 24, 1976, twenty-three-year-old Randi Carson went to see Teicher for some dental work. Carson was anxious, as most people are when they see a dentist, but she had little reason to expect what was in store that day. Teicher sedated Carson and completed the dental procedure without a hitch. But then he added another step to his patient's care: With the groggy Carson slowly coming out from under the sedation, Teicher took her hand and placed it over his penis. He asked her for a "head job."

Carson left the dentist's office in an anesthetic daze, confused and frightened. She later complained to the police.

It so happened that two other young women had also complained about Teicher. None of the three women knew about the others. The police didn't take the first complainant very seriously, believing she had imagined an incident of sexual abuse due possibly to mind-altering side effects from the dental anesthesia. They did, however, equip the second woman, twenty-five-year-old Susan Hyman, with a hidden microphone and recording device before her next appointment with Teicher and told her to ask him about the alleged abuse. The police hoped he would support her claim, and that an acknowledgment would be recorded on tape. But Teicher wouldn't admit to anything.

Then when Carson contacted the police, they decided to look again into what was beginning to seem like a pattern of sexual deviance. As with Hyman, the police equipped Carson with a microphone and recording device before her next appointment. They dusted her bra and panties with fluorescent powder to reveal if Teicher touched them. However, even though Carson was unconscious while the dentist again treated her, he did not abuse her. On her last monitored visit to Teicher's office, Carson also tried to get him to admit that he had fondled her while she was sedated. But Teicher denied that and simply told Carson that the drugs had made her imagination run wild.

In New York, a woman's word that a man abused or raped her is enough to bring an indictment. But in the Teicher case, the complainants' credibility was highly questionable because the women, in each instance, had been sedated. In the Teicher case, their word alone was not sufficient.

The police knew they'd need some creative sleuthing to obtain reliable confirmation of Teicher's aberrant behavior. The dentist was well respected in his field, and he even lectured professionally. He lived a traditional home life in Westchester with a wife and three children. And he gained community recognition for his starring roles in local amateur theater productions, including musicals. Teicher was a charming man, and no one suspected him.

His distinguished appearance and voice, and his presence, helped him play perfectly his respected-dentist role when police investigators directly confronted him. Teicher explained repeatedly, in his self-assured way, how and why patients under sedation could imagine something as absurd as what they reported. He even showed the police a package insert for the sedative he used that warned of possible hallucinatory side effects.

If the police asked an undercover officer to pose as a patient to try to prove Teicher's sexual activity, the officer would be rendered unconscious by his medication and would thus be unable to observe what he did to her. And even if she carried a tape recorder in her purse, the audiotape would not reveal the abuse. (The undercover officer would also be at great personal risk, a risk the police department was not willing to take.) So, in an unprecedented move, the Manhattan DA's office requested a warrant to hide a video camera in Teicher's office. Warrants for surreptitious audiotapes were a common investigative tool back in 1976, but the DA's office could not find a model—anywhere in the country—for requesting court approval to videotape covertly a suspect in the privacy of his own home or office. It would have been legal to videotape anything in a public place, explains Fairstein today, but it was not legal to tape secretly without a warrant an individual's activities in a private situation. Yet after the Manhattan Sex Crimes Unit proved that the detectives had exhausted all other investigative means and that the prosecutor had cause to believe that Teicher was guilty, the court authorized a break-in to install a hidden video camera in Teicher's office.

The judge's warrant had a catch. It mandated that the camera only be used when an undercover policewoman was the "patient" in Teicher's chair. The police could not violate the privacy of other unsuspecting patients.

Thus the investigators faced their next hurdle: finding an undercover policewoman to volunteer to be sedated by a suspected sexual pervert. No one on the Manhattan police force stepped forward. Finally Dorothy Beineix, an attractive twenty-one-year-old brunette with the Westchester County sheriff's office, said she would be the decoy. She made an introductory appointment with Teicher, and then a second to have a wisdom tooth pulled, as he recommended. Teicher's office scheduled Beineix as the dentist's first patient on July 28, 1976.

Late the night before, police engineers stole into Teicher's office and installed a camera in an air-conditioning duct over his dental chair, its lens facing downward. They wired the camera to the light switch so that when Teicher flipped it on in the morning the camera would start recording. Thus the camera would record Beineix's treatment, and the detectives could turn it off when she was done.

Beineix did have some protection. Detectives in the building's basement monitored a screen showing what the camera was recording. Another detective, posing as Beineix's boyfriend, sat in the office waiting room with a hidden earphone allowing his coworkers in the basement to communicate with him. The plan was for the basement team to signal the "boyfriend" as soon as the video monitor showed Teicher abusing his "patient," Beineix. Then the "boyfriend" would rescue her.

But this was in 1976, before detectives knew how to use videos effectively, and before today's advances in video technology. What the police and the DA's office hadn't planned on was that after Teicher had performed the dental work on Beineix, he would lift her out of the chair before fondling her, thus removing her from full view of the camera.

Under sedation Beineix was unable to stand by herself, so Teicher lifted her into an upright position and held her between his opened legs with her front pressed against him. The door was shut, and Teicher's unsuspecting assistants had left the room after the dental procedure was completed. "Raindrops Keep Falling on My Head" was playing over the music system piped into the office. With Teicher and Beineix partially out of range, the camera only showed Teicher's legs and Beineix's back as he stroked and caressed the various parts of her body. It recorded Teicher lifting Beineix's blouse in the back and groping her buttocks and sliding his hands around toward her front. But from its position, the camera didn't show whether Teicher actually touched Beineix's breasts.

Even so, the detectives in the basement had seen all they

needed. They signaled their colleague upstairs, who ran down the hall and pushed open the treatment room door. There he saw Teicher massaging Beineix's breasts as he supported her, in a drugged state, leaning against him.

"What are you doing?" asked the detective.

"I'm ventilating her. She's in respiratory distress," responded Teicher calmly.

"You're under arrest," said the detective.

Two police detectives led the still-dazed Dorothy Beineix, who despite her undercover training was frightened and shaking, out of Teicher's office. One on each side, the assisting officers supported her under her arms and comforted her.

The Teicher trial illustrates some valuable techniques for prosecuting a professional man accused of a sex crime, as well as highlighting more general courtroom strategies for handling any type of case.

First, the technique that made Fairstein's success possible when prosecuting Teicher was the use of an undercover camera. Fairstein wasn't surprised by the dentist's self-assured reaction to the police officers' questioning, both before and after the taping. It was a common response. "We have many cases of doctors and dentists abusing [women] in their offices," says the prosecutor. "One of the reasons that the taping technique is a very good investigative technique for this kind of crime," she continues, "is that professionals and most articulate assailants, as opposed to street criminals, deal with confrontation very well. Because they think they're more intelligent than the people they're dealing with—both victims and police—they are often very comfortable talking and have a ready explanation for whatever it is that they've been proficient at doing." Sex offenses are one of the most recidivist of crimes, says Fairstein, and it tends to be very rare for offenders to be caught the first time. "So we often find with professionals that if they are accomplished at doing what they are—in a medical or dental office where there are other support personnel present, often outside the door—they've probably been doing it for a long time." The professional "might try the first time a little fondling with the door closed," continues Fairstein, "but I think you don't get to the point of undressing a patient or undressing yourself until you've established a pretty safe routine and the confidence of doing it." The videotape of Teicher's sexual activity pierced the dentist's glib explanations and the confidence he had developed in his repeated abuse of female patients. In the trial, however, Fairstein had to argue the videotape's legality, and she kept in mind that if she won, the issue of the covert taping would surely come up on appeal. And while the video camera did help Fairstein construct an argument against Teicher, its limited field of view prevented her from showing the abuse in its entirety.

Second, the dentist's defense that Beineix was in respiratory distress following her treatment, and that his maneuvering was an attempt to help her, led Fairstein to rely on another trial tactic that is uncommon in typical sexual abuse cases. In Teicher, Fairstein researched a complex scientific field—dental anesthesia—and relied heavily on expert witnesses to prove her charges. Most rapes are street crimes and typically involve one-witness identification, explains Fairstein. But in Teicher's case, his insistence that he was engaged in an acceptable medical practice—holding Beineix upright with his arms around her chest to help her breathe—turned the trial into a battle of experts giving their views on sedation and respiratory distress treatment.

Third, Teicher's 1978 trial provided a parade of character witnesses, making it a paradigm of Fairstein's prosecutorial challenge when a sex crime defendant is an established, respected professional. Teicher, whose wife sat in the courtroom daily during his twelve-day trial, brought in professional colleagues and an array of patients, including two nuns and a priest, to testify on his behalf. The respectability they radiated far overshadowed that of Fairstein's complainants. Fairstein had to drop as a complainant in the case the first woman who reported Teicher's abuse because the DA's office could no longer locate her. Of the two other complaining patients, Hyman was a single woman who worked part-time in a veterinarian's office; Carson was attending accounting school.

Fairstein overcame the defense experts and the character witnesses, and even the defendant's charm, by relying on two staples of top trial work—preparation and perseverance. "I am by nature very compulsive and thorough," says Fairstein. "Those are traits which serve me well as a litigator." In the Teicher trial, Fairstein demonstrated her skill in getting victims to tell her everything she possibly wanted to know. She found, after a long search, the leading scientific expert in Teicher's sedation technique. Fairstein plotted her response to every turn the Teicher defense could take. When she made her closing statement, she addressed all the details in the case to prove that every fact and every argument supported her accusations.

In this trial Fairstein also demonstrated how she can take advantage of a strategic mistake by an opposing lawyer. Early in the case both Fairstein and defense counsel Henry B. Rothblatt noted that the judge assigned to preside over the trial—Judge Dorothy Cropper of the Supreme Court of the State of New York—had a reputation as a defender of individual liberties. Many lawyers, in fact, considered Judge Cropper to be a defendants' judge. Both lawyers suspected that Cropper, whom Fairstein describes as "a very large, very handsome woman with a real poker face and no chitchat," would scrutinize critically the DA's investigative techniques, particularly her use of the videocamera. Rothblatt was so confident that he had drawn a favorable judge that he waived his client's right to a jury, opting instead for a verdict from the judge herself. (In New York this is an option for the defendant, but not for the prosecutor.) With the women's liberation movement coming into its own, the defense also reasoned that only a woman would have the courage to rule in Teicher's favor. "If anybody could acquit without being accused of being a chauvinist pig, she was the one," says Stephan H. Peskin, the lawyer in Rothblatt's firm who handled the pretrial work. But Rothblatt and Peskin were wrong, and Cropper listened carefully to both sides of the case. Fairstein argued the facts and the law, appealing to the judge's knowledge and fairness rather than to any preconceived notions about her personal biases. In the end Rothblatt's reliance on a judge whom he did not understand, and his decision to turn down a jury that might have been more inclined to believe Teicher, proved to be the defense lawyer's biggest mistake.

The Teicher case shows how Fairstein handles a condescending and chauvinistic opponent by relying on her own straightforward, matter-of-fact style of argument. When Fairstein faced Rothblatt as her adversary, she was only twenty-nine, and one of a mere handful of women lawyers in the DA's office. Rothblatt obviously could not adapt to the circumstances that had provided him with both a female prosecutor and a female judge. The American courtroom, with more and more women lawyers and judges, has lost its ambiance of years past when the legal profession admitted only men into its ranks. Thus the bar is in flux as men and women lawyers together seek a new equilibrium in attitudes toward each other and toward standards of courtroom behavior. While women lawyers find their way in a previously all-male system, perceptive male lawyers do acknowledge, both in demeanor and speech, a new courtroom scene, one with unfamiliar actors. The men can feel the strain of combining traditional gestures of courtesy and gallantry toward women with their typically aggressive, no-holds-barred approach to quashing courtroom opponents. It's a difficult challenge for many, and as in the case of Teicher, not all succeed.

When he represented Teicher, the sixty-year-old Rothblatt was a formidable presence in the New York bar and a member of the old school of law practice. He had won many cases and coauthored books on trial technique with F. Lee Bailey. As an old-line, traditional courtroom lawyer, Rothblatt had cultivated a grandiose and bombastic style. Tall and lanky, he sported as his hallmark a pencil-thin mustache, and he wore a luxuriant black toupee. In keeping with his old-line demeanor, Rothblatt (who died in 1985) used paternalistic and condescending terms of endearment when he spoke to Judge Cropper. "Darling" and "dear" sprinkled the defense lawyer's remarks. "There were very few [women] practicing criminal law," says Fairstein of that time, "and I was used to being called 'honey,' 'sweetie,' 'dearie,' not ill-meaningly, particularly by older men who were not used to working with women in the court system. But [Rothblatt] made the same kind of characterization to the judge."

The defense lawyer also minimized the seriousness of the abuse charges. His attitude, recalls Fairstein, was as if "it was no big deal. It was just a little bit of her breasts, a little of her rear end. There were constant innuendos of 'I know more than the court does because I've been practicing for a number of years, and Judge, you're just a young woman.' Of course, he thought I was just a baby," adds Fairstein.

Finally, the Teicher case illustrates how different courtroom styles can affect the outcome of a case. Rothblatt argued the case in the grandiose manner that had brought him so much success before juries. He did not bother to modify his style to one more suitable for a judge. With great theatrics the defense attorney shouted at times, whispered at others, and occasionally pounded his fist on the defense table. Cropper was unimpressed. "This guy was just barking up the wrong tree," says Fairstein, noting that Cropper was "all business and very closemouthed."

The prosecutor, on the other hand, made a reserved yet forceful presentation specifically tailored for a judge. An attractive, five-foot-eight-inch woman who carries herself well, Fairstein offered little show. And she visibly ignored the fact that both she and the judge were women participating in a sex crimes trial. She paid strict attention instead to her case, and to the law she was working to uphold. It is an approach that she follows to this day.

The prosecution began, of course, with an indictment. In this case, however, the defendant was indicted twice. In August

1976, Teicher was charged with four counts of sexual abuse in the first degree. Each count represented a different complainant (that is, three women patients and the undercover female police detective). But because that indictment, which was prepared before Fairstein joined the Sex Crimes Unit, alleged that Teicher had subjected each complainant to sexual contact "by forcible compulsion," it had to be withdrawn. None of the women was, in fact, forced to engage in any activity with the dentist: They all were too medicated to resist.

A second indictment in January 1977 charged Teicher with three counts of sexual abuse in the first degree. It listed only three complainants, leaving out the first woman who could no longer be located. This time, the indictment alleged that Teicher had subjected each of the women to sexual contact when they were "incapable of consent by reason of being physically helpless." Fairstein later compared the dentist's behavior to a form of necrophilia—except here the bodies were warm.

The blond-headed Fairstein, who has modeled many subsequent investigations on the kind of undercover operation used in the Teicher case, didn't actually take over until after the second indictment. District Attorney Morgenthau named Fairstein sex crimes chief in 1976 after her predecessor, Leslie Snyder, had moved on to another office. While preparation for the Tiecher case began under Snyder's direction, it ultimately became Fairstein's to try in court.

The trial began on June 2, 1978. It played to a packed courtroom—Judge Cropper even had to move the proceeding to a larger room. The New York tabloids were out in full force. "Every day our local papers had this on page one," says the prosecutor. The attention was not lost on Rothblatt. Even though he had no jury before which to argue his client's case, he did have the spectators and the press. Rothblatt was so used to grandstanding that when he would have spoken to a jury had there been one, he simply addressed the audience. "It made things lively for the press," says Fairstein, but "it fell dead on the judge. It was another example for me of 'Just try your case. Enough of the theatrics.' "

Fairstein, by contrast, tried to draw little attention to herself. She was careful to dress conservatively, both because she is a prosecutor and a female. "I think it's probably very different for a prosecutor than for a defense attorney," says Fairstein, who advises younger women prosecutors on their dress. "We are not in private practice," she tells them. "It's not that you're representing an individual client who may approve or disapprove. We are public servants—we represent the public—and I don't think extremes or dramatics in appearance in the courtroom are appropriate." Fairstein never wore pants when they were popular in the 1970s, nor will she wear very short skirts. "One of the things juries do is to chat about appropriateness or inappropriateness of dress," Fairstein explains. Once, she recalls, a juror even wrote the DA and told him to tell his female assistants (not Fairstein) how to dress. "I don't think half the time in the jury room should be spent discussing whether or not an assistant DA has underpants on," wrote the juror. Still, Fairstein "hates lady lawyer clothes," those monochrome female takeoffs on men's suits. She chooses instead to be natural but uncontroversial, favoring a soft suit or a subdued dress with a blazer, and taking off all her jewelry except a wedding band.

Sometimes Fairstein worries that being an attractive woman prosecutor in a sex crimes case can work against her. Juries might think she's keen on retribution because, like the plaintiff, she's a woman. This response is particularly likely in cases of date rape. To insure that a jury accepts the gravity of the matter, Fairstein sometimes assigns date rape cases to a male prosecutor. "When *he* gets impassioned about it and argumentative and tries to bring it home to a jury, it's not one of the girls saying [how serious the crime is]," says Fairstein.

In a jury trial Fairstein tries to "flush out" in voir dire jurors who have generally negative attitudes toward rape or sexual abuse victims, or those who can't understand what a date rape is. However, jurors sometimes tell the trial lawyer only what they think that lawyer wants to hear, rather than sharing their honest opinions. So Fairstein tries to identify general attitudes or mindsets, such as those of people who would in a date rape case blame the victim for inviting the man over to her house. Fairstein doesn't ask the juror about this situation directly, but asks instead "questions in which the same conservatism might surface." A blue-collar worker, for example, who tells Fairstein that his daughters are housewives and that he believes women belong in the home would not make a good juror for the prosecution in a date rape trial.

In the Teicher trial, however, Fairstein didn't have to worry about juror attitudes. On the first day, when Rothblatt waived his client's jury right, Fairstein breathed a sigh of relief. She had been concerned that a jury might not believe that Teicher behaved against his patients in the way she alleged. "Our biggest fear, which never was known to the defense attorney," says Fairstein, "was the fact that female jurors often have a great deal of difficulty understanding why an attractive, articulate man would sexually abuse women." University of Colorado jury studies involving two identical-fact situations surrounding rape by a professional man—with an attractive, well-dressed, clean-cut individual playing the defendant in one, and a physically unattractive, unkempt, unclean individual playing the defendant in the other—have shown that the attractive defendant is usually acquitted. "Throughout our investigation of this case, I found people saying to me [about Teicher]: 'He's so handsome. I can't imagine him having to do anything like that to get women.' Our biggest fear was picking a jury and having women—facts aside—sadly base their verdict on liking or not liking the defendant, finding him attractive and finding the women less attractive."

Before Rothblatt waived the jury, says Fairstein, "he had a great shot, from my experience with professional defendants, of either an acquittal or at least a hung jury with a lot of sympathy for the defendant, who had no criminal record, and who was going to take the stand [himself]." A jury was also likely to be more confused by a battle of experts than a judge would be, Fairstein adds. "On many, many levels that was the defense lawyer's biggest mistake." Instead of convincing twelve lay people of the dentist's crime, all Fairstein needed to do to get her verdict was to convince a knowledgeable and legally sophisticated judge.

What's more, Rothblatt based his bet that Cropper would favor his client, the defendant, on an incomplete picture of the judge. The defense lawyer saw only her predilection for protecting defendant rights. He didn't consider that Cropper might be more offended by a sex crimes case than by the drug crimes frequently tried before her. More importantly, "the thing he forgot," chuckles Fairstein today, "is that Judge Cropper is a woman." The prosecutor thought that she had a judge who, because she was female, might be more inclined to view the Teicher case equally, from the female patients' point of view as well as from the defendant's.

After the two lawyers' opening statements Fairstein kicked off her case with her strongest witness. She called undercover police detective Dorothy Beineix to the stand. Beineix had been considered a good undercover in the Teicher case in part because of her appearance. She was of the physical type that Teicher had gone for before. At one time Fairstein had even been concerned that the scanty and provocative clothes Beineix wore when she visited Teicher—a very short denim skirt and a tank T-shirt top—would bring charges of entrapment. But the dentist's lawyer never offered that defense. It wouldn't have helped fight the earlier patients' charges anyway. The defense chose instead to deny any abuse to any of the complainants.

Unlike Fairstein's opponent in the Chambers trial, Jack Litman, who is known for his energetic movement around the courtroom, Fairstein tends to remain still when questioning witnesses, preferring to stand at the far end of the jury box during direct and cross-examination. Her strategy is to draw the judge's and the jury's attention away from herself, and to the witness. "I want to be out of the picture," says Fairstein.

As Fairstein questioned Beineix, the undercover officer testified that she made an appointment with Teicher for July 20, 1976. She said that, after examining her, Teicher recommended a wisdom tooth extraction. The dentist checked Beineix's pulse, lifted Beineix's blouse off her braless breasts, and listened to her heart with a stethoscope.

When Beineix said she was concerned about possible pain with the extraction, Teicher told her he would sedate her so she would be "totally unconscious" and that she would experience "an erogenous experience" and would feel "very high." He asked her to bring someone with her to the appointment for the extraction because she would be unable to walk home alone.

Beineix arrived at Teicher's office wearing no bra, her pubic area dusted with fluorescent power, and a recording device in her handbag. She was taken to Examination Room No. 2, where Teicher usually performed his dental procedures. He again listened to her heart under her blouse and told her she would have "a very erotic experience." After he injected her in the arm, Beineix lost consciousness.

Teicher extracted Beineix's tooth.

As Beineix slowly regained consciousness, she recalled, Teicher told her to stand up and put her arms around him. She couldn't do so because of the medication, so Teicher lifted her out of the dental chair and stood her between his legs facing him. Teicher began to gyrate the lower part of his body against Beineix's. She testified that she was "scared to death." She started crying, she said, and she couldn't stop shaking. She remembered the other detectives entering the room to help her, and arresting Teicher, but she was overcome by her own sense of helplessness in coming out from under the sedation.

When Fairstein had finished questioning Beineix, she called to the stand two of the bona fide patients who had first complained about Teicher. "One of the things that I've always done in getting [initial] information from victims in sex offenses is explaining that I need to know as much about them, as much about what occurred, as the best defense attorney could know or find out," says Fairstein. She begins easing into those necessary revelations by asking the victim about herself. "In order for me to understand what occurred I need to know about you," she tells them. "I need to develop a relationship so you trust me, so I can ask you questions that are extremely personal in nature, about information that you might not normally be willing to give me—particularly because you don't know how it's going to be used." Fairstein, who gives her home phone number to victims suffering severely from their trauma, tries to explain the reasons for each question, particularly the embarrassing ones. "If you can explain to a victim why a question is being asked, you'll get cooperation," Fairstein notes. Sometimes the victims do call her at home to express their anxieties, to share more information, and to ask questions.

She also explains that under New York's rape shield law, a defense attorney cannot ask a victim about her past sexual experience. Fairstein will indicate which of her questions the defense attorney is allowed to ask, and which he is not. But she adds, "I need to know as much as he can find out. I can't protect you," she tells victims, "I can't keep things out of the courtroom unless I know about them." If, for example, a woman has recently moved to New York from Alabama, and the defense lawyer, after sending his investigator to Alabama, finds out that the victim had been convicted of prostitution and had had three abortions, he might ask her about that in court. But the information may not be relevant to the rape trial, says Fairstein. "I may be able, because of the shield law, to exclude it, but I can't do that after the question's been asked. The damage is done if his lawyer finds out what I don't know and says in front of the jury 'Isn't it a fact that last week before you got on a bus to come here . . .' "

If Fairstein knows the victim's background ahead of time, she can present certain information to the court herself, pretrial, and move to preclude the defense attorney from asking any questions related to it. Or if a written report—such as a gynecological report—contains irrelevant but potentially damaging information, Fairstein will move that the court edit the report to remove those portions before the defense attorney sees it.

Some might think that because Fairstein is a woman, she would be more successful than a man in questioning sex offense victims. Fairstein strongly disagrees: "One of the things I do in lecturing and training about this work is say that it is not the sex of the person who is working on the cases that's important, but the manner in which we treat the victims. My [male] deputy, a person who has worked with me for ten years, is one of the most successful people at this kind of work. There are a lot of male assistants in the office, and I really think it's their compassion and ability to relate to the victim that's important, and not the sex. Yet," adds Fairstein, "from time to time there are victims who do come in and make a point of saying 'I'm so much more comfortable talking to a woman than I am to a man.' "

Because Fairstein took over the Teicher case after the indictment, she did not handle the initial questioning of his victims; but she did prepare them for trial. When Fairstein called Susan Hyman, she testified about her visit to Teicher's office in September 1975. The dentist told Hyman she would need a wisdom tooth extracted and said that she would be sedated so she needn't worry about pain. According to Hyman's testimony, when she returned for the extraction, Teicher raised her blouse to examine her with a stethoscope (Hyman also wore no bra) and then injected her with a sedative in the arm. She lost consciousness.

Hyman testified that when she awoke she saw a penis in front of her face, closed her eyes, and after reopening them, saw a pair of trousers being zipped shut.

Hyman recounted to Judge Cropper her complaint to the police, and her efforts under their guidance to obtain an acknowledgment from Teicher of the abuse. (Investigators suggest that victims return to the alleged perpetrator of a sexual crime, equipped with a hidden microphone and recording device, explains Fairstein, "only when the victim is emotionally capable of carrying on a conversation with someone at whose hands she suffered a traumatic experience.")

Randi Carson, the third dental patient to notify the police of Teicher's abuse, followed Hyman on the stand. She testified that she had gone to see Teicher for her dental work in May 1976. She returned to have her tooth extracted on May twenty-fourth.

As Fairstein questioned Carson, she told Judge Cropper about her experience in Teicher's office. She explained that because she had not brought a friend to take her home, one of Teicher's assistants walked with her. After she arrived home, Carson testified, she noticed that she "had a soreness to the left side of the vagina." She also found that her underwear was wet. Carson explained to the judge her unsuccessful attempts to get Teicher to admit to his behavior while she wore the police department's hidden recorder.

Although Fairstein typically sits by herself at the counsel table, she does rely on a female paralegal or detective sitting behind her in the courtroom to keep eye contact with testifying victims and to offer them moral support. "Many victims come to us with family or friends," explains Fairstein, "but just as many come without." Sometimes the person closest to them is actually a witness in the trial and therefore cannot sit in the courtroom. Or sometimes Fairstein makes a strategic decision not to let family sit in because it affects the victim's ability to testify. They're embarrassed, or they don't want their families to know how bad the crime was. "Sometimes the victim, seeing her mother start to cry in the courtroom, will also start to cry," says the prosecutor. "I prefer she get through it without crying so the defense attorney won't say the next day, 'Look, the DA had her break down in the courtroom.' "

The press presents another challenge to the sexual abuse victim who is trying to maintain her composure in court. Fairstein regularly counsels sex crime victims not to deal with reporters.

"Too many issues are created before a trial," she says, and a victim's answers to press inquiries "could be used by the defense in cross-examining her," to the prosecution's detriment. To help with this problem, Fairstein's office never releases the name of a victim before a trial, and a "gentleman's agreement" with the press keeps them from printing the victim's name once a trial starts. However, the Teicher case attracted unusual media attention because of the stature of the defendant, and reporters did photograph the women who testified against the dentist. Fairstein tried as much as she could to arrange for the women to enter and leave the court in a way to avoid photographers and reporters. "It was one of the things we prepared them for," the prosecutor says of the press attention. "They were told it would be almost inevitable."

However, none of Fairstein's concerns about victims' feelings keep her from being direct and graphic in court. Several times during the Teicher trial she played the videotape of Teicher abusing Beineix. As expected, Rothblatt challenged its use in the investigation and the way in which the tape's content was relayed in court. In a colloquy before Judge Cropper, Rothblatt questioned whether the detective who sat in the basement of Teicher's building watching the video monitor as the camera recorded the dentist and his "patient" could testify as to what he saw. Rothblatt said that the detective, a police department electronics technician, should not testify about his observation on the monitor because the recording didn't represent the entire truth:

Rothblatt: This, in my judgment, is the most critical evidence in this case. My client's liberty literally stands or falls on what is on that film, and I said this in my opening, Your Honor, and I reaffirm it now. We are not ashamed and we would have been delighted if there were better pictures that took place. We want whatever was recorded to be seen with all its implications, and it is a worse distortion of evidence to have a police officer who has a bias and looking at the videotape, to give his version of what he sees. That's what I want Your Honor to see, and that's what we are—

The Court: I don't see that. I don't see that that is any more of a bias than any other witness who would testify to whatever it is that he saw.

Rothblatt: Well, Judge, if the officer were in the room testifying to what he observed, obviously he is in a better position to tell us what took place than anyone else. People who are physically present in the room can give an account. What is this officer proposing to do or what is this testimony proposing to do? This officer proposes to explain what you and I will see on a film. He sees no more and no less; he sees precisely that, and he is giving his interpretation of . . .

Fairstein: It is the primary signal which then became permanently recorded on the tape, that's what he was looking at. . . . The analogy that I used earlier would be . . . to officers testifying to a conversation which they heard as it occurred, although it was also being audiotaped. . . .

Rothblatt: What I am saying is that not only is his version of what took place not a total picture of what took place in the room, but it is less than that, and he is giving you his version of less than what you will see. . . .

Fairstein: The testimony elicited will not be opinion testimony. This is the officer's observation and includes testimony concerning the entry and exit of other persons into and out of the dentist's treatment room.

Rothblatt: It doesn't show the whole room, he doesn't have—

Fairstein: You are talking about two different things [the use of the detective's testimony and the completeness of the video image].

The Court: The objection is overruled.

Fairstein presented the rest of her case by calling the detective to the stand, and four other detectives who took part in the camera installation and monitoring. Repeatedly asking each of the detectives what he or she saw, Fairstein drove home her message for the judge. For example, Fairstein asked Lieutenant Louis De Martinis what he observed on the monitor:

De Martinis: I observed Dr. Teicher bare [Beineix's] chest, expose her breasts, place the stethoscope on her chest. I observed him take her off the dentist chair, hold her between his legs.

Fairstein: Were any part of either of their bodies touching each other?

De Martinis: It appeared that the lower part of their bodies were touching. . . .

Fairstein: And was Miss Beineix facing the doctor or was she facing away from him?

De Martinis: She was facing the doctor. The doctor had his arms around her. His hands then went up underneath her blouse, in the back, and came around to the front portion. His hands were then—then went down to her buttocks. At that point I called for the backup man to come in.

Fairstein: And did you continue to make observations on your monitor?

De Martinis: Yes.

Fairstein: Could you tell us how much longer, approximately, you did make observations and what, if anything, you observed?

De Martinis: For a short period of time, possibly a minute, two minutes, three minutes, I observed him caressing her buttocks, and then I noticed—

Rothblatt: I object to that. I submit that we ought to have a description of what he determines as caressing and not a confusion, I mean—

The Court: Webster's?

Rothblatt: There seems to be—

The Court: What did you see, Officer?

De Martinis: I saw him with his hands on her buttocks, on her, on her cheeks, if it would, and I saw him sort of making a gyrating motion with the lower part of his body.

Fairstein: Was he doing any dental work at the time?

De Martinis: Not at this time, no.

When the defense's turn came, Rothblatt relied on Teicher's dental colleagues and friends to support the defendant in court. Rothblatt first called Teicher's partner, and then three of his dental assistants. The first defense expert, a dentist specializing in dental anesthesiology named Dr. Harold L. Hamburg, testified about Teicher's method of anesthesia, a fairly rare procedure called conscious sedation. (The rarity of the sedation technique "led to a lot of problems in our finding an expert," recalls Fairstein today.) Teicher administered to his patients Valium and Seconal so they remained conscious as opposed to being anesthetized and losing consciousness. But at the same time, the patients were not aware of what was happening and appeared to be conscious. After the Valium and Seconal injection, Teicher gave his patients a local anesthetic for the dental work.

Hamburg and another defense expert, Dr. Norman Trieger, testified that they had watched the videotape of Teicher with Beineix and that the dental work itself appeared to be proper. Both also said that recovery procedures for conscious sedation vary from dentist to dentist.

When Fairstein cross-examined Hamburg, he admitted that the procedures Teicher had apparently developed appeared actually to be a combination of two techniques. Neither had been medically approved for fifty years:

Fairstein: Can you tell us, please, the name of that dental or anesthesial or recovery procedure that you saw for that four-and-a-half-minute period in that film?

Hamburg: You know, resuscitation—I'm going to be just a drop long with it. Then I'll answer your question. Resuscitation has filled up to recent years with so many techniques, there's six thousand techniques and if there are seven thousand dentists, there are seven thousand techniques.

The Court: Well, Doctor, let me interrupt your long-winded explanation. Do you think there is a name for that technique that you saw, and if you know, what is it?

Hamburg: To me it looked like a modification, because all you could see was a back side. A modification of a Sylvester and the old Howard technique. . . .

Fairstein: Now, Doctor, in performance of that technique is the patient facing the physician or dentist who is performing this procedure?

Hamburg: The patient is facing—well, the technique was done on a collapsed body that was, you know, prone.

Fairstein: The technique was done on a body that was in a prone position, is that right, Doctor?

Hamburg: Yes.

Fairstein: Did you ever see or know of that technique done on a patient in a standing position?

Hamburg: Not personally, but there are dentists—but dentists develop so many techniques.

Fairstein: Doctor, do you know of that technique ever being done on a patient standing?

Hamburg: I, personally, don't know.

Following Hamburg, Rothblatt called out his character witnesses, including two nuns and a priest who had been Teicher's patients. As with the anesthesiology expert, Fairstein went straight to the point when she cross-examined Sister Patrice Murphy. Fairstein wanted to make it clear that Teicher treated the nun after he had been arrested and charged; and that the dentist then applied the resuscitation method he had claimed to use on Beineix precisely because it would support his defense. Even then, Fairstein showed, it wasn't exactly the same procedure:

Fairstein: Sister, on what date did you have dental work performed?

Sister: I don't remember the exact date. I remember that it was early February.

Fairstein: And that was your first visit to the doctor?

Sister: Yes.

Fairstein: And could you tell us how you were dressed on that date?

Sister: I think I had slacks and a blouse, possibly a blouse and jacket because it was winter.

Fairstein: Were you wearing a bra on that date?

Sister: Yes. . . .

Fairstein: You testified that you remember coming to, awakening from the drugs, is that correct?

Sister: Yes.

Fairstein: And at the point which you awakened, the doctor asked you to stand or assisted you from the chair, is that correct?

Sister: Yes. . . .

Fairstein: How long was the encounter that you had with him, from the time that you got out of the dental chair until he assisted you out of the room?

Sister: Two minutes, maybe.

Fairstein: During that two-minute period, was he ever seated on his stool with his legs around your body?

Sister: No.

Fairstein: Did he ever hold your body against his?

Sister: No.

Fairstein: Did he ever put his arms around your back as in a hug?

Sister: No.

Fairstein: Did he ever place his hands on your buttocks?

Sister: No.

Fairstein: Did he ever put your lower portion of your body against his groin area? . . .

Of course, the tanned and gray-haired Teicher spoke on his own behalf, both eloquently and at length. "He spoke with great sincerity," recalls Fairstein, "and I knew I had an actor on the stand. He had far more experience on the stage than I had in the courtroom at that point."

Teicher explained his early schooling and training in dentistry and anesthesia, and he explained the development and desirability of conscious sedation. "We have been able for more than half a century to eliminate pain in dental treatment," testified Teicher. "The problem is, will that patient voluntarily come into our office and sit down and allow us to perform this painless technique? We have found out that there is a whole hoard of people requiring massive dental work, who will not come into a dental office because of their fear of the injection, the needle and our dental service." With conscious sedation, Teicher explained, patients are not unconscious and unable to respond—but they feel nothing and lose their fear. Teicher explained his training and technique in such detail and with so many digressions that the judge repeatedly stopped the dentist to ask him to stay on course. "Marvin's biggest problem," says his assisting defense attorney, Peskin, "was that he had a big mouth. He talked too much and said inappropriate things. That came across as being his *bête noire.*"

The dentist went on in his testimony to describe the way he handled his patients, and how he introduced them individually to the procedure of conscious sedation:

Teicher: I tell them that they will have a feeling of euphoria, and the patients will look at me and it is totally Greek, and so, I will tell them that they will have a feeling of well-being. They may feel that they are flying. In modern jargon, with youngsters, I will tell them they will space out a little and have good vibrations. I will tell them that they will have no recollection of the experience, and basically they will have an amnesia; that they will not have any recall of the dental experience as such. . . . I will tell them that they should not be alarmed if they should have any other type of dreams; they can have a melancholia, they can come out depressed, they can wake up crying. They can have confusion, hyperexcitability, they can hallucinate.

The Court: You tell them all that?

Teicher: I tell them that.

Then Teicher explained how he brought patients back from the sedation, asking them to stand up, to face him while he is seated, to stand between his legs, and to lift their arms breathing in and out while he compresses their rib cage and repeatedly tells them to breathe deeply. Teicher even demonstrated the technique on his wife in the judge's robing room. When Fairstein replayed the videotape of Beineix, Teicher narrated it, explaining his every movement.

Teicher also testified that Valium can cause patients to hallucinate—a ready explantion for the patients' "sexual fantasies"—and he produced the patient inserts for the drug that indicated this possibility. But when Fairstein cross-examined Teicher, he could not identify for the court any patients other than the complainants who had experienced hallucinations following treatment, even though he had administered Valium and Seconal more than five hundred times.

For her rebuttal, the prosecutor called her expert, Dr. C. Richard Bennett, a professor of anesthesiology at the University of Pittsburgh. Bennett had studied and worked with one of the originators of the conscious sedation procedure. When that doctor died, Bennett took his position at the university.

"I was very concerned, not wanting a "you pay, I say' witness," recalls Fairstein. Unlike defense counsel, state attorneys can't afford the best hired-gun experts, anyway. "I thought a good solution would be to have an academic," continues the prosecutor. "I tried the local dental schools, [but] Teicher had been affiliated with NYU, and nobody from NYU wanted to be involved. Nobody from Columbia wanted to be involved because it was NYU."

Fairstein had found chapters in several dental texts about the conscious sedation technique, but she located only one entire book particularly devoted to it. It was written by Bennett, and when Fairstein called to ask his advice on experts, he agreed to testify himself. Young and articulate, Bennett was very supportive of the conscious sedation technique, but also very offended that someone could give it such a bad name. Bennett also agreed to help Fairstein prepare her cross-examination of Teicher. The anesthesiology professor helped her anticipate what Teicher might say, and plan how to combat his answers through her cross. Together, Bennett and Fairstein went over her questions, Teicher's possible answers, and her follow-up questions. Although the DA's office normally pays its expert witnesses about $125 a day, Fairstein recalls paying Bennett only the cost of his airfare and hotel accommodations.

When the prosecutor stood in the courtroom and announced, "The people call Dr. Charles Richard Bennett," she enjoyed one of the few "Perry Mason" moments of her life. It so happened that when Fairstein had cross-examined Teicher, she asked him who the leading experts in the conscious sedation field were, and who he relied on for his education and advice. Unexpectedly, among the names Teicher provided was Fairstein's own expert. Fairstein remembers that, two days later, she called Bennett to the stand: "I looked to see what the reaction was from the defense table—and the bottom fell out."

Fairstein had little difficulty showing that her expert was better qualified than the defendant's. All of those who testified on Teicher's behalf, says the prosecutor, were his friends. They all had connections to Teicher. Fairstein's expert, on the other hand, had no connections to the victims nor to the prosecution. In cases where the battle of expert witnesses is more challenging, Fairstein seeks to find academics who are specialized in a small field of expertise, rather than people who have more general knowledge and who testify regularly on a number of issues. The latter tend to be viewed as "professional experts," and their opinions may not be taken as seriously as those of someone who participates less regularly in court proceedings. Fairstein's preference in experts sharply contrasts with that of many personal injury lawyers, who feel that experts who testify regularly make the strongest impression.

In the Teicher trial, anesthesiology professor Bennett testified that he had administered or supervised the use of conscious sedation between 30,000 and 40,000 times. Not one of these patients had developed respiratory problems, said Bennett. It wasn't possible because the patients were conscious and their respiratory systems were active. A recovery procedure such as the one Teicher uses is therefore superfluous, Bennett testified.

Nor was it medically recommended. Bennett explained that placing a sedated patient upright can cause blood to drain from the brain, making the patient unconscious. And compressing the rib cage prevents air from entering the lungs, rather than helping to fill the lungs with air as would be mandated in cases of respiratory distress.

"If in fact she had been in respiratory distress, which we disputed," explains Fairstein today, "[Teicher] was doing the thing that would most endanger [Beineix], lifting her out of the chair and preventing her from getting oxygen."

Furthermore, continued Bennett in his testimony, single doses of Valium do not cause hallucinations:

Fairstein: Could you tell us, please, in your experience working with Valium, whether you have had any patients report to you his hallucinatory effects?

Bennett: Never.

Fairstein: Are you aware of any patients, cases that you have administered or supervised, who have experienced erotic hallucinations?

Bennett: Never, no.

Fairstein: Is Valium in your experience, when it is given on a single-dosage basis, a hallucinatory drug?

Bennett: No.

Fairstein: Could you explain that?

Bennett: Well, there have been hallucinations reported, following withdrawal of orally administered Valium that had been administered over a protracted period of time. When a patient is suddenly taken off the Valium, they may have some hallucinations, dreams, what have you. There are to the best of my knowledge only three cases reported in which intravenous Valium was implicated in the production of hallucinations. The three cases occurred when the drug was in the clinical testing phase, prior to the release for use by the general medical profession. In these instances Valium was being used to treat delirium tremors, to treat alcoholic patients. And you no doubt know, delirium tremors are frequently accompanied by hallucinations in their own way. . . . I believe it became mandatory at that point for the package insert to state that Valium can produce hallucinations. It is my understanding that if one episode of anything occurs when the drug is in the clinical-testing phase, it must be included in the package insert.

Fairstein: And you say those three experiences known to you, are they known from your own clinical experience with the drug? . . .

Bennett: I have not seen any patient experience hallucinations after having been administered intravenous Valium. As a matter of fact, the drug is used quite often as an antihallucinogen, to treat patients that have psychosis, neurotic syndromes, acute alcoholic withdrawal, and so forth. . . .

Fairstein: And would you tell us, please, if the effect of Valium when it is administered to a patient for conscious sedation is to cause that patient to hallucinate in any sense?

Bennett: No, it is not.

Fairstein: Do you tell your patients before you administer the drug to them that they will experience dreams, hallucinations, space dreams, a fantasyland, anything like that?

Bennett: Nothing of the sort. The only—the mention that I make to a patient of how they will feel is that they will be comfortably relaxed, awake, aware of their surroundings, essentially that's it.

Fairstein: I have no further questions.

In his closing Rothblatt tried to argue that regardless of the validity of Teicher's treatment, it was a treatment that worked for him and the one he used on all of his patients. "Now, Your Honor, I don't think that this is a case where Your Honor has to decide whether the resuscitation technique of Dr. Teicher, the pressing of the rib cage and the oral suggestions that followed, are of the most ideal techniques, that the top people in the dental profession could practice, this form of sedation, or whether or not his resuscitation techniques are a little antiquated or obsolete. From his training as an anesthesiologist—that went back in years, in his career—I think that is completely irrelevant.

"The fact that—the fact of the matter remains and everybody agrees, including Dr. Bennett, the prosecution's expert, that in the final analysis, with every doctor or dentist, anybody in the healing arts, the final analysis of what technique is best for the individual practitioner is what he finds from his clinical experience over the years works for him."

As for the video, Rothblatt argued that there was no evidence from the film that Teicher's hands were on Beineix's breasts, they were on the side of her back, and that the areas he had touched were not private parts and did not constitute sexual abuse.

Rothblatt also argued that Carson's allegation that Teicher had put her hand on his penis was not sexual abuse under the law. The statute specifically said that the abuse was from the actor touching the private parts of the victim, and not the victim touching the actor, or the defendant.

Fairstein's turn came. The prosecutor sums up last in a state criminal case, which is a tremendous advantage, she says, because her words and arguments are freshest in the jurors' minds when they begin to deliberate. Fairstein stands very close to the jury box for her closing. "You want that jury to be paying attention to nothing else," she explains. "You don't want them looking over at the defendant, whose lawyer has him looking like he will cry, shaking his head no."

In the Teicher closing, Fairstein painstakingly chronicled the dentist's behavior with each of the three women complainants. A compulsive note-taker, Fairstein had every point of her summation listed on a yellow legal pad before her, with different points marked in different colors, depending on their importance. "I always feel I don't want to take a chance that the one thing I leave out" will lose the case, she explains. In this respect Fairstein differs from some lawyers who try to narrow the issues in a case, thinking that too many ideas will confuse a jury. Jurors sometimes attach great significance to really insignificant things, something that seems to be a total red herring or a minor part of the case, says Fairstein of her approach. "We've all found that if you don't address it, you've got eleven people who are right on target, and you've got juror number twelve saying, 'Well, she never talked about the color of the defendant's underwear. Why would a women like that be wearing leopard print underwear?' " Fairstein does balance her thorough coverage, however, with an awareness of "the danger of putting the jury to sleep," and she works at maintaining juror attention through eye contact and some movement. "Fortunately," says Fairstein, "sex offenses are a little more interesting than car thefts." And over time, Fairstein has cut back on her crib sheets, and she may even look at them infrequently while speaking, concentrating instead on her eye contact. But she wasn't always so facile. During Fairstein's first trial, a robbery case, the judge called her to the bench and admonished her under his breath: "This isn't a book report. You don't read it like a book report. It's a summation."

Teicher, began Fairstein in her closing for that trial, talked his way out of an investigation after the first reported abuse, but nonetheless he abused another patient. "Mr. Rothblatt claims that this is absurd; that no one in his right mind would commit the same act, if that's in fact what he was doing, so close in time, one month after the [first] incident," said Fairstein to the judge. "Quite the contrary, Your Honor, it shows the nature of the defendant's sickness. He was able to talk his way out of the first incident. The police believed him. He had literature [inserts from the Valium packaging] which used the word 'hallucinations.' He had beaten the system and he was quite free to try it again on Susan Hyman."

Fairstein then recounted Teicher's behavior with his patients, supporting the women's versions of what happened, and refuting the dentist's. She attacked the defense witnesses, one by one, noting that Teicher's partner had never seen the videotape; that his assistants who doubled as receptionists were not competent licensed dental assistants or hygienists, nor were they familiar with his treatment; that the character witnesses were meaningless. "We assume that any professional man at the age of fifty-three, [who] practiced for thirty years, would have a slew of friends and acquaintances who would attest to his good reputation," said Fairstein, "but obviously not a single one of them was present with him in the office on the date that these things occurred." All of the patients whom the defense called were treated after Beineix, added Fairstein, so their testimony was arranged for the purposes of the trial. And none of them had been ventilated after their dental procedures as Beineix had been, if in fact, said Fairstein, any of them were ventilated at all.

"I submit, common sense and intelligence would convince any of us," concluded Fairstein, "that a dentist's hands belong in our mouths."

Fairstein won. Teicher was convicted of two counts of sexual abuse; the judge acquitted him of the third count, involving Susan Hyman, because the prosecution did not prove beyond a reasonable doubt that Teicher had acted toward Hyman as he did for the purpose of his own sexual gratification. But Judge Cropper did say in her opinion that she found Teicher's testimony "contrived, self-serving, completely unconvincing, and not worthy of belief." She later sentenced him to only four months in prison, which wasn't surprising because he had no prior criminal record. More importantly, says Fairstein, Teicher lost his dentist's license. Who knows how many women he had mistreated over the years—or how many he would have mistreated, she wonders.

As Fairstein had suspected, the defense lawyers challenged

the videotaping, among other issues, in their appeal. The Appellate Division upheld the videotaped investigation in its opinion of February 21, 1980. The following year New York's highest court, the Court of Appeals for the State of New York, also affirmed the conviction.

Said Fairstein of the final outcome: "I think we've made our point." And she recalls to this day that one of the highlights of her career was when Judge Cropper told her after the Teicher trial "that that was the best cross-examination of an expert witness and a defendant that she had heard."

HOWARD L. WEITZMAN

Wyman, Bautzer, Kuchel & Silbert, Los Angeles

Greg Gorman

At six-thirty on a Friday morning in October 1983, with John Z. DeLorean's trial on charges of conspiring to sell and distribute $60 million of cocaine scheduled for the following month, attorney Howard Weitzman's answering service rang his Pacific Palisades home. The answering service said that *Hustler* magazine publisher Larry Flynt was trying to reach Weitzman.

"I took the phone call, thinking of course that Larry Flynt had been arrested on some porno case in California," says Weitzman, "and Flynt told me he had the videotapes." Weitzman knew Flynt was referring to the government's undercover videotapes, including one showing DeLorean drinking champagne before an open cocaine-filled suitcase.

"Great, I have them also," the forty-nine-year-old Weitzman recalls responding, deciding at the same time that the caller was a crank. "One of the things you do get as a result of a high-profile case is a lot of calls from strange people," notes the attorney. When the person on the other end of the line invited Weitzman and DeLorean to his house to review the tapes, Weitzman refused and hung up. "I got five phone calls that day from a 'Larry Flynt.' I returned none of them," says Weitzman.

That evening Don Hewitt, executive producer of CBS's "60 Minutes" news program, also called. He had met with Flynt and previewed the videotapes. When Hewitt described to Weitzman what he had seen, DeLorean's lawyer knew he had a problem. Hewitt told Weitzman he was going to put the tapes on the air that very Sunday night. Weitzman argued with the newscaster. DeLorean would never get a fair trial with such a public airing because it would bias potential jurors, insisted Weitzman.

"He says to me, 'Look, I'll give you the opportunity of going on "60 Minutes" and explaining what happened,' " recalls Weitzman. "I said, 'Jeez, I've got a better idea, Don. Maybe you can get two 800 numbers—one for guilt, one for innocence—and we can just try the case Sunday night.' "

It was typical Weitzman. Feisty, irreverent, refusing to be bullied by anyone, the University of Southern California physical education major and baseball player takes to a case like a street kid fighting off his rival gang. Despite his traditional lawyer's business attire, the five-foot-seven-and-a-half-inch Weitzman even has a roughish, boyish look about him. But Weitzman's everyday relaxed style and casual banter, youthful face and easy smile, only mask his willingness to fight—and his eagerness to win.

Weitzman's sports background has helped him in this way. "The main characteristic Howard has which is part of his success, apart from his intellectual capacity," says DeLorean, "is that it probably hurts him more to lose than anybody in the world—because he is so intensely competitive—and he is able to channel that, in a rational way, into constructive purpose in the courtroom."

"I'd much rather be the lawyer that won, than the lawyer that lost, the DeLorean case," agrees Weitzman, who was in New York preparing to run in the 1982 New York marathon when he was first called to defend his famous client.

When DeLorean hired Weitzman, the attorney was practicing with his own firm, a small five-lawyer practice called Weitzman & Ré. At the time, Weitzman already had an impressive record as a criminal defense lawyer. He had successfully defended Mary Brunner, who according to Weitzman's resumé is the only [Charles] Manson family girl charged with and not convicted of murder. Weitzman's resumé also lists Louis Tom Dragna, alleged southern California crime leader, who was acquitted of charges that he ordered the murder of a government informant; Jimmy "the Weasel" Frattiano testified in that case. Weitzman represented Barbara Mouzin, the alleged head of the "Grandma Mafia," in a highly publicized trial involving cocaine and millions of dollars of money laundering. While Weitzman initially lost the Grandma Mafia case, the verdict was reversed in part on appeal, and Mouzin's sentence was reduced from twenty-five to ten years.

Despite the damning "60 Minutes" videotapes, Weitzman won an acquittal for DeLorean and became himself an instant international celebrity. When DeLorean was charged later in Detroit with racketeering, fraud, and income-tax evasion, Weitzman also agreed to represent the automaker in that trial. Again, Weitzman was victorious, and this time he cemented his place in legal history.

But before the Detroit case actually went to trial, Weitzman left his small firm and joined as a senior partner a large corporate practice, now called Wyman, Bautzer, Kuchel & Silbert. "I had begun [in my own small firm] to represent clients in areas that required some different expertise, and I needed some different support," says Weitzman, who occupies a spacious executive office in Wyman, Bautzer's Century City high-rise building and who sits on the firm's executive, management, and compensation committees. "I know a lot of people in this town, and I've been asked for a number of years to do certain things and represent certain people," continues the lawyer, describing himself as "a man who works all of the time at a pace a lot of people don't care for." But with a small firm Weitzman had found that he "consistently turned [new business] down. I don't have to do that anymore," he now says.

Along with DeLorean, Weitzman's recent famous clients include Valerie Terrigno, the declared gay activist and first mayor of West Hollywood, charged with embezzling grant money from the U.S. government, and Cathy Evelyn Smith, who injected actor John Belushi with heroin and cocaine during the week before he died and who pleaded no contest to involuntary manslaughter. Smith was recently paroled from prison. Weitzman also represented rock singer Ozzy Osbourne in a case alleging that lyrics to two of Osbourne's songs caused a teenager to commit suicide. That case eventually was dismissed. Actors Marlon Brando and Sean Penn and palimony lawyer Marvin M. Mitchelson also retain Weitzman to represent them.

With a big firm, says Weitzman, who has a young son with his third wife, Margaret, as well as a teenage son from his second marriage, "I don't have to worry about the overhead. Although you don't translate that into dollars and cents, emotionally and pressure-wise it's a major difference."

Weitzman claims that he doesn't make a lot more money than he did with his own small practice, although working with his new firm is "very rewarding" financially, and the opportunity to make even more is there. For Weitzman's work on the cocaine trial, and for much of the preparation on DeLorean's Detroit trial, DeLorean paid his lawyer with a San Diego ranch—valued at $2.5 million. Wyman, Bautzer billed DeLorean for Weitzman's additional work on the Detroit trial, work completed after the attorney had joined that firm.

Even with his broader practice and power base, Weitzman

to this day primarily sees himself as a trial attorney. "What you have going for you if you are an experienced litigator, and if you've been fortunate enough to have some success," says Weitzman, "is the fear from the other side that you have no qualms about walking into a courthouse, putting twelve people in the box, and going to work. And I, of course, have no problem doing that. I kind of like that."

John DeLorean concurs. "If you ever get in trouble," he says when asked about his lawyer, "hire him."

To this day, the public still doesn't understand fully John DeLorean's cocaine trial. Lasting from early March up through mid-August 1984, the proceeding attracted nationwide publicity, in part because DeLorean, a General Motors exeuctive before founding his now-defunct, Northern Ireland–based DeLorean Motor Company, is himself a colorful figure, and in part because the government tracked and prosecuted the rags-to-riches automaker with the zeal and tactics befitting a best-selling crime thriller.

DeLorean—with his statuesque, aristocratic mien and shock of silver-white hair—captured the imagination of the American public. He and his third wife, glamorous fashion model Christina Ferrare DeLorean, lived a wealthy, flamboyant, jet-set existence, with homes and business ventures in the U.S. and abroad. DeLorean had broken away from his fast-track but controversial career at General Motors to charge ahead on his own. In 1978 he convinced the British government to provide financing and subsidies for manufacturing his innovative gull-winged sports car in a Northern Ireland plant. But DeLorean Motor Company was soon plagued by strife and financial difficulties. The automaker grew increasingly desperate to find new ways to keep his dream and his lifestyle intact.

In June 1982, James Timothy Hoffman, a former neighbor near DeLorean's San Diego vacation ranch, whose young boy at one time played with DeLorean's son Zachary, paid a call on

DeLorean. DeLorean did not know that Hoffman was a convicted narcotics smuggler, turned government informant.

DeLorean says that Hoffman contacted him to suggest investments in his motor company; during the trial Hoffman maintained that the calls were strictly social. Whatever the nature of their initial discussions, in July, Hoffman introduced DeLorean to Benedict J. Tisa, an FBI agent posing as James Benedict, a crooked banker who laundered drug profits. In mid-September, Hoffman also introduced DeLorean to William Morgan Hetrick, an aircraft company owner whom the government suspected of transporting illegal drugs. Hetrick would later plead guilty to narcotics charges.

According to trial testimony, Hoffman said that DeLorean—who was facing extreme financial pressures from his failing motor company—asked about entering into a large drug deal. DeLorean's conversations with Tisa, AKA "James Benedict," and Hetrick and still another undercover agent, who posed as an underground drug dealer named John Vicenza, allegedly grew more serious. Ultimately, the government agents claimed, DeLorean conspired with Morgan Hetrick to smuggle cocaine from Colombia into the U.S.

In preliminary filings and during the trial Weitzman gave DeLorean's version of the story. Weitzman argued that Hoffman, who knew about DeLorean's financial crisis, had specifically targeted DeLorean for an undercover operation. Weitzman said that Hoffman contacted DeLorean just to set him up in a drug deal to help pay off Hoffman's obligations to the government that came with being an informant. Weitzman accused Hoffman of lying to the government about how he commenced his conversation with DeLorean: James Timothy Hoffman had called DeLorean pretending to talk about potential investments in DeLorean's motor company, Weitzman insisted. The lawyer proved that DeLorean even mailed company documents to the man.

And while DeLorean thought Hoffman was offering to arrange investments in the DeLorean Motor Company, James Hoffman was telling his government superiors that the discussions were drug-related, said Weitzman. "In carefully guarded conversations between July and September 1982, Hoffman continued the double entendre," wrote the defense lawyer in documents filed with the U.S. District Court in Los Angeles. "To DeLorean, the discussions concerned legitimate investments and floor planning (short-term loans). Hoffman explained these conversations to his superiors as narcotics related." When DeLorean's neighbor tried to turn the conversation with DeLorean directly to narcotics as another alternative for raising money, DeLorean tried to steer the discussion back toward legitimate investment through a bank, added Weitzman. According to Weitzman's court filings, DeLorean at one point even tried to back out of the discussions, to which both FBI agent Tisa, posing as banker "James Benedict," and James Hoffman responded with threats. Eventually the undercover agents convinced DeLorean to give "Benedict's" bank, as a show of interest, a worthless assignment of nonexistent DeLorean Motor Company stock. All the while the agents still promised to find him new investors.

In the end, concluded Weitzman when describing his view of the case, Hoffman did finally orchestrate a drug deal, but it was one that bypassed DeLorean completely. The money was to be flown from the banker "Benedict," who pretended to believe that DeLorean's worthless stock was collateral for a loan to make the drug purchase, to cocaine trafficker William Morgan Hetrick. In turn, the cocaine would pass from Hetrick to a government investigator posing as underground drug dealer "John Vicenza." Then the coke would go to the informant Hoffman for distribution. Despite all the discussion surrounding DeLorean, he was to put up no money for obtaining the drugs, nor was he to participate in selling them, insisted Weitzman during the trial. DeLorean hadn't agreed with Hetrick to go in on any kind of deal—much less a drug deal, says the lawyer.

The strongest evidence favoring the government's version of

the transaction was the October 19, 1982, videotape of DeLorean and the undercover agents with the suitcase of cocaine. But Weitzman told the jury that the government arranged for the videotaping just to cement its case against DeLorean. The undercover investigators called DeLorean to say that Hetrick had come through with funds for the motor company, and that the first $10 million was ready. The agents insisted that DeLorean fly to Los Angeles to pick up the money personally and to celebrate with them. So DeLorean met them in a room in the Sheraton La Reina near the Los Angeles International Airport. As he sat there, the undercover agents carried in a suitcase of cocaine and opened it before DeLorean, with hidden cameras rolling. The resulting videotape showing the automaker sitting before the suitcase of cocaine topped off more than one hundred earlier undercover video and audio tapes. It was immediately after this last filming that DeLorean was arrested.

At the trial, through sixteen weeks of dramatic testimony, almost all of the witnesses appeared on behalf of the prosecution. Weitzman, assisted by his partner Donald Ré, only called a handful to speak for his client. The government took about four months to present its case; Weitzman took about a week and a half.

What won the day for DeLorean was Weitzman's cross-examination of the prosecution witnesses. In fact, when DeLorean bumped into one of the jurors sometime later, she told him about her reaction to Weitzman's aggressive questioning. "She said by the time [Weitzman] finished the first witness, the FBI agent Tisa [who played the part of the crooked banker Benedict], that the case was all over, the jury knew that the whole thing was a fabrication and that I would never be convicted," relates DeLorean. "It was absolutely clear, and everything after that was a formality."

The jury, when deliberating, actually broke down on its first vote as follows: Seven found DeLorean not guilty because no crime had been committed. Five could not make a decision as to whether a crime was committed. But all agreed that no matter what happened, they would have found DeLorean entrapped. "Therefore, before they ever got to that issue," explains Weitzman, those five "decided to agree with the majority because they believed either way they would find him innocent."

Still, most people today think that DeLorean was acquitted because Weitzman proved his client had been entrapped. What the jury verdict said, however, was that DeLorean, whose automobile company later declared bankruptcy, was not guilty of the charge against him. The jury found DeLorean not guilty of conspiring to distribute cocaine; the jury decided that DeLorean had never committed the crime in the first place. Therefore, explains Weitzman, DeLorean was not found innocent simply because he had been entrapped: "To be entrapped you have to have committed the criminal act—and then the theory is that somebody made you do it." In the cocaine trial, says Weitzman, "we proved that John never engaged in a conspiracy to import, distribute, possess, or sell drugs."

It took the jurors eight days to reach their decision, says Weitzman. "Asked why it took them that long, they said they wanted to be as fair as possible to the government."

In the DeLorean case Weitzman shows how he begins winning an acquittal long before a prosecution witness ever takes the stand.

For one, Weitzman papered the court with pretrial motions. Some of the fifty or sixty he filed were procedural in nature; others were discovery requests, including Freedom of Information Act motions, enabling Weitzman to obtain valuable but previously unavailable documents. Among these documents were telephone toll records that proved there were a number of calls not recorded even when the government said they were, and other papers showing how the government preplanned the taped meetings with DeLorean. Weitzman learned, for example, that the informant Hoffman's toll record listed fifty-two unrecorded telephone contacts. "If their case was airtight, what in the world would they care if we got the toll records or not?" Weitzman queries of the government's initial refusal to turn over that information. "When they fight you tooth and nail, you've got to think there's something there."

Actually, the judge hearing the case, U.S. District Judge Robert Takasugi, denied the majority of Weitzman's pretrial motions, a result Weitzman says is not unusual for any lawyer. Still, every pretrial effort was fruitful, at least in small ways, says Weitzman. "Motion practice such as we were engaged in, and in any big case, does provide you with another positive aspect," explains the attorney. "It requires the government to respond in writing. With each government response you begin to get some insight into where they are coming from."

Also before the trial began, Weitzman fought desperately to counter negative publicity, which he thought was damaging to his client. The "60 Minutes" fiasco was just one skirmish in that battle. Weitzman also moved to seal from public view all of the government's pleadings as they were filed because he disagreed with what they said. "The press was printing it all, and it just got worse and worse against John," explains Weitzman. On this pretrial motion Judge Takasugi did rule in Weitzman's favor—indicating that he would review the pleadings himself and decide which ones would not prejudice DeLorean's case and could, therefore, be released publicly; but that ruling was later overturned by the Ninth Circuit Court of Appeals.

Weitzman similarly sought to negate the onslaught of bad press when he began the voir dire, or jury selection. The defense attorney tried to find jurors who weren't biased by the publicity, relying in part on their answers to a lengthy juror questionnaire. And when questioning the potential jurors, Weitzman openly tried to convince them that they could reach a verdict contrary to their initial inclinations after seeing the "60 Minutes" videotapes.

Once the trial did begin, Weitzman used his forte, cross-examination, to its fullest. "Howard has a tremendous analytical mind," says DeLorean. "He can take this diversity of facts and somehow recognize an anomaly when it comes along. This has made him probably—at least [from] everything I've ever seen—the best cross-examiner alive." By the time a witness takes the stand, Weitzman knows everything about that person and his involvement in the case—so if the witness shades the truth or hedges, Weitzman is quick to pick up on that point.

Weitzman was "just awesome in the way he would sense that somebody was not telling the truth or that the story didn't hang together," continues DeLorean. "He'd look for the little crack between the pieces and then penetrate it. Especially in [this case] where a number of people were fabricating a story—they always get the main part of it straight, and maybe the second level straight—well, then Howard would get down to a point where he'd find the first clear inconsistency. From then on they'd just fall apart one after another." They fell apart because once Weitzman found an inconsistency in the testimony of a prosecution witness, he'd hammer away at it during the cross-examination, asking the witness over and over again about that particular information, attacking the testimony from a variety of different angles, until the witness finally caved in, admitting that his initial statements did not, after all, represent the truth.

"What I do best, if I do anything best," agrees Weitzman, "is cross-examination." It was through Weitzman's cross-examination that he proved DeLorean never engaged in the alleged cocaine conspiracy. "We proved that, during the cross-examination of the [drug enforcement] agents, out of their mouths, as well as [the mouth of] the informant," stresses the attorney.

While many lawyers might have defended DeLorean by claiming entrapment, Weitzman's trial strategy dictated staying clear of that argument. In fact, Weitzman mentioned the concept of entrapment only briefly during the trial, in his closing argument. He sought instead to prove that the case had nothing to do with entrapment—that DeLorean hadn't committed the crime he was accused of in the first place—so the issue of entrapment did not apply. But just to make sure his client would be on the winning side, Weitzman also showed during his cross-examination of the prosecution's witnesses that the government *tried* to entrap DeLorean. The press, Weitzman says today, focused primarily on the entrapment issue because it "allows the public to better understand the proceedings, and it paints a different picture of the case that generates more reader interest."

The chief prosecutor in the case, Assistant U.S. Attorney James Walsh, disagrees with Weitzman's depiction of his defense argument. "Basically, I think that the jury was given a great deal of information regarding the way in which the government conducted its investigation—and was invited to pass judgment on whether it was entrapment," says Walsh. In fact, Walsh maintains that Weitzman misrepresented the theory of entrapment, focusing on the investigators' behavior, rather than on the federal court criteria that emphasize the defendant's frame of mind and willingness to engage in crime. Under an entrapment defense in federal court, a defendant is guilty if he was already inclined to commit the alleged crime. Instead, "the [DeLorean] jury was bombarded over the months with information related to police conduct," says Walsh of Weitzman's courtroom questioning. "Since the judge allowed all that information in, the jury probably felt it was supposed to use that." And even though Weitzman didn't offer a formal entrapment defense, the judge instructed the jury on entrapment law and allowed the jurors to consider entrapment during their deliberations.

Weitzman knew that his first major battle in the DeLorean trial would be countering the prosecution's image of a guilty defendant, an image engineered by the government through its sting operation procedures. Weitzman had to fight in every way possible the widespread, resulting public acceptance that DeLorean was indeed guilty.

The day Weitzman received the phone call asking him to

work on the case, DeLorean was in jail, with bail set at $20 million. That bail, says Weitzman, was part of the government's setup. "To put a twenty-million-dollar bail on John DeLorean and try him as a major drug smuggler was part of the public relations campaign so that any potential juror would remember that. It has a certain shock effect. The inference is that only major criminals have a twenty-million-dollar bail on them. Jurors subconsciously adopt that perception." Often Weitzman files a motion to have his client's bail lowered; in DeLorean's case he argued that the bail was not fair because it was so high, and that it tied up DeLorean's property, which had to be posted as collateral. Ultimately the court reduced the bail to $2.5 million. It's "part of the job," says Weitzman of his bail negotiations.

While working on the case, Weitzman gave DeLorean an office next to his, and until the end of the trial the automaker was a regular at Weitzman & Ré. DeLorean spent about twenty percent of his time back east—where he had a farm in New Jersey and an apartment in Manhattan—but when he was in Los Angeles he stopped by to work with his lawyer almost every day. "Usually the client subliminally knows more about the case than anyone else," says DeLorean. "And Howard has the ability to get that out of you and to understand it." He does so, explains Weitzman, by getting "very specific" in his questions and discussions with the client. "I talk about what I think took place to jog their minds," says the defense attorney. "I ask a lot of questions to help clients recreate conversations and events. And I go over it over and over and over again."

Weitzman likes working closely with his clients. "I believe clients have a right to have some input into their case," he says. "It's their life." But when such input leads to disagreements, adds Weitzman, he insists on being the one to call the shots. If a client keeps arguing, Weitzman returns the person's money, even when, on rare occasions, he had had to borrow himself to make the refund.

Weitzman had about a year and a half to prepare for the

DeLorean trial; he spent one hundred percent of his time on the case during the last twelve months. The lawyer had a lot to work with—videotapes and audiotapes, and a government informant's testimony proffered as seemingly convincing proof of DeLorean's guilt. Additionally, Weitzman "personally went through literally thousands and tens of thousands of pages of records," including telephone logs, says DeLorean, "so he really understood" the case.

As Weitzman grew closer to DeLorean, DeLorean's cause loomed larger in his lawyer's mind. He decided that his client was a victim. "Perhaps one of the greatest crimes committed by the government was that it permitted an admitted perjurer, a drug dealer, a con man informant, to relate his version of ambiguous conversations without corroboration as a basis for beginning one of the most insidious and misguided law enforcement operations in history," Weitzman wrote passionately in his unsuccessful pretrial motion to dismiss the case because of "outrageous government conduct." The government targeted John DeLorean, a person who had no prior involvement with narcotics, and lured him on with promises of legitimate large-scale investments, concluded Weitzman.

Weitzman was initially victorious in some important pretrial motions, only to lose them later in appellate rulings. First, Weitzman argued that the government's pleadings should be sealed from public view because they contributed to a public perception that DeLorean was guilty. Every time the press reported on alleged facts in one of these pleadings, they added to DeLorean's negative publicity, which Weitzman said harmed his client's chances for a fair trial. While Judge Takasugi agreed with Weitzman, indicating that he would preview all pleadings before releasing them publicly, the Ninth Circuit reversed the trial judge's decision. The appellate court said that the special review process would be too time-consuming and would lead to delay.

Second, Weitzman filed a motion with the judge to obtain all the documents the government had on the DeLorean case, citing DeLorean's right to the documents under the federal Freedom of Information Act. In response the government argued that releasing the correspondence between the U.S. State Department and the United Kingdom about the cocaine case would violate foreign policy considerations and could have an effect on national security. Other documents were said to be protected because the DeLorean investigation was still ongoing, and the trial pending. Despite the government's refusal, the FOIA request confirmed for Weitzman that certain documents did in fact exist. "If the documents don't exist, the response is 'There aren't any documents,' " Weitzman explains. "To say that correspondence between the State Department and the United Kingdom dealing with the investigation of the drug case against John DeLorean deals with national security and foreign policy is just ludicrous. So what that response says is 'We can't give you that because it will hurt our case.' " While Takasugi ruled in Weitzman's favor, the Ninth Circuit also overturned that decision. The appellate court said that supplying the documents to the defense would be too burdensome on the government and would have delayed the trial.

The "60 Minutes" brouhaha led to Weitzman's third critical pretrial defeat before the Ninth Circuit. Evidently Larry Flynt had obtained copies of the undercover videotapes from a clerk employed by a firm that initially worked on the DeLorean case with Weitzman. That firm had borrowed the tapes from the prosecution to make copies to help prepare for the trial. But the firm's clerk also made copies of the video for himself, and he in turn sold these to Flynt. Although the defense lawyers did not file charges against the clerk, he was fired.

After learning that fateful night in October 1983 that Flynt had passed the tapes on to "60 Minutes," and that the popular CBS television show was going to air them, Weitzman called Judge Takasugi. He asked him for a Saturday-morning hearing to request a temporary restraining order against the airing of the tapes. Weitzman worked all night and early the next morning to prepare the necessary documents. And Takasugi, with both the government and Weitzman in agreement ("one of the few times we agreed on anything in this case," notes Weitzman), issued the restraining order.

"I call CBS from chambers," recounts Weitzman, "with the judge there, with the prosecutor. We inform them the restraining order has been issued and [ask] who do we serve it on. They give me a name, I get in my car at two o'clock Saturday afternoon, I drive to CBS. Of course, by the time I get there, there's forty cameras there, they film me, and of course the head of the 'net' comes out for service on the TV, and I go away." With an evidentiary hearing set for the following Monday to determine whether airing the tapes would in fact hurt DeLorean's ability to have a fair trial, Weitzman breathed a sigh of relief, knowing that at least he and his client were safe for the weekend.

At eight-thirty the next morning, Sunday, Weitzman's phone rang again. It was a lawyer representing CBS. Weitzman recalls the conversation:

"Howard, how are you doing?"

"Fine." (Wondering to himself "What in the world is this guy doing calling me at eight-thirty on a Sunday morning?")

"Listen, there's a hearing scheduled for noon today before the [U.S. Court of Appeals for the] Ninth Circuit."

"You're obviously mistaken. Today is *Sunday.*"

"I understand that."

"What's the purpose of the hearing?"

"Well, CBS is contesting the restraining order that Judge Takasugi issued preventing us from showing the tapes."

"You got the Ninth Circuit to convene on Sunday?"

"Yeah, I called Judge [William A.] Norris and he agreed to do it."

(*That's* when," Weitzman interjects at this point in his story, "I really learned what big [law] firms were all about.")

Weitzman headed out for an eight-mile morning run. He came back home, and without showering put on his jeans with his T-shirt and running shoes, and left for downtown L.A. "I don't think they respected John DeLorean's rights or mine by calendaring the hearing on a Sunday," says Weitzman of his attire, worn to indicate his outrage.

It was noon when he arrived at the courthouse. "Sure enough," he recounts, to this day showing his disbelief, "the media's all there. The CBS lawyers are all dressed up in suits and ties. The prosecutor is there, dressed similarly to me because he had already left for the office before they contacted him. I get handed a stack of papers [Weitzman's first indication of the CBS lawyers' arguments], and at twelve oh five three judges wearing robes come out and they're on the bench. It was incredible.

"CBS made this big presentation about First Amendment and all this kind of stuff, and '60 Minutes' and share ratings and percentages of the market, and how important it is that the public see all this."

Then the judges looked at Weitzman. He stood up and gazed around the courtroom. "You know, this is kind of like being in Fantasyland down in Anaheim," Weitzman recalls saying. "I'm not exactly sure what I'm doing here.

"Now let me see if I can just narrow down the issues: It's John DeLorean's Sixth Amendment right to a fair trial versus CBS's right to get a certain share rating and percentage of the market. Have I kind of focused in on the issues?" Weitzman asked scornfully. "Somebody steals these tapes, CBS buys them from the thief, John DeLorean is about to lose any chance he has to get a fair trial because you're going to allow these people to run the tapes, edit them, splice 'em, dice 'em, put on whatever they want and comment on them—and their argument is now that they have the tapes they're entitled to it because '60 Minutes' is one of the biggest-viewed shows in the market?

"Nobody's talked about the defendant here. I've got to be missing something." Weitzman was livid.

"Well, how do we have the power to order CBS not to do this?" Weitzman recalls one of the three judges asking.

"That's what you're *supposed* to do," responded the exasperated lawyer. "That's your job. If you think they're wrong, that's why you're wearing the robes. You *tell* them that they're wrong and they can't do it."

"Well, do you have any cases [as guiding precedent]?"

"Judge, when's the last case you think took place when you have an international figure in one of the most highly publicized cases ever, have the media buy stolen videotapes of the undercover investigation and try to play them nationally? I don't think there're a whole lot of cases that have been similar to this."

But by then, DeLorean's lawyer sensed he was fighting a losing battle. It was "a stacked deck," he says. The court ruled for CBS, citing the network's First Amendment rights. Frantic, Weitzman and the government prosecutor telephoned Supreme Court Justice (at that point, not yet chief justice) William Rehnquist at his home. Rehnquist suggested that Weitzman contact the chief justice, and he gave Weitzman the phone number for Warren Burger's law clerk. But Burger's clerk simply said that the Supreme Court doesn't do anything "unless it's in writing."

That evening, only a few hours after the Ninth Circuit's ruling, the entire nation could watch on television John DeLorean's toasting the future over cocaine, exclaiming, "It's better than gold." Other stations quickly picked up the tape and replayed it many times over. Judge Takasugi was furious, says Weitzman, and in an attempt to lessen the negative impact on potential jurors, postponed the trial until March the following year.

"What's interesting in all of those cases," says Weitzman after describing the Ninth Circuit reversals of his key pretrial district court victories, is that "what the Court of Appeals did was ignore the rights of the individual—which supposedly is what our constitution is all about—and ruled in favor of the establishment power, which is the media and the government. What difference did it make if the public saw those pleadings the day they were filed—or four days later," asks Weitzman, still arguing his points. "The truth is that it made no difference except that [releasing the documents] could have a devastating effect on the individual" and any opportunity for a fair trial.

As much as Weitzman says he hated pretrial publicity, claiming it could irreparably harm DeLorean's chances in court, Weitzman also used the press to broadcast his own version of the case. "A lawyer has a responsibility to attempt to neutralize negative pretrial publicity by responding responsibly and positively to allegations," says Weitzman. Contrary to most lawyers, Weitzman doesn't avoid the media or offer the traditional "no comment." Instead, he tries to bring to reporters' attention positive points about his client and his client's case. Yet he also says that in the DeLorean trial, he held his own news conferences only after evidence was introduced, and after the jurors were in place and isolated from the media, so that Weitzman himself couldn't be accused of tainting them.

DeLorean himself spoke publicly only once, in granting an interview to *Rolling Stone* magazine, and that was done against Weitzman's advice. Christina DeLorean granted three interviews—to *Better Homes and Gardens, People* magazine, and "20/20," the ABC news program—with the approval of Weitzman. Again, says Weitzman, the interviews were granted "to neutralize [negative publicity] the best I could so John got almost a fair trial."

But the prosecutors simply accused Weitzman of publicity hounding. He shrugs that off. "They didn't lose the case on the courthouse steps," Weitzman responds. "They lost it in the courtroom."

To confirm the results he feared from negative pretrial publicity, Weitzman asked the two hundred prospective jurors for the trial to complete an extensive forty-two-page questionnaire. "You are expected to sign your questionnaire, and your answers will have the effect of a statement given to the Court under oath," read the covering instruction page. In the questionnaire Weitzman asked the jurors about their occupations for the past five years, about any previous training in law, accounting, or business finance, and about direct or indirect involvement with federal courts, law enforcement agencies, or automotive companies. The defense lawyer also asked about the jurors' views and experience with narcotics and narcotics laws, and about their exposure to pretrial media coverage on the case. In fact, about half of the questionnaire focused on pretrial publicity. Ultimately, more than ninety-two percent of the prospective jurors believed DeLorean was guilty, or more likely guilty than not, says Weitzman. Fifty-three percent of the jurors were excused because they conceded that they could not overcome their anti-DeLorean bias.

During the actual voir dire questioning, Weitzman also tried "to neutralize" harmful publicity about DeLorean. "I wanted to ask the jurors what they thought they saw, and then tell them 'If it turns out that isn't what you saw—that the government brought that [suitcase of cocaine] in and it had nothing to do with a drug deal—would that change your frame of mind as you sit there right now before the trial starts?' " Weitzman describes his exchange:

Weitzman: You saw that videotape these people showed on television?

Juror: Yes.

Weitzman: What you thought you saw was John DeLorean in the middle of a drug deal, right?

Juror: Yes.

Weitzman: And as you sit there now having seen John DeLorean captured on television by the government in the middle of a drug deal, you presume he's guilty, or more likely guilty than not, don't you?

Juror: Yes.

Weitzman: Would it make any difference if I told you what you saw was not a drug deal—that the government set it up so it looked like a drug deal?

"Objection," the government attorneys cried out. Summoned to sidebar by Judge Takasugi, Weitzman insisted he was "just telling the truth." He explained to the judge that the tape was not a drug deal, that Hetrick had already been arrested, and that DeLorean had no idea that the cocaine was going to be there. "They brought it out merely for show. Ask them," Weitzman challenged the judge.

The government prosecutors replied that they brought the cocaine out "just to get DeLorean's reaction," recalls Weitzman in describing the discussion. The judge overruled the objection and the lawyers returned to their jury selection.

"The first juror," continues Weitzman, "said words to the effect of 'Well, why would they do that?' And I said, 'Ask them that. I don't have the answer. My question to you is would it make a difference?' "

"Of course it would make a difference," responded the juror.

The press "went crazy when that happened," says Weitzman, "because of course what the government had to do was to cop to [doing] that. They basically had to take the position, which they did the whole trial, that it was okay to do that because it would show DeLorean's reaction—that he was calm, cool, collected, and therefore he knew all along what was going on."

Not all of the jurors were so openminded. Weitzman's ability to identify a juror's [negative] mindset is uncanny, says his former law partner, Donald Ré, adding that jury selection is one of Weitzman's strong suits. At one point during voir dire for the DeLorean trial, "a group of us were talking about Howard's ability to size up jurors," Ré recalls. A potential juror, a woman, was next to take a seat in the jury box. "Howard stood up and looked at this lady and said, 'You really don't want to sit on this jury, do you?' She said, 'That's right, I don't,' and Howard excused her. All she had said was her name. A lot of lawyers would have explored and diffused her feelings," says Ré, "but just by watching her body language Howard had an instinct there was something wrong," that something about the nature of the case bothered her, and that she didn't even want to sit around for jury selection.

Weitzman can be just as ruthless during voir dire as he is sensitive, adds Ré. Another potential juror, whom both Weitzman and Ré felt was biased against DeLorean, steadfastly refused to admit his true feelings. As a result, Weitzman had no grounds on which to excuse him. So Weitzman grew more and more aggressive in his questioning until finally the man "stood up and started crawling over the rail," recalls Ré. He "said to Howard, 'I'm going to come over there and punch you.' " And that response was enough to disqualify the juror.

"He can go soft on people to get them to come out of their shells, and he can go hard on people to get them to come out of their shells," summarizes Ré. If the first technique doesn't work, Weitzman switches to the second. The switching is "partly [due to] his personality," adds Ré, "because he gets fed up."

Actually Weitzman thought that all the jurors started out biased against DeLorean. Yet he still says DeLorean got a fair trial. "I really believe the man wouldn't have been acquitted if the government would have proven that he did it," says Weitzman. "You don't let people like John DeLorean off if you think he did it. It's human nature—you like to take down the big guy." Nor was juror sympathy a factor in DeLorean's acquittal. "What's sympathetic about multikilos of cocaine?" Weitzman asks. "There's nothing sympathetic about the man. So there's a reason why he was acquitted." That, says Weitzman, is innocence.

In his opening statement Weitzman began his campaign to prove DeLorean's innocence. The government here created everything you see in this case, he told the jury. Weitzman stressed that an informant, James Timothy Hoffman, ran the investigation, and that Hoffman was nothing more than a criminal, a convicted cocaine dealer with a debt to the government. As he described the development of the government's case against DeLorean, Weitzman's indignation grew visibly, reaching its peak in what he described as his own "quiet outrage."

Weitzman excels when he's talking to a jury, sharing his views and ideas. "The key is that he relates very well to the ordinary people sitting in the courtroom," says Terry N. Christensen, a former partner at Wyman, Bautzer. "He comes across as a regular citizen himself—he moves around, he isn't stuffy and stilted. He's physically a regular guy, a likable guy, who's comfortable with himself." Because Weitzman can be natural in the courtroom, his own personality shines through; he can use humor when appropriate and show indignation when appropriate.

"The jurors," adds DeLorean, "all basically felt strongly about Howard. A number of women on the jury wanted to marry him," he says, laughing. "Howard comes off as a very good person who's interested in justice."

Weitzman made it clear in his opening statement that he was going after justice, that he was going to prove to them that DeLorean was interested only in financing his ailing automobile company, that DeLorean was vulnerable because his life's dream was at stake, and that promises of new financing provided the government hook with which the informant Hoffman pulled DeLorean into discussions in the first place. Before Hoffman's contact, Weitzman emphasized, the government did not even suspect DeLorean of narcotics dealings.

The attorney equated the DeLorean case to the shooting of a movie. "It was made to look like something else was happening, just the way you make a movie, so it would come out looking the way it wasn't," he reiterates today. Weitzman says he tried to recreate the DeLorean scenario for the jurors, explaining how the events involving DeLorean were made to transpire. "It is best to approach a good part of the present as if on a set," he explains, "and take the jurors behind the scenes" where the drama is planned. During the trial Weitzman also reinforced the notion of playacting by analogizing the FBI agents in the investigation to actors.

The only character who didn't know he had a part in the play was DeLorean himself, continues Weitzman. The government was responsible for all the other players. "It was important to make the jurors understand that the subject of this tape recording was the only one who didn't know what was going on," Weitzman says. Yet at the same time, "the agents spent days figuring out how to manipulate the conversation." And in their presentation of the case, he adds, the prosecutors further manipulated the appearances of DeLorean's meetings with the undercover agents by recording only some of the conversations that took place.

Undercover agent Benedict Tisa, who played the part of the crooked banker "James Benedict," took the stand first. The courtroom was packed with electronic equipment—loudspeakers, television sets, and audio headphones. "They thought he was their best witness," says DeLorean, looking back on Tisa's testimony. "He was a very credible, good-looking guy, ex-football-player, a marine, twelve-year accountant with the FBI."

Assistant U.S. Attorney Robert Perry, who assisted Walsh and the prosecutor, handled Tisa's direct examination. Perry asked the undercover FBI agent about his role in the DeLorean cocaine investigation:

Perry: Did you have occasion on or about July twelfth of 1982 to have a conversation with [the informant] Mr. Hoffman about John DeLorean?

Tisa: Yes, I did.

Perry: Was this a telephone contact or in person?

Tisa: No. Mr. Hoffman called me.

Perry: What, if anything, did he say about John DeLorean?

Tisa: Mr. Hoffman called me and indicated that he had just had a meeting with Mr. DeLorean the previous day. . . . And during the course of that meeting, he had been in a discussion with Mr. DeLorean, where Mr. DeLorean wanted to invest approximately two million dollars in a narcotics transaction that would generate approximately forty to fifty million dollars sometime within the next sixty days. . . .

Perry: Based on your conversation with Mr. Hoffman, did you determine or was there indication as to whether or not you might be hearing from John DeLorean?

Tisa: Yes, there was. I was to expect a call from him.

Perry: In what capacity were you to expect a call from Mr. DeLorean?

Tisa: I was expected—I was to receive a call from Mr. DeLorean at Eureka Federal Savings and Loan, my undercover banker role.

Perry: What, if anything, were you to do when you got that call?

Tisa: I was to provide credibility for Mr. Hoffman, insofar as his financial capabilities at the bank, in other words, verify that he had a lot of money on deposit.

Perry: . . . did you have occasion to receive a telephone call from John DeLorean?

Tisa: Yes, I did.

According to Tisa and the prosecution's interpretation of DeLorean's taped conversations, DeLorean was to purchase the illegal drugs through Hoffman, and then sell it for a much-needed profit. Perry asked Tisa why the agents introduced DeLorean to [the suspected cocaine smuggler] Hetrick:

Perry: Did there come a time when a decision was made to attempt to combine the investigation of Mr. DeLorean with the investigation of Mr. Hetrick?

Tisa: Yes, there was.

Perry: When did that time come?

Tisa: That was in early August of 1982.

Perry: How were the investigations going to be combined?

Tisa: Well, what I was to do was to go to Mr. Hetrick and Mr. DeLorean separately and ask them if they would be interested in meeting each other from the standpoint of mutual desires, needs, and intentions. If they were agreeable to that, then I would go ahead and arrange a meeting for them to sit down and discuss their mutual interests.

Perry: What was the purpose in trying to put Mr. DeLorean and Mr. Hetrick together?

Tisa: Well, on one hand, I had Mr. DeLorean, who, based on my understanding at that point in time, wanted to invest approximately two million dollars in a narcotics transaction to generate money for his company, and also having an immediate need for a lot of cash, and on the other hand, we had Mr. Hetrick, who had expressed his capability of supplying narcotics, cocaine, and also having this offshore cash from his cocaine trafficking in the Cayman Islands and needing that to be brought back into the United States in some usable form. So, what I had was a willing investor, apparently, and a willing supplier, and by putting those together, they might come to some agreement . . .

On the stand, Tisa explained that the government had been wanting to get Hetrick's drug trafficking money into the U.S. so the agents could intercept it. The government thought that offering DeLorean's companies as an investment avenue would provide the necessary enticement. Similarly, if DeLorean purchased Hetrick's drugs, the government could seize the cocaine.

"In other words," concluded Perry, referring to the anticipated meeting of DeLorean and Hetrick, "you felt that it would be an opportunity to gather evidence of the intent of both men. Is that right?"

"Yes," replied Tisa.

When Weitzman stood up to cross-examine Tisa, the defense lawyer told a different version of DeLorean's conversations with the undercover agents and with Hetrick. "One of the things I was able to do," says the attorney, "is I took the jury through each tape—which is why the examination took so long. I wanted to show that there were two different conversations [between DeLorean and Hetrick] and that the government was attempting to put these guys together, and the only two people who didn't know what they were trying to do were DeLorean and Hetrick.

"In a single meeting that DeLorean and Hetrick had that was videotaped, a two-and-a-half-hour meeting, DeLorean is told prior to the meeting that Hetrick believes that DeLorean is going to invest in his cocaine deal. And even though DeLorean isn't, the government (of course DeLorean didn't know it was the government) has told Hetrick that, and [told John] that [he] shouldn't tell Hetrick he's not going to invest in the deal because Hetrick will back out" of any investment discussion. And "Hetrick was a fellow that the government had represented to DeLorean was a cocaine smuggler who wanted to invest up to thirty million dollars in DeLorean's company," Weitzman adds.

When the two men got together, they had one conversation—but about two different topics. "The agents told Hetrick," according to Weitzman, to "tell John about what it's like to fly the planes in Venezuela and about the cocaine, and would encourage all that conversation. And DeLorean basically talks about the company and about Ireland, and the car. It was pretty bizarre," concludes Weitzman. If someone listens to the tapes and is told they're about a cocaine deal, that's their mindset, says Weitzman, "which is what they did with the jury."

When Weitzman replayed the tapes, controlling the sound with a pause button, and at the same time putting the transcripts on a big screen with a projector, he walked the jury through the conversations, word by word, line by line. On cross-examination "I basically replayed everything, piece by piece, and I would take the agent [and later the informant Hoffman] through it. 'Well, DeLorean didn't say this; you said it, right?' " Weitzman said he asked the government witness.

"In video- and audiotape cases, sting-type cases," explains Weitzman, "where you know the government has a program and it's a case where you have a client who is clearly not guilty, the lawyer has to go behind the tapes and determine how the conversations progressed, who carried the conversations, who introduced the subject matters, what the responses were."

For example, as a suppliant, DeLorean did not want to offend the man he thought was James Benedict because Benedict was a banker and therefore a potential source of money for DeLorean's company—and DeLorean was desperate for investors. "When you look at the tapes, you can see it," explains Weitzman. "You can see every time they talk about cocaine, John kind of pushes that aside and then he talks about the money. And they bring it back in and he [says] yes, and he kind of pushes it aside and talks about the money. You have to take the time to point that out to the jury."

In any conversation, business or social, Weitzman notes, one party is more powerful than the other and can manipulate the discussion. "If you understand the powerful/powerless, the need-versus-want-versus-control concept, the psychologies of communication, you can begin to see how the powerful people can manipulate the less powerful." Weitzman's goal was to show how the government agents and informant, as the more powerful party based on their prior knowledge of what was going on, manipulated their conversations with DeLorean. "What this jury had to understand—and what other juries need to understand—is who the person is, or what they are, or how much money they have doesn't make them the more powerful person in any given setting.

"When you are the entrepreneur attempting to raise money, you are the person out there asking, and the person with the money is the person who can really control the conversation," Weitzman concludes. "The skill of the entrepreneur is to change the roles, so that the person with the money is real thankful that the entrepreneur is giving him the opportunity" to invest his money. But with the government, in DeLorean's case, there was no opportunity to change roles. DeLorean remained the suppliant, unable to play any other part in the transpiring scenario than the one the government assigned him.

When cross-examining Tisa about the events on that fateful day of October nineteenth—the day DeLorean was videotaped with the cocaine—Weitzman painted a picture of his client as totally powerless, a man in circumstances far beyond his control:

Weitzman: Mr. Tisa, we were discussing I think October the nineteenth a little earlier this morning. The decision was made that John should be arrested before he came to Los Angeles, correct?

Tisa: Yes.

Weitzman: When was that decision made?

Tisa: Sometime right just prior to the—I guess the eighteenth or nineteenth. . . .

Weitzman: You had already concluded that he had been involved in and committed a crime, correct?

Tisa: Yes. . . .

Weitzman: You will agree with me, won't you, that Mr. DeLorean did not know the cocaine was going to be in the room?

Tisa: Yes. . . .

Weitzman: Regardless of how he reacted, he was going to be arrested anyway, wasn't he?

Tisa: Yes. . . .

Later in the cross-examination Weitzman forced Tisa to admit that DeLorean had tried to back off from suggestions of a drug deal, but Tisa prevented him from doing so:

Weitzman: Now, you told me as of September fifteenth, when John DeLorean told you that he didn't have the money, you thought it was part of your responsibility to create an alternative for DeLorean to stay in the ["drug"] deal, right?

Tisa: I don't believe I said create an alternative.

Weitzman: Suggest an alternative?

Tisa: No. I believe I said, in my undercover role, I was reacting to what I perceived as his intentions and desires based on his statements. . . .

Weitzman: So you believe it is part of your role as the [FBI] agent, not the undercover crooked banker, but as the agent, working on a case, when you investigate a case, to get right down and help create situations to allow somebody to continue acting what you believe to be criminal conduct, right?

Tisa: No.

Weitzman: When John DeLorean said to you, "I don't have the money," and you interpret his responses to be, well, you—Benedict, crooked banker—come up with another alternative, even though he says that he would leave word in your office—are you telling us when you hang up the phone and put back on your FBI-agent coat and tie, part of your investigative role is to sit down and come up with some alternatives?

Tisa: No.

Weitzman: That is what you did in this case, right?

Tisa: No. . . .

Weitzman: And when you say to John DeLorean at page eleven of 23.1, line ten [of the undercover tapes transcripts]: "Well, all right, I'll, I'll . . . if you hear of anything or if you can work something out, let me know and I will see what I can do, but . . . It doesn't look that good," what did you mean?

Tisa: From the standpoint of him asking me to come up with some suggestion to keep him in the drug deal.

Weitzman: So it didn't look good at that point, that it would work out, right?

Tisa: In my undercover role I was trying to express my displeasure with this thing he was trying to do.

Weitzman: What was he trying to do? Back out of the deal?

Tisa: No. He was trying to continue in the deal with no money. . . .

Weitzman: Do you think John DeLorean was saying to you: "Look, Tisa"—I beg your pardon—"Benedict, I don't want to put any money in this deal. If you want me in this deal, come up with some alternative where I can do it without any money." Do you think that that is what he was saying to you?

Tisa: Yes.

Weitzman: So instead of just sitting back and waiting to see what John DeLorean did, to see what he wanted to do, you participated in suggesting alternatives to him, right?

Tisa: Based on what he was saying to me, yes.

Weitzman: So the answer is "yes"; is that correct?

Tisa: Yes.

"By the time Howard got through with Tisa, he was totally destroyed," says DeLorean. DeLorean credits both Weitzman's understanding of the case, based on months of tedious, dedicated preparation, and his analytical ability for making him such a strong cross-examiner. "Howard understood the case, and I don't think the prosecutors did or anyone else," says DeLorean. Because of his preparation, "Howard had a clear idea of where he wanted to go, and they didn't understand that. He used that ability to pull out of these people the pieces of evidence and the testimony that he required to accomplish the result he wanted."

In cross-examination, summarizes Weitzman himself, a lawyer first needs to be prepared in what he or she believes happened and what he or she believes can be accomplished. "You need to have a goal in mind of what you want to show the jury. You need to understand what cross-examination is—showing your side of the story through questions, and eliciting the answers. It's more than just the question. It's your only way of communicating your defense in a criminal case, your position in a civil case to the jury or to the judge."

The lawyer's questions have to be phrased in such a way, says Weitzman, that the response is not only what the lawyer wants, but one that tells a story to the jury. This is possible in cross-examination because different rules apply than during direct examination: A lawyer can, for example, lead a witness by suggesting certain ideas and can impeach a witness with prior testimony.

In all, Tisa's cross-examination lasted about three weeks, and that of Hoffman, the prosecution's other star witness, who followed, slightly less. With Tisa, says DeLorean, of course, "he killed their case, but [afterward] the revelations were even more dramatic—just one after another after another." For example, Weitzman reiterated time and time again, during his cross-examination of Hoffman, that the informant, around whom the entire case was built, had lied repeatedly in the past. In fact, Weitzman also showed that Hoffman at one point had demanded a share in the cocaine the agents seized from the deal they anticipated before he would agree to continue working on the investigation.

By the time he finished cross-examining the two chief prosecution witnesses, says Weitzman, "I got both [Tisa and Hoffman] to concede, in my opinion, that no crime was ever committed and that DeLorean was set up."

Subsequently the prosecutors ran through about twenty more witnesses in about two weeks, including some surveillance witnesses, and other government agents. Walsh and Perry never called Hetrick to the stand, says Weitzman, "because he couldn't testify that DeLorean did anything wrong."

"Don't you think," said Weitzman, that "if Morgan Hetrick could come in here and say that he committed a crime with John DeLorean, the government would have called him?" The jurors had heard the tapes, Weitzman stressed, and nothing on them indicated that Hetrick and DeLorean had made a deal.

When Weitzman's turn came to present his case, he called to the stand, with one exception, only government employees, including an ex-DEA agent named Gerald Scotti, who had worked on the case. Weitzman called Scotti, he says, to show that "the agents really didn't believe that DeLorean had committed a crime, that the reason for bringing the cocaine in was to make the jury think he knew what was going on and he was involved with the cocaine, even though they knew he wasn't." Scotti testified that Walsh, a veteran prosecutor with extensive experience in narcotics cases, had proposed a toast after one of the DeLorean videotapings—a toast to a future cover of *Time* magazine. This case is not about a drug conspiracy, emphasized Weitzman. It's about publicity, ego, and career enhancement. DeLorean, Weitzman says, represented a big catch for the federal drug enforcement program, a catch that the government badly wanted to pull in. Walsh denies the toast.

The one nongovernment defense witness, DeLorean's secretary, served only to confirm Hoffman's testimony on cross-examination that certain letters were typed and that a telephone log recording calls between Hoffman and DeLorean was in her handwriting. DeLorean himself never took the stand because, Weitzman is reported as saying, "we didn't need him."

It was critical for Weitzman to keep the jury focused during the trial on the circumstances preceding DeLorean's arrest, not on DeLorean himself. Otherwise, the attorney explains, "if they focused on the individual, they would have overlooked what was happening. Over and over and over again, I basically pushed their faces in it so they could see what was happening."

When the trial was over, newspaper headlines across the nation screamed DeLorean's acquittal. "Automaker takes a walk," read the August 17, 1984, *Los Angeles Herald Examiner.* "DeLorean is freed of cocaine charge by a federal jury," proclaimed the more sedate *New York Times.* "Praise the Lord," declared DeLorean. And his wife cried.

Though Weitzman admits that his client was guilty "of real poor judgment," he was, says the defense lawyer, "a man in a desperate frame of mind."

Adds Weitzman, "This case is living proof that the government can, will, and does, given the situation, get involved in giant cover-ups and will systematically withhold evidence if it suits their needs."

DAVID M. HARNEY

Harney, Wolfe, Shaller & Carr, Los Angeles

Claude Ellis Photography

It was a nightmare come true. During a November 1982 San Francisco business trip, sixty-two-year-old Harry Jordan, a successful and popular insurance broker, noticed blood in his urine. He called his old friend and longtime physician Dr. Carlton H. Waters in Long Beach, California, where Jordan lived. Waters told Jordan to come see him after returning to town. But before Jordan could do so, he awoke at home one night with severe abdominal pain. Jordan's wife, Miriam, took him to the emergency room at the local hospital, the Long Beach Community Hospital. When Dr. Waters arrived at around eight that morning, he ordered X rays. They showed on Jordan's right side—on his right kidney—a cancerous, baseball-sized tumor.

Waters contacted a urologist, Dr. Marshall Grobert of Grobert-Sawyer Medical Corporation, who in turn called in a younger doctor who worked for him, Dr. Barton Wachs. The physicians' consultations continued throughout the day, and that evening Wachs proceeded to operate to remove Jordan's cancerous, and almost nonfunctional, kidney. But instead of taking out the right kidney, Wachs removed Jordan's normal left kidney.

Jordan survived, primarily because his family fired the doctors at the Long Beach Community Hospital and transferred Jordan to the University of California Medical Center. There another urological surgeon removed the lower eighty percent of the cancerous kidney and reattached the salvaged top portion to function as best it could. Today, Harry Jordan exists by living—although not comfortably—on one-tenth of his total kidney capacity. Had the cancerous kidney been removed, Jordan's left kidney would have been able to handle all of his body's needs, and he would have had a normal life. Ironically, at the time of his operation Harry Jordan was on the board of directors of the Long Beach Community Hospital Foundation.

David M. Harney, Jordan's lawyer, who sued the hospital and all the doctors involved, still gets mad when he talks about this case. Because of the faulty operation and Jordan's severely reduced kidney capacity, says Harney, Jordan "has to be given medications, including prednisone, which is a corticosteroid, which has side effects, including osteoporosis or breakdown of the bony content, the calcium, of the bone. As a consequence, Mr. Jordan is suffering collapses of his spinal vertebrae, requiring him to be in a body cast and in a wheelchair." When he walks, he hobbles with the use of two canes. Jordan could well be forced in the near future to begin dialysis and continue on it for the rest of his life. On top of this, Jordan, who before the operation suffered from heart problems, no longer qualifies as a candidate for successful heart surgery. He is unable to work, says Harney, who argued in the malpractice suit that the kidney operation obliged Jordan to sell his insurance business and grapple instead with mounting financial problems.

Harney's indignation is characteristic of this feisty third-generation Irish American's fight to help clients harmed by medical malpractice. More than ninety percent of Harney's cases fall in the personal-injury and wrongful-death fields, and seventy to eighty percent of those involve medical malpractice. A California native, law review graduate of the University of Southern California School of Law, and former president of the International Academy of Trial Lawyers, the sixty-four-year-old Harney has won nine multimillion-dollar verdicts in his career of almost four decades. A doctors' trade journal once named him "the best plaintiff's lawyer in the land," based on a poll mainly of defense lawyers.

Harney's firm maintains a low case-per-lawyer ratio to allow a full financial and time commitment to each client. Harney tries only about four or five cases a year, significantly fewer than he tried years ago when courtroom battles were generally shorter and less complicated. He also is trying, for logistical reasons, to limit more of his practice to southern California.

In fact, Harney turns away twenty-nine out of every thirty lawsuits that come his way. "Out of the twenty-nine, I reject twenty-five out-of-hand based on phone conversations or interviews" because the claim isn't valid or strong enough to make litigation worthwhile, explains the lawyer. Harney investigates and evaluates the remaining five lawsuits to determine if they have merit, or in the case of alleged medical malpractice, to determine if the medical care provided the plaintiff was negligent, and if that negligence caused the plaintiff's injury.

To help determine if such a case has merit, Harney relies in part on three full-time physicians on his staff, all retired from their own medical practices. One physician is a pediatric neurologist, one a general surgeon, and the third an internist and vascular disease specialist. Harney also relies when necessary on other outside medical professionals for their advice. The doctors offer opinions based on their professional experience and expertise.

Even if a case does have merit, Harney may turn it away; it's a matter of degree. "In order to invest in a case you have to have a serious injury—and a reasonable chance of winning," he explains. Harney often looks for the "shock value" of a case, suggesting that a plaintiff's lawyer first must be shocked himself or herself upon hearing the client's story. Only then can the lawyer expect a jury to be shocked and to award a large sum in damages.

In addition to looking for cases with merit and a strong chance of winning, Harney prefers those that are financially worthwhile, that is, with potential for large awards. "The medical and legal profession cannot afford the prosecution" of all cases, Harney says, defending his decision to turn down some meritorious suits. "If we took and prosecuted every case, we would clog up the court system and would increase insurance costs and medical fees.

"The ability to argue to get the proper measure of damages is important," stresses Harney. He works to obtain for his clients what he thinks is fair compensation for their injuries—compensation that is always more than the defendants in a lawsuit want to pay. But during different trials, Harney relies on different strategies to get the damage awards he seeks. For example, when one of Harney's partners tried a case against Ford Motor Company alleging defective brakes, the jury awarded the brain-damaged plaintiff about $1 million. The case was appealed and sent back for a new trial, but by then the partner had left the firm. So Harney took over—and won a new $11.6-million verdict. He got that verdict, upheld on appeal, in part by asking the jury to award the plaintiff $3.6 million for economic loss and $4 million for pain and suffering, both of which Harney explained for the jury in great detail. To support these requests, Harney chose a different expert witness than the one his partner had used; Harney's expert, whom he called early in the case, automatically won the affection of the jury. Harney also told the jury to send a message to the Ford Motor Company by additionally awarding the plaintiff punitive damages. But here, Harney did not name an amount. He told the jurors he left that amount up to them. Harney simply asked the jurors not to award "too much because it would be hard to keep" since a trial judge would be likely to reduce what seemed to be an excessive amount. But Harney also asked the jurors not to award "too little because it would not send a message" to the Ford Motor Company. On its own, the jury settled on a sum equal to the award for pain and suffering—$4 million—bringing the total award to $11.6 million. However, after the jury had announced its award, the trial judge reduced the amount of the compensatory damages, lowering the total to $9.2 million.

Although Harney looks for sizable monetary awards for his clients, he isn't deterred from taking a case just because a doctor has no insurance to cover a jury verdict. "If someone goes without insurance, I'll go after him," says the trial lawyer with conviction. "I believe it's immoral to allow people to run around capable of injuring someone else and not be able to pay the damages." In one case, for example, Harney represented a nurse who had a face-lift and awoke from anesthesia to find her plastic surgeon fondling her. The surgeon, who had performed the operation poorly to boot, had no insurance. But after Harney won a $500,000 malpractice verdict, he was able to collect $350,000 from the doctor—by forcing the sale of his office building and of his home.

Finally, Harney also considers when reviewing cases whether they have "jury appeal." "Traditionally," he explains, "juries are not interested in giving anything—not one dime—unless the residual permanent injury is visible." Second, the plaintiff's lawyer must consider the presence and the appearance of the plaintiff himself or herself. "If you have somebody who is kind of a bum, even if malpractice resulted in a injury, the jury is not interested in awarding damages," says Harney. "The attorney," he explains, "can look at the family in a wrongful death and say, 'I like the family; the jury will like the family,' or in a personal injury case, can look at the plaintiff and say, 'This plaintiff has jury appeal.' " Finally, the appearance and the credentials of the defendant doctor or defendant hospital, represented by its administrator, cannot be too strong, or the jurors will find it impossible to believe that the doctor or hospital was capable of malpractice. A Marcus Welby–type doctor destroys the jury appeal of a plaintiff's case because "if the person looks like he couldn't possibly commit any bad practice, the jury won't buy it," says Harney. An unattractive, "schlocky" doctor who looks as if he could have done what was alleged makes a much more appealing defendant.

Harney says he often relies on psychology in the courtroom, that is, understanding how jurors think and knowing how to make them view facts and circumstances in a certain light. Harney sometimes tries to make jurors personally identify with his clients. To do so, the lawyer must get to the jurors' level, advises Harney, a child of the Depression who worked as a janitor at age twelve.

Harney points to one challenging case he tried and won in late 1985 as a prime example of how he uses jury psychology. A man, his wife, and two children had been driving in a twenty-five-year-old VW van from California to east Texas when, on a Texas freeway, the van overturned and caught fire. One of the children was badly burned. It so happened that shortly before the accident, the father had decided that the van's fuel system was not working properly. "So," explains Harney, "he took the gas cap off the car and ran a line from the outside of the car to the back where the engine is, and stuck that line into the gas input to the engine. Then he put a bunch of rags around the area were the gas cap had been." Thus the car burst into flames when it turned over. Not many trial lawyers would have taken the case, but Harney agreed to represent the family, and he sued the Volkswagen company. During the trial, the company argued that the father was wrong to tinker with the van's fuel system. Harney was able to show, however, that the vehicle was defective, leading to engine starvation. "The poor man, who didn't have any money, is out there in the desert with his wife and two children, and he's got to get them to his final destination point, and he did the best he could. He was no genius" recites Harney, describing his argument to the jury, but "I said that my client probably did a better job than the Volkswagen engineers over in Germany did when they designed this piece of junk." The jury found in favor of the VW driver for $3 million on the theory, says Harney, "that this car was defectively designed with reference to stability, and the fire that occurred was the result of the instability and not what the father did." Unfortunately the judge overturned the verdict because he didn't think the evidence supported it. Harney appealed and is optimistic that in the end he will prevail.

On the other hand, continues Harney on the topic of jury psychology, "jurors have a lot of imagination and a lawyer should not get carried away with having the plaintiff explain too many things that are obvious." Once, for example, Harney represented a race car driver who had crashed into a racetrack guardrail and lost both his legs. Harney argued that the guardrail was defective—that a different design would have prevented such a serious injury—and he sued the raceway. When the client took the stand at the end of the trial, Harney refused to let him elaborate on how terrible it was to have no legs. Harney simply asked the young man about the race and how the crash happened. Then Harney asked the young man, "How are you doing now?" "I'm doing great, Mr. Harney," the former racer replied in an upbeat voice. The jury had been deliberating for about three days when the raceway's insurance company representative finally contacted Harney. He admitted that before the trial the company never thought that the plaintiff had a chance. But then the insurance representative offered Harney's client a $400,000 settlement.

"You learn all this sort of thing even before you go to law school," says Harney about the use of jury psychology. "I think every great lawyer I've seen was born with this ability to apply psychology." Even with his current success—evident in his Los Angeles condominium, his San Diego County home, his Idaho cattle ranch, and his eighteenth-century estate in Ireland—

Harney has obviously not lost his touch for communicating with everyday jurors.

When Harney does decide to accept a case—based on merit, financial potential, and jury appeal—he doesn't always win. But Harney has built his reputation as a lawyer willing to take risks when he thinks he has a chance. "I've taken a lot of long shots," he admits. "If you think the total ingredients—the plaintiff, the law, the facts, the total mixture in the bowl of soup—will have sufficient appeal, then you can go ahead and take it even though it may be a long shot," suggests Harney to other plaintiff's lawyers.

Once Harney makes that decision, he zealously plows ahead, his determination matched only by the large amounts of time and money he pours into a case. "The defense knows Harney is willing to gamble and to spend a lot of money and a lot of time," says his former law partner James J. Pagliuso, who after working almost two decades with Harney recently began his own practice.

Along with his three in-house doctors, Harney relies on other key staff members to help him win in court. Five private investigators take on much of the research required to understand and document fully facts and events leading to a client's lawsuit. In one case, for example, it was one of the law firm's investigators who found the "smoking gun" that cinched a victory for Harney's client. The client was a woman, a patient of a successful Los Angeles psychiatrist. When in San Francisco on a trip, the woman accidentally encountered her psychiatrist while she was walking down the street. He invited her to have a drink at his hotel, and they ended up in his room in bed. She later became extremely emotionally upset about the incident and confessed to her husband, who left her. When Harney sued the psychiatrist on behalf of the woman, the doctor said he was in San Francisco on business, traveling alone without his wife, but he denied any involvement with the patient. However, Harney's investigator got the psychiatrist's American Express bill from the hotel, with a room-service charge for "Dr. and Mrs. . . ." Harney simply mailed a copy of the bill to the psychiatrist's lawyer, who, knowing that his client had a $200,000 malpractice policy, immediately telephoned Harney. "Would you settle for one hundred and ninety-five thousand dollars?" the other lawyer asked.

Another eight lawyers and about twenty assistants and clerical workers also work for the four partners at Harney, Wolfe, Shaller & Carr. Among the firm's personnel is Harney's younger son, David, a law clerk there while completing his own law school training. (Harney's older son, Brian, is an anesthesiologist in private practice in Fallbrook, California.) Harney, Wolfe occupies the thirteenth floor of a modern new office building in downtown Los Angeles, "the closest [office] building to the courthouse," says Harney, referring to the main Los Angeles County Superior Court building. His condominium home is conveniently across the street from the office.

At the office a special room houses trial evidence and courtroom props, enough in fact to fill a small museum. In this "evidence room" are two genuine full-body skeletons, an artificial but full-scale skeleton with detachable organs and muscles, an assortment of medical instruments, and rows upon rows of medical illustrations and photographs. Other large posters depict accident action sequences: "About 1970 we started having artists recreate how accidents [leading to a particular lawsuit] happen," explains Harney of the full-color pencil drawings. Outside the office is a garage full of cars and motorcycles, more evidence from previous lawsuits.

One of Harney's most valuable tools at work is his extensive medical library, more than 1,000 volumes, housed with the firm's total law library of 8,000 to 9,000 volumes. In the medical collection is Harney's own text, *Medical Malpractice,* published by The Michie Company in Charlottesville, Virginia. Basically it's a book of "thou shalts," explains the trial attorney, adding that his text probably is used as often by doctors and insurance companies as by lawyers. For example, in chapters relating to each of the specialized fields of medicine, Harney advises readers on acceptable standards of practice. Before the book was first published in 1973, and before publishing supplements and the second, 1987, edition, Harney sent every chapter for review to a doctor specializing in the field on which that chapter was written. "I don't want to be a medical doctor under false pretenses," he explains, "and I don't want to put out a product that is inaccurate." The book also includes a chapter for other lawyers on how to handle a malpractice case. "There's a lot of him in the book," adds Donald E. Selby, Michie's director of professional publications. "He makes all that law come alive."

Harney, whose plaques, certificates, and awards span the hallway walls outside his office door, works on a contingent-fee basis equaling between one-third and forty percent of a jury verdict, after first subtracting off the top any expenses incurred when preparing and trying a case. "The clearer the case, the lower the fee," Harney explains of his billing policy. Harney won't represent insurance companies "on principle"; he considers working for them "to be somewhat in the slavery department because lay people are telling you how to practice law," and he doesn't "want some insurance adjuster telling me what to do." But he does represent a number of physicians, whom he usually does not charge. "To be selfish about it, it's always nice to have doctor friends," says Harney. "You'd be amazed at how much of our work is referred by doctors" whose patients have suffered from malpractice in the hands of their previous physicians.

While Harney does not charge doctors he represents, he also points out that he does not bill for the time he gives to evaluating, investigating, and offering opinions on cases that he doesn't accept. Nor does Harney charge for any case he loses.

Despite his workload, Harney seems unconcerned about maintaining a strict regimen focused on one case at a time, with no outside diversions. "He can be trying a case and have breakfast and lunch meetings on different cases," says Pagliuso. "I've been in trials [with Harney] where he's gone to different functions every night," including Democratic Party functions. Harney, says

Pagliuso, is a "big political contributor." In fact, Harney was a member of the California delegation to the 1968 Democratic Presidential nominating convention at the Ambassador Hotel, and he says he was the last person to see Bobby Kennedy before he was assassinated.

Despite the intensity of Harney's lifestyle and his dedication to work, he is philosophical about winning and losing lawsuits. "Of the cases we take, nine out of ten will settle," he explains. "We never know which will be the one." Of the one case out of ten that does go to trial, Harney says his success record is "close to fifty-fifty. It's the highly debatable case that ends up being tried," he explains. And Harney points out, plaintiffs nationally are winning only twenty percent of those cases. Then again, tough cases are the ones that Harney most enjoys. "Some trial lawyers will only try winners," he is quick to note. "I usually settle the winners because my clients are usually better off with a good settlement than a gamble and all those years on appeal." As for the others? "My theory," he says, laughing, "is that you can't lose them all."

Harry Jordan's case first came to Harney through Jordan's business lawyer, John Argue, a well-known tax and business attorney who organized the 1984 Olympics in Los Angeles. Originally Jordan had asked Argue only to collect past and anticipated medical expenses for him, an amount Argue estimated to be about $1 million. In early 1983, Argue called Harney to ask for help down the road should Jordan's doctors not agree to pay that sum.

It was nearly a year after Jordan's operation that Argue finally came back to Harney to take on the case. In the meantime, Argue had raised his estimate to $1.5 million, and the doctors and hospital steadfastly refused to meet the demand. Harney knew that Jordan's circumstances presented a malpractice claim with merit, potential for a sizable award, and most importantly, jury appeal. The plaintiff's lawyer thought that Jordan, a very outgoing, active, and popular man, would make a sympathetic figure for any jury. A World War II fighter pilot, he had earned the nickname "Lucky Jordan" because the enemy hit his plane so many times and he always survived. He was a temporary Air Force general during the Korean War when his own general was killed. Married to his wife, Miriam, for about forty years, Jordan began his career after World War II in his father-in-law's Long Beach insurance brokerage business, about thirty miles south of Los Angeles. Eventually Jordan took over the agency, where his wife and two of their three children also worked. Jordan "belonged to the Kiwanis, the Rotary club, he played golf, he was a big fisherman, did a lot of traveling, entertained, had a beautiful house and a large boat—everything was going fine," says Harney when describing his client before the ill-fated surgery. He even had raised $3 million for the Long Beach Community Hospital, adds Harney with an appropriate note of irony.

So Harney agreed to take on Jordan's case even though he knew at the time that a 1975 California law limiting recovery for pain and suffering, or noneconomic damages, in medical malpractice cases to $250,000 was pending before the state supreme court. Harney was certain that the law would be declared unconstitutional. "The right to sue for personal injury is a common law right, and the U.S. Constitution and most state constitutions say in common law cases the parties are entitled to trial by jury—and that right should remain inviolate," asserts Harney. Some other states had already held such medical malpractice caps to be unconstitutional. Furthermore, Harney recognized that the California cap did not apply to awards for economic loss nor to punitive damages, and he thought Jordan's case deserved both.

Typically when other lawyers refer clients, Harney negotiates a fee-sharing agreement on a case-by-case basis. Such a forwarding or referral fee "has to be hammered out," he says, adding that "sometimes it's the most difficult part of getting these things moving." Frequently lawyers referring cases to Harney have no desire to share in his fee, nor do they stay involved in the case. But when the referring lawyer wants to continue participating,

Harney usually gives that lawyer one-fifth of the contingent fee earned. Sometimes the referring lawyer gets only ten percent, and never more than half. When the referring lawyer does stay involved, explains Harney, that lawyer also serves as a "hand holder" for the client. "Some clients need a lot of hand holding," says the plaintiff's lawyer. Argue's participation in the Jordan case was unusual for a referring attorney in that he actually appeared at the trial as a witness, testifying about Jordan's loss of income.

Once the two lawyers decided to work together, Harney had very little time before the California one-year statute of limitations ran out on the Jordan case. He quickly put together a complaint for filing with the court, suing on Mr. and Mrs. Jordan's behalf Carlton Waters, Jordan's internist; Barton Wachs, the urologist who acted as chief surgeon; Marshall Grobert, the urologist who acted as assistant surgeon; Grobert-Sawyer Medical Corporation, Wachs's and Grobert's employer; William Stanton, the general surgeon who also acted as an assistant surgeon; Robert Odell, the anesthesiologist; Rudolph Chaney, a radiologist, and his employer, Community Radiology Medical Group, Inc.; and Long Beach Community Hospital, where the surgery took place. Harney named as defendants all of the physicians involved and the hospital in order to spread the blame for the faulty procedure and to collect a greater total award for his client. In particular, Harney sued the hospital for allowing the operating urologist Wachs on its staff. The plaintiff's lawyer maintained in the suit that Wachs, the son of a wealthy, prominent Long Beach physician and newly hired by the urologist practice of Grobert-Sawyer Medical Corporation, had a poor and disjointed educational and training record. Harney said that Jordan's internist Waters had even tried to reach other urologists in preference to Grobert-Sawyer, but Jordan's surgery was on the Friday after Thanksgiving, a time when many doctors are vacationing or hard to reach. "A lot of malpractice occurs around holidays" when many of the competent doctors aren't available, says Harney.

Harney sought compensatory damages against all the named

defendants, plus punitive damages against Waters, Wachs, Grobert, and the Grobert-Sawyer Medical Corporation. Definitions for compensatory and punitive damages vary somewhat among states, but in California, compensatory damages include two categories: special damages that are generally economic and relate to medical expenses and income loss, both actual and potential; and noneconomic damages for pain and suffering. Punitive damages are awarded in addition to compensatory damages to punish the defendant or to make an example. In California, plaintiffs are not allowed to specify in a complaint the amount of damages requested because of possible negative press consequences for the named defendants.

In response to the charges, Wachs, Grobert, and the Grobert-Sawyer Medical Corporation responded that the operation was simply "an honest mistake" that was not their fault. The two urologists said that when they looked at Jordan's X ray in the hospital viewbox, it had been placed in the viewbox backward so that Jordan's tumorous right kidney appeared to be his left one. The doctors further misinterpreted right and left markings on the X ray, leading them to misdiagnose the location of the cancer and order the removal of the left kidney. Grobert, Sawyer, and Grobert-Sawyer Medical Corporation held firm to the offer they had made to Argue for a $1 million settlement.

The other defendants also denied any malpractice. The radiologist, for example, said he had written on the X ray jacket the abbreviation "NEO R KID," short for neoplasm or cancer of the right kidney. He said he had written the words in red—indicating an abnormality—rather than in black, the standard indication for normalcy. Yet all the other doctors said they never saw the X-ray jacket.

Several months after filing suit, Harney asked the judge for an expedited trial because of the seriousness of Jordan's injury and his decreased life expectancy. Under California law, if the plaintiff is more than seventy years old, the court must grant an expedited trial, and if the plaintiff's life expectancy is substantially diminished, the judge may grant one. The defense lawyers, says Harney, "always oppose" these requests. The judge in Jordan's case, Robert C. Nye, held a hearing on Harney's request for an expedited trial eight to nine months after he first filed suit. Armed with depositions to show that he could go to trial quickly and with evidence on Jordan's diminished life expectancy, Harney won his motion, and the judge set the trial for a few months later. The average time for getting a case from filing to trial is close to five years, says Harney of this feat.

The three-month, multidefendant trial beginning in December 1984 was an acrimonious one, with Harney accusing the physicians of carelessness, neglect, and even stupidity, while the defendants' lawyers attacked Harney's trial tactics. The judge refused to let Harney pursue his argument that the hospital should have refused the urologist Wachs staff privileges; Judge Nye also struck from the trial record any testimony supporting Harney's claim to punitive damages. But in the end, after deliberating for six days, the jury found the internist Waters, the urologists Grobert and Wachs, the general surgeon Stanton, and the Grobert-Sawyer Medical Corporation guilty of medical malpractice. The jurors exonerated the hospital, the radiologist, and the anesthesiologist. In all, the jury awarded Jordan $2 million in past noneconomic damages, $2.5 million in future noneconomic damages, $6,600 for past medical expenses, and $97,000 for future medical expenses. The jury awarded Jordan's wife $250,000 for past noneconomic damages and $375,000 for future noneconomic damages. The entire verdict totaled $5,228,600.

But as fate would have it, one day before the jury had finished its deliberation, the California Supreme Court held that California's law placing a cap on compensation for noneconomic damages in medical malpractice cases—a cap of $250,000—was indeed constitutional. As a result, Judge Nye, who earlier in the trial had said that he thought the $250,000 cap was unconstitutional, spontaneously reduced the jury's $5.2-million verdict to $256,000, which included $6,000 for Jordan's unreimbursed medical expenses. "It was kind of a Pyrrhic victory," says Harney of the jury's initial award. Harney has appealed the reduced damages award, the lack of any award for punitive damages, and the exoneration of the hospital.

Despite the outcome to date, Harney maintains that the Jordan case has been, and is, worth the effort. For one, the jury trial attracted nationwide press attention—ranging from the Atlanta-based cable television network CNN to PBS's "MacNeil-Lehrer Report"—publicizing Jordan's plight and inflamming debate on malpractice award caps. Harney is hopeful that the higher California courts will find in his favor, especially given that several new judges have replaced those on the state supreme court since that court ruled that the malpractice cap was constitutional.

The urologists Grobert and Wachs, the attending general surgeon Stanton, and the business entity Grobert-Sawyer Medical Corporation settled after the trial for $300,000 each, totaling among the four parties $1.2 million. They agreed to pay more than the $250,000 cap, says Harney, because the president of one of the insurance companies, Doctors Insurance Company in Santa Monica, California, said the company didn't intend to apply the cap to a case such as Jordan's, and because those defendants wanted to wrap the matter up. Harney agreed to the settlement, he says, because Jordan badly needed interim funds. The internist Waters appealed.

Despite the still-undetermined final outcome, the Jordan trial already offers valuable pointers for preparing and trying a medical malpractice lawsuit, including selecting a winnable suit as Harney did. The $5.2-million verdict, despite the California Supreme Court ruling and the judge's reduced verdict, still indicates that Harney successfully convinced a jury that Jordan's doctors had been negligent and that their negligence was what led to Jordan's permanent injury. The jury felt that Jordan deserved the $5.2-million award.

In the Jordan case, Harney also successfully demonstrated his heavy reliance on investigators, even sending them all the way to Mexico to check out Wachs's medical training record. The investigators alleged, for example, that Wachs had to go out of the country, to Mexico, to enroll in a medical school before he could transfer to one in the U.S., and that he performed poorly on his medical boards. These allegations could help support Harney's claim, now cited in his appeal, that the hospital should never have permitted Wachs to operate.

Similarly noteworthy was Harney's trial strategy of spreading liability for the malpractice. Doing so enabled him to seek maximum damages for his client because each physician's malpractice insurance coverage was limited, either to $500,000 or to $1 million. Harney was successful in this tactic, convincing the jury that not only the operating surgeon Wachs was at fault, but also three other doctors involved in the surgery, and the Grobert-Sawyer Medical Corporation. "The real foul-up was with the urologists," explains Harney today. It was "tough trying to spread the liability" to the general surgeon and the internist.

Harney also helped boost the jury award by suing several of the doctors for punitive as well as compensatory damages. When Harney sued for punitive damages, the doctors could not admit liability because their insurance policies did not cover punitive damages. Thus the doctors lost the psychological advantage with the jury of admitting guilt and offering to pay damages; generally, such demonstrated remorse brings jury sympathy around to the defendants rather than to the plaintiffs, so it was to Harney's advantage to prevent that from happening.

Still another strategic tactical decision entailed calling the defendants themselves as adverse witnesses before any other plaintiffs' witnesses testified. Under California law an attorney is able to question adverse witnesses as if cross-examining them, including asking leading questions. A "leading question" is one that suggests an answer in the wording of the question, such as "You went to the theater last night at eight?" This technique of calling the defendants as adverse witnesses allowed Harney to put in front of the jury early in Jordan's case the defendants' versions of the kidney operation. Thus the defendants could not alter their testimony after hearing what their own experts said on the stand, nor could the defense experts try to explain away the defendants' behavior in advance of the defendants' testifying. After Harney had questioned the defendant doctors, he called his own experts to offer their critical views on the doctors' care, as the doctors themselves had described that care.

Finally, the Jordan trial exemplifies an aggressive courtroom style. Throughout that trial Harney elected to appear caustic and biting. "In the Jordan case the defendants were very arrogant," explains Harney. In response, he opted for an attitude of outrage. Harney hoped that by choosing this particular demeanor and style he would elicit in the jurors the same indignation and repulsion that he felt toward the doctors. And he did.

Harney spent three solid months preparing for the Jordan trial, including taking fifty-two depositions. His investigator Joseph M. Beringhele devoted a couple of months, traveling from San Francisco to Guadalajara, Mexico, where the operating urologist Wachs attended medical school. Beringhele asked a second freelance investigator—a former U.S. State Department employee—to accompany him to Mexico as an interpreter. Once there, Beringhele, who has worked for Harney for twenty years, also hired a local private detective. Among his many stops, Beringhele visited the dean of foreign students at the Universidad Autonoma de Guadalajara to research Wachs's medical school record. (Wachs had been refused admission by all U.S. medical schools to which he applied, says Harney.) Back in the States, Beringhele also obtained documentation from the California Board of Medical Quality Assurance in Sacramento to show that Wachs had failed his state boards three times before he passed, says Harney.

Much of the investigation preceeding the trial, both in Mexico and in the U.S., centered on Harney's belief that Wachs had used illegal drugs. (The court would later, however, exclude any evidence related to this.) Beringhele even tracked down in prison one of Wachs's former associates who was convicted of murder. "Harney believes in leaving no stone unturned," says Beringhele when describing the extent of his activities and efforts to locate Wachs's associates and friends from years past. "If there's something out there, we make a diligent effort to find it."

When it came time to present his case, Harney explained to the jury that Harry Jordan's pain preceeding the operation was on his right side. The doctors could even feel the tumorous mass by pressing on Jordan's right side. "And the evidence will show," Harney told the jury sarcastically, "that in medicine all designations, right or left, pertain to the patient, not to anybody else. And if a lady, for example, has something wrong with her right foot, it is her right foot, not the physician's right foot, not the radiologist's right foot, but the patient's right foot, and not somebody else's left foot." As he spoke, Harney wore two round buttons on his lapels—one with a large "R" and the other with a large "L."

After Wachs removed Jordan's left kidney, with both the urologist Grobert and the general surgeon Stanton assisting, continued Harney, the three doctors failed to recognize immediately their mistake, even though they cut the removed kidney in half to confirm the presence of cancer cells.

When Harney finished addressing the jury, the eight defendants' lawyers stood one by one to make individual opening statements on behalf of their clients. The attorney for Wachs did not try to argue that the operation was successful. "Indeed Dr. Wachs admitted from the moment that he was aware that the incorrect kidney had been removed that he had made a mistake," said Robert C. Baker, "and he admitted to it November twenty-seventh [the day after the surgery], and he admits it today." Wachs "never acted in any disregard but only regard for the patient, and he, like all mortal human beings, can, and unfortunately did, make a mistake."

When it came time to call his witnesses, Harney relied on a technique that, although generally atypical for other lawyers, had served Harney well in the past. Harney put every defendant—all the doctors and the hospital administrator—on the stand as adverse witnesses. "The defendant does not want to admit he made a mistake," says Harney. The defendant "will be defensive. You have to drag out of him what happened." This is critical, Harney explains, because "less than ten percent of what really happened is contained within the medical record which surfaces. The medical record is always under the control of the defendants, and the injured party or the family of the deceased in a malpractice case never [kept independent] medical records. So consequently you have to start off with the ability to cross-examine the defendant or defendants in order to bring out [for the jury] the true facts if possible, and then go from there. Your own experts have to have that information in order to give their opinions." Under the California code, as permitted in some other states and in federal courts, Harney asked the defendants leading and suggestive questions, which are not permitted during direct examination of a lawyer's own witnesses.

The internist Waters, for example, was one of Harney's first witnesses, and because he was a defendant, he was an adverse witness. To get a full description of Waters's involvement in Jordan's kidney operation, Harney grilled the doctor about his preoperative notes and reports. One dictated report was not even transcribed until four days after the operation:

Harney: And did your history and physical, as finally transcribed four days later, indicate the side of the body on which there was a lesion in Harry Jordan's case?

Waters: Yes.

Harney: And what side is that?

Waters: Right.

Harney: Now, in addition to the dictated history and physical, did you write in the record a so-called progress note in your handwriting?

Waters: I wrote an admission note and a presurgical note.

Harney: And would you read into the record your admission note, please? First of all, tell us the time of day when you wrote the admission note.

Waters: Right after I did the history and physical.

Harney: Around eight-thirty to eight forty-five [A.M.]?

Waters: Yes. Before the dictation. . . . Here it is. Would you like me to read it?

Harney: Please. Read it into the record verbatim. . . .

Waters: "Hematuria in right flank and costovertebral angle pain for four days. Patient has severe coronary heart disease and has been on Coumadin for two to three years. There is normal sinus rhythm. Blood pressure is one forty-four over eighty-two. The chest is clear. There is no pedal edema. There is marked tenderness to percussion over the right costovertebral angle."

Harney: Would that be in the area of the kidney on the right side?

Waters: Yes. . . .

Harney: . . . your second progress note, could you find that for us, please?

Waters: Yes.

Harney: Excuse me, Doctor. It is right here. What did you write in your second progress note, and please, read that into the record verbatim.

Waters: "Bleeding and clots continue and IVP [intravenous pyelogram] shows a baseball-sized tumor in the left kidney. Dr. Grobert has seen and will do a nephrectomy tonight. The patient still has a normal sinus rhythm; chest is clear; chest X rays negative for metastasis. Blood pressure one twenty over eighty." And that is dated six, twenty-six, '82.

Harney: June twenty-sixth?

Waters: Yes.

Harney: And you have got the mass on the left side?

Waters: Right.

Harney: And when you say "right," do you mean "correct"?

Waters: Correct.

Harney: You have already talked to Dr. Chaney [the radiologist who first read the X rays], who categorically said it was on the R-I-G-H-T side?

Waters: Right.

Harney: And you talked to Dr. Grobert who had pointed out this large mass on the right side to you?

Waters: Right.

Harney: And you have told Dr. Grobert the patient has pain in the right flank and that he had tenderness in the right flank area?

Waters: Yes.

Harney: Now, where did you get this word L-E-F-T for that note?

Waters: That is fatigue talking. The wrong date, the wrong side.

In questioning an adverse witness or in cross-examination, Harney tries to highlight facts supporting a plaintiff's claim, especially when the defense is hiding that information. "You have to have a very good memory to be able to trap the witness," explains Harney, who never uses notes when speaking in court, and who writes little during a trial. "He has a fantastic memory," says former partner Pagliuso, who worked extensively on the Jordan case with Harney. "He takes no notes in a trial. He just sits there. He can be in a lengthy, lengthy trial and never take any notes."

"I'm kind of a juggler. I take a lot of mental notes," explains Harney.

Sharp listening skills paid off, for example, in one of Harney's earlier cases, a lawsuit involving a boy who had a cancer in his foot. The boy's family claimed that his teacher had dropped a round metal bar on the boy's foot, aggravating his condition and requiring that the foot be amputated. In defense, the teacher said that he dropped the bar on the floor and it slowly rolled into the foot. A cancer specialist named Ian Macdonald testified for the defense that there was no relation between the iron bar and the boy's cancerous condition. The doctor offered as a basis for his expertise his observations of a man with a similar cancer in his arm at the New York Sloan-Kettering Hospital in the 1930s. This man's cancer, said Macdonald, was extremely slow-growing; he observed its slow growth because the patient refused surgery. But later in his testimony Macdonald—to support his opinion that the growth rates of this cancer are "variable"—said he had seen one "fast-growing" cancer, and he described the patient as a man in New York in 1936 with a cancer in his arm.

When Harney cross-examined Macdonald and asked him to describe more fully the "slow-growing" cancer he had mentioned earlier, the doctor referred to the very same man in New York. Through his sharp listening skills, Harney had caught the redundancy in the examples and pointed out the doctor's mistake. Thus Harney completely discredited Macdonald as an expert witness. "That," says Harney, "is an example of how a witness—even though very prominent—will get on the stand and say many things out of the blue to justify a certain position being taken." Harney was merciless in his cross-examination, so merciless that in their appeal, the defendants' lawyers wrote: "Dr. Macdonald was subjected to the most unwarranted cross-examination and personal attack witnessed by trial counsel. The viciousness of the attack cannot be overstated or overemphasized."

The defendants' appellate challenge failed, but the trial record shows that Harney was, in fact, an aggressive cross-examiner. His technique even caused the cancer specialist to lose his composure, and hence his respectability before the jury:

Harney: Doctor, do you have any personal dislike of me?

Mr. Haight [opposing counsel]: Your Honor, I don't think that is material.

The Court: Yes.

Harney: Just to show bias.

The Court: Yes. I think it is permissible. Overruled.

Macdonald: I—I have no idea why this should be interjected.

Harney: No. I just asked you, Doctor—

Macdonald: Would you think that this would affect my estimate of a synovioma's [the cancer's] size, Mr. Harney?

Harney: No. Would you answer my question, please, Doctor.

Macdonald: No. I feel neither dislike nor any emotion about you at all, sir. I am here to do a job, and so are you.

Harney: Do you recall the occasion where you got off the witness stand, Doctor, and called me a name—the last three words of which began with the letters, respectively, *s,o,b*?

Macdonald: Yes. And you had earned that, Mr. Harney. . . .

Another Harney tactic is to build up speed while questioning a witness until the witness trips up under the growing pressure and gives an answer Harney wants, but one the witness hadn't planned to provide. "The cross-examination of a witness by an opposing party has been described as 'the greatest legal engine ever invented for the discovery of truth,' " says Harney. The continental European legal system, he adds, doesn't have cross-examination. "I wouldn't be able to practice under that system at all," says the plaintiff's lawyer.

In the case of Harry Jordan's kidney surgery, an acid-tongued Harney similarly took out after another expert, Mitchell S. Karlan, a surgeon testifying in support of Stanton, the general surgeon who assisted Wachs when he operated on Jordan:

Harney: Would you assume in this case the chief surgeon [Wachs], the captain of the sinking ship, testified that this was absolutely not an emergency?

Baker [Wachs's attorney]: I move to strike the preamble of Mr. Harney.

The Court: The motion is granted. You may reframe the questions.

Harney: Would you say that Dr. Stanton was a member of the crew of his ship?

Karlan: I have never considered my operating team as a crew. I think he was a second assistant.

Harney: Like a second mate on a ship?

Karlan: No, sir. A second mate has some delegation and authority. He has rank. The second assistant has a job to do and that is to assist. . . .

Harney: Was he acting as a general surgeon, sir?

Karlan: He was functioning in the capacity of a surgeon who was serving as a second assistant.

Harney: And did Dr. Stanton have to have some kind of game plan in the event there was involvement of the vena cava or the heart or the aorta or the spleen or the liver or the stomach or the bowel?

Karlan: I would say yes.

Harney: And how could he ever get a game plan if he never found out which side the tumor was on?

Karlan: He was told which side the tumor was on.

Harney: Which hand is this ball in [holding ball in right hand]?

Karlan: Mr. Harney, if you told me that ball was in your left hand, I would have the utmost respect for you and say it is in your left hand.

Harney: Sir, which hand has the ball in it?

Later during his cross-examination of Karlan, Harney's sarcasm reached its peak. Harney asked Karlan about Wachs's performance of the surgery:

Harney: When you talk about a captain of the ship [Wachs], were you talking about a qualified captain who could sail the ship without sinking?

Karlan: May I point out, Mr. Harney, he took this kidney out and did a radical nephrectomy? He did it with expertise. He did it well. He took the wrong kidney out. But he did it.

Harney: Do you think he ought to get the Nobel Prize?

Harney isn't always so scornful. He modifies his courtroom technique when he thinks a hard-hitting style will work against him. For example, when in 1987 Harney tried the case of nineteen-year-old Terri Tyus, who at thirteen had had almost her entire intestine erroneously removed during surgery for a benign abdominal tumor, Harney was more low-key. While one of his experts—a specialist in rehabilitation nursing—testified about Tyus's annual medical and specialized feeding costs, Harney casually leaned back against the courtroom wall next to the jury box, his arms lightly folded across his chest. He clearly recognized that the opposing lawyer representing the defendant doctor in this trial was extremely soft-spoken and gentlemanly, an attorney whom jurors typically find so likable that Harney knew he had to adopt the same demeanor or lose juror sympathy to the opposing side. The Tyus trial ended with a $500,000 settlement offer from the defendant, who was the doctor assisting in the surgery. Harney had previously settled, out of court, with the operating doctor and with the hospital.

In another trial, Harney says the opposing lawyer did not know when to pull back and to be less aggressive. This case grew out of an incident when a man left a bar at about two-thirty A.M. He drove into a house being moved on a trailer and was killed. The moving vehicle "had something like twenty-seven lights across it," says Harney, who represented the man's wife and children. "I put on a case that this moving outfit was deficient with regard to the amount of illumination that they provided. People were returning from bars at that time, and [they] might have had quite a bit to drink," so the moving vehicle should have had more lights to warn other drivers. But it so happened that in this case the man had run into the moving vehicle on his way to visit his mistress. During the trial, the moving company's defense attorney actually brought the mistress into court—in front of the wife and children. The impact on the jurors was psychological backfire, says Harney. They awarded the family $100,000.

In the Jordan trial, after Harney had finished aggressively questioning the defendants, he called to the stand a number of other witnesses for direct examination. These included the surgeon who operated on Jordan at the UCLA Medical Center, Jordan's new urologist, his new internist, a leading kidney transplant expert, nurses on duty the day of Jordan's surgery, an economist, Jordan's business attorney John Argue, and Jordan's wife and three children. Harney didn't count on a set order for his witnesses, one planned before the trial began. Rather, he determined on a day-by-day basis whom he would call to the stand. For one, the doctors' and experts' own unpredictable work schedules mandated this flexibility. Also, judges' calendars change, jurors get sick, arguments on legal matters consume more time than had been anticipated, says Harney. "I'd prefer if I ever could to put witnesses on the way I want to," adds the plaintiff's lawyer, but "I don't think in my entire career I've ever had it work out according to plan."

Once Harney got his experts in court, he had no trouble working with the doctors and helping them make their medical opinions clear to the jury. Harney was "very, very good with the medical terms, and being able to talk to the doctors," observes Jordan when asked about his malpractice lawsuit. "He researched extremely well. He knew his way around and how to deal with the people."

One of the better medical experts testifying on Jordan's behalf from Harney's list of witnesses was John S. Wilson, a prominent Los Angeles surgeon. Wilson explained why he thought the internist Waters was guilty of "conscious disregard" of Jordan's safety, a prerequisite for awarding punitive damages in addition to compensatory damages. "As far as the progress notes," testified Wilson, "Dr. Waters . . . knew or should have known what his admitting note said. He had talked to the patient and it was on his right side. And to have it suddenly shift to the left, it would—it should have caused him great concern . . ."

Harney: Assume that Dr. Waters testified to this effect: that when he arrived in this room [the senior urologist] Dr. Grobert was there with one film in the box and Dr. Grobert had it in backward. But be that as it may, whether there were ten films or just one film, Dr. Waters testified that his consultation with Dr. Grobert before going up to see the patient was only five to fifteen seconds, and the consultation was with the film or films in the box backward. Is that below the standard?

Fidler [Waters's attorney]: Standard of whom? I object to the question.

Harney: Of the interns, of the interns.

Wilson: The fifteen seconds or the films in backward or all of the above?

Harney: Both. In other words, doing an X-ray review for impending major surgery with the urologist, without talking to a radiologist who is within a few feet of this box, within a few feet, and he doesn't talk to the radiologist. He spends five to fifteen seconds talking to a urologist who has the films in backward, where he, Dr. Waters himself, has them in backward. Now, is that below the standard?

Wilson: Yes.

Harney then took Wilson through all the steps preceding Jordan's surgery—asking Wilson to assume that the doctors intentionally followed each and every step from discussing the diagnosis, to scrubbing up, to removing the kidney. "The connotation of all this stuff," explains Harney, "puts it together that in order to do all of this deliberately and intentionally, then there had to be a conscious, awake disregard." Harney sought to prove conscious disregard for Jordan's safety to get a punitive damages award from the jury because the California legislative cap on medical malpractice awards applies only to noneconomic compensatory damages, not punitive damages. There is "a built-in punitive amount for medical malpractice cases," says Harney, "because of the fiduciary obligation between the physician and the patient."

But Judge Nye struck from the record all testimony that might have justified the jury's awarding punitive damages. The judge "had the attitude that 'Wachs was the guy who really fouled us up, so I don't want anybody else found liable for what Wachs did,' " explains Harney. "And as far as Wachs is concerned, [the judge reasoned] 'since he's willing to admit [to the damage], then why should I let punitive in?' " Harney maintains that if the judge hadn't struck the testimony supporting Jordan's punitive damages claim, the jury "would have nailed those guys [the defendants] for maybe ten million dollars punitive."

"The judge was very much against me for some reason," says Jordan.

As the three-month trial progressed, all the parties grew more hostile. Verbal skirmishes were breaking out regularly. One centered on the consent form Jordan signed before his operation, with the plaintiffs maintaining that the form was blank, indicating neither "right" nor "left," and the defendants arguing that the form was clearly marked for a left nephrectomy. The defendants also said that Jordan had had pain on his left side (he had recently fallen while boating and had hit his left side), and that he was so obese that they could not feel the cancerous mass. With accusations flying, personal animosity among the lawyers only continued to grow.

At the end of the trial Harney tried to turn the ugly tone of the proceeding to his client's advantage. "It is a pleasure to be here to try to wind down this long proceeding," Harney announced in his closing statement. "And as I was vilified and attacked by these eight wonderful masterminds of the law [the defense lawyers], I thought of the old ploy that if you have no case yourself and you can't attack the other case, then attack the other lawyer because he may be defenseless. And the more I got attacked, the more I thought my client should be defended.

"And it was interesting during the course of these eight brilliant arguments that started out with Mr. Baker [the operating urologist Wachs's lawyer] making what I thought was a vicious attack on Harry Jordan that he was a perverter of the truth, not telling the truth. And I thought how undignified can it be that Harry Jordan is attacked physically and his normal kidney is removed and he has been subjected to everything we know about, and then to add insult to injury, reopen his wound and drop in hydrochloric acid, and just to make him feel worse, why not attack his character; why not attack his veracity; why not attack his honesty?

"Let's have everybody go down in this maelstrom of confusion and negligence and disregard of Harry Jordan," concluded Harney. "Why not let's everybody be together?"

The jurors did not let Jordan go down. Although they exonerated the hospital, the radiologist, and the anesthesiologist, the jurors did find the other doctors—Grobert, Wachs, Waters, Stanton, and the Grobert-Sawyer Medical Corporation—guilty of medical malpractice. The jurors gave Jordan, and Harney as his lawyer, their whopping verdict of $5.2 million in compensatory damages.

Yet there were disappointments in that victory. For one, the judge had denied Harney the right to introduce evidence showing that the hospital should not have allowed the operating urologist

Wachs on its staff. This argument was one Harney had hoped to use to convince the jury that the hospital was also liable for Jordan's condition. Second, the jury did not award Jordan for his loss of income as part of the compensatory damages. "There was a big fuss about Harry's loss-of-income claim," explains Harney. The defendants alleged that Jordan sold his business to his son only on paper and actually stayed in control himself. Harney pointed out that the son paid for the business. Probably, speculates Harney, the jury "figured Jordan was going to get paid for the business from the son and therefore didn't really lose any money on it" to merit an additional amount in the final award. And third, the judge had not allowed Harney to seek punitive damages.

Even worse was Judge Nye's decision to strike Jordan's $5.2-million award and to set a new award at $256,000, including $6,000 for unreimbursed medical expenses, following the California Supreme Court's ruling upholding the constitutionality of the state $250,000 cap on medical malpractice awards. If the jury had given Jordan compensation for loss of income, that portion of the verdict would have been secure because the cap doesn't apply to it. The cap applies only to awards to compensate for noneconomic loss, such as pain, suffering, inconvenience, physical impairment, and disfigurement. Nor would punitive damages have been limited if the jury had included them in its award.

Harney appealed the final outcome, challenging the judge's rulings forbidding Harney from trying to prove that the hospital was negligent in granting the urologist Wachs staff privileges, preventing Jordan from recovering punitive damages, and reducing Jordan's compensatory damages award.

It was while the appeal was under way that Grobert, Wachs, Stanton, and the Grobert-Sawyer Medical Corporation each decided to settle for $300,000, giving Jordan a total of $1.2 million. Harney's pending appeal now applies only to Jordan's former internist Waters and to the Long Beach Community Hospital.

The law firm can absorb the financial disappointment at this point. "In some instances," explains Pagliuso, "Harney enjoys a challenge. And sometimes the challenge may be more important than the economics. He looks at these cases in a bigger picture," concludes Pagliuso. "I would have liked to see this case settled. I think Dave looks at this case [recognizing] in part that the defense—the whole defense industry of the malpractice case—wasn't very well served by this case going to trial. It was in the newspapers all the time. It was on television. After it was over, everybody was taking about this case to show how the cap limitation on damages is so unfair."

Harney, who firmly believes that caps on damages are unconstitutional, hopes that the discussion continues, convincing many to feel as he does. States have differed in their rulings on the issue. Courts in Idaho, Illinois, Minnesota, Montana, New Hampshire, North Dakota, Ohio, Texas, and Virginia have found the caps unconstitutional. But as in California, courts in Florida, Indiana, Nebraska, and Wisconsin have upheld the constitutionality of these limitations.

The Jordan case, says Harney, demonstrates with finality that the cap "is ridiculous." Even officials at the American Medical Association and a major insurance company for physicians have stated publicly that they didn't intend for the cap to apply to cases such as Harry Jordan's, says Harney. And in his home state of California, Harney hopes that the case of Harry Jordan will be "the vehicle to knock out the cap."

ARTHUR L. LIMAN

Paul, Weiss, Rifkind, Wharton & Garrison, New York

Americans most likely remember Arthur Liman, fifty-five, as the chief lawyer for the U.S. Senate select committee that investigated the Iran-contra scandal in the summer of 1987. Liman questioned Lieutenant Colonel Oliver North and others on national television about their role in the U.S. sale of arms to Iran, and the diversion of proceeds to the Nicaraguan contras.

It was a challenge Liman remembers well. "Oliver North was clearly one of the best prepared, most articulate, and most charismatic witnesses that any lawyer would ever have to confront," says Liman. "Moreover, he was on television where his very facial features took on heroic proportions. He was sitting at counsel table with only one lawyer, facing a committee consisting of twenty-six members, plus counsel for the committee, plus assistants of the members, so it looked like the whole world was against this young marine with his medals."

Liman knew that he couldn't attack North through his questioning; he had to pull back. "Anyone who would have persisted in questions of a witness like North, without a judge there, where all that you would get would be speeches [unrestrained by a judge], is simply asking to evoke more and more sympathy for North, and not get the facts and create the impression of bullying him. Common sense had to prevail. You cross-examine a witness like Oliver North differently from the way you cross-examine some other witness."

So Liman, who can be as tough and determined and hard-nosed as any lawyer, behaved kindly toward North, adopting an almost avuncular approach when addressing the congressional witness. "When he's trying to elicit the truth," says another lawyer of Liman, "he uses the style that most fits the circumstances."

Liman's contribution to the Iran-contra investigation, along with his oversight of the lengthy Senate report that followed those hearings, was simply one more undertaking in a long list of distinguished achievements. Liman is the ultimate corporate lawyer, one whose multiple successes on numerous fronts have made him prominent at his prestigious midtown-Manhattan law firm, throughout New York City, and in the nation as a whole.

A sizable number of Liman's noteworthy accomplishments were done in public service. In 1972, New York's Governor Nelson Rockefeller named Liman chief counsel to the New York State special commission investigating the Attica prison uprising. Governor Hugh Carey asked Liman to serve on an executive committee on sentencing reform and to head his Executive Advisory Committee on the Administration of Justice. In New York City, Mayor Edward Koch asked Liman in 1985 to chair an investigation into allegations against the city's medical examiner.

At the same time, Liman was completing a two-year volunteer term as president of New York's Legal Aid Society, the organization that provides legal services for the city's poor.

When Liman is not laboring on behalf of worthy causes or governmental investigations, he's raising the banner of justice for those either wronged or under attack. They are no less newsworthy. Liman represented fugitive financier Robert Vesco when he was charged with embezzling; businessman John Zaccaro, husband of former Vice Presidential candidate Geraldine Ferraro, during the controversy over his real estate holdings; investment banker Dennis Levine, who was charged with insider trading; and junk bond pioneer Michael Milken. One of Liman's favorite courtroom victories was in 1980 when he helped New York City recoup $72 million from Rockwell International Corporation after that company provided defective parts for the city's subway cars. This was a trial, says Liman, that showed his skills at their best. Other Liman clients who readily seek his advice include corporate raider Carl Icahn; Warner Communications; Becton, Dickinson and Company; Time Inc.; and Lazard Frères & Company. Liman also helped Pennzoil win its $10.5 billion judgment against Texaco, sending that company into Chapter 11 bankruptcy.

Liman's high-profile public service and well-publicized client matters have kept him in the spotlight. And his stellar record on a variety of fronts has attracted even more business. In fact, Liman earns the kudos of his partners as rainmaker par excellence—a highly desirable tribute in the increasingly competitive realm of big-time corporate law.

Despite his rainmaking skills, it is litigation that Liman loves best. In the courtroom he finds the utmost thrill of his profession: the challenge of legal combat. "You have to enjoy it," says Liman of his passion. "You have to enjoy the battle. You have to get satisfaction out of it."

Early in his career Liman took a leave from Paul, Weiss, Rifkind, Wharton & Garrison to join the U.S. Attorney's Office in Manhattan. There he hoped to appease his initial curiosity about trial work. "I didn't know I was going to have a career as a trial lawyer," says Liman of the move. "I had enough doubt about it that I went to the U.S. Attorney's Office in order to try cases to see, one, whether I liked it, and two, whether I could be effective at it." From 1961 to 1963, Liman worked as an assistant U.S. attorney for Robert Morgenthau, building prosecutorial experience with all the trials he could handle. Ever since, Liman has kept his agenda at Paul, Weiss both full and varied. Clients hire him to handle cases on appeal just as often as they hire him to try them in the first place.

Ironically, it is in the courtroom that Liman finds the tranquillity of concentration, the peace of fully focused pursuit that eludes him in his everyday, high-intensity world. "Once the trial starts, it's like an operating room for me," says the trial attorney, who lives on Fifth Avenue in Manhattan with his wife, Ellen, an art advocate and author. The courtroom protects Liman from the pressures of his office, he says, where the phone rings constantly with clients calling for advice. "That is pressure," says the magna cum laude Yale Law School graduate. But "the courtroom is like an operating theater. No client, no matter how pressing the problem, would ever think of trying to reach me in a courtroom when I'm trying a case. I'm able to concentrate on that one thing. That's an enormous luxury."

In the courtroom Liman is renowned for his intelligence and preparation, for his superior judgment and adaptability when developing and implementing case strategy, and for his cross-examination technique. He usually seems genteel and courtly, but can nonetheless engage in brutally pointed examination of witnesses when the situation warrants. *The National Law Journal* once titled a feature article about Liman "The Gentle Lion of Litigation," evoking the contradictory image of kindness and consideration mixed with unchallenged strength and superiority. It is precisely this combination of traits that makes Liman so effective before a jury.

Yet even today Liman humbly admits to "stage fright" before a trial. "Every lawyer has stage fright," he says. "You accept the fact that you're going to have a degree of anxiety. It's natural to have that. But you have to know that you can live with it, or you're going to be miserable." Then, says Liman, instead of being satisfying, trial work will be punishing. After Liman stands up in the courtroom, however, his stage fright leaves. "Stage fright occurs the minute before you stand up to speak," he explains. Once on his feet Liman bears down on the work at hand and progresses, undisturbed, in his legal "operating room."

But he's still not overbearing. Liman hardly evokes the image of the carefully manicured, polished litigator, impeccably dressed and impeccably suave. He is, instead, unassuming and appears to be a willing friend of the court rather than a lawyer insisting on proving a point. Liman presents himself as someone who wants to help jurors find the truth. "Trial law is no more than being able to convince people of facts," says Liman. "That's what trial law is about. You have to use common sense. You can't be on a high horse. You can't talk down to people. You have to use plain language. You have to say to yourself, 'What would impress me?' And you have to be natural."

On occasion, appeals courts have overturned Liman's trial victories. One notable case was that of Chris-Craft Industries Inc. when it sued Bangor Punta Corp. after a failed tender fight over Piper Aircraft Co. Through a novel application of a particular provision of securities law, Liman argued in 1977 that Bangor Punta owed the disappointed bidder, Chris-Craft, monetary damages. Liman convinced a jury to award Chris-Craft $36 million, at the time a record for securities cases. But the U.S. Supreme Court overturned the award, disagreeing with Liman's interpretation of the law. The two companies ultimately settled. "I do my work as professionally as I can," responded Liman when asked about such reversals. "My experience with the appellate courts is that it's a rare case that you're going to win when there isn't some support for it that will stand up on appeal. The cases where I have been overturned were cases on the frontier of the law."

Only about a third of Liman's cases scheduled for trial actually make it to court. He believes in settling when it's advantageous to his client. "I don't really think there's weakness [in offering to settle] unless you convince yourselves you're weak," says Liman. "I've never hesitated to make an offer of settlement, and if it's not accepted, to withdraw it." Whether Liman will make another settlement offer in that case depends on the circumstances, he says. Future offers may be higher, lower, or nonexistent. "I have had cases where people refused [a settlement] and called ten days later and wanted to accept. But I said, 'Too late. I'm taking the case to verdict.' "

If a lawyer regularly "ups the ante" and makes increasingly better settlement offers as a case progresses, that lawyer loses credibility for future cases, explains Liman. "You get a reputation of lowballing in the first place," he says, and opponents learn to wait you out. Good lawyers, says Liman, "put the figure on the table, and if it's not accepted, they're willing to take the case to trial."

Liman settled two cases recently. "In both of them," he says, "the juries [later] told me that they were disposed to our point of view." In one of these cases Liman defended Christie's after a company dealing in art sued the auctioneer, claiming that Christie's had mishandled the auction of eight Impressionist paintings. After the case settled mid-trial, the jurors said that they would have returned a verdict for Christie's. Liman acknowledges that he "felt that [result] from the moment I engaged in the voir dire," but he still thinks the decision on whether to proceed is the client's. Christie's decided to settle during the trial, says Liman, because it didn't want the continued lawsuit publicity, which Christie's felt was being exploited by the other side. A verdict three weeks down the road was not as important to Christie's as ending the suit then on terms that were acceptable. "That was the client's decision. It was a source of disappointment to my colleagues and me. No doubt about that," concludes Liman.

The second case, involving client Continental Grain Co., settled because "the potential for an adverse verdict and the consequences it would bring made it prudent for the client to get the case behind it," says Liman. "The client has to decide whether they really want to put their business fortunes in the hands of jurors," he explains. "It's a risk." In such cases Liman views his role of trial lawyer as watching how the evidence is going in, helping his client understand the risks of trial, and seeing "that the result is satisfactory—not that I have a scalp on my belt.

"I think that lawyers who say 'I never settle' are allowing their ego to get in the way of their professional responsibility," concludes Liman. "That's something that's very, very dangerous for trial lawyers. It's very tempting when you've prepared for a case, you've put a great deal of effort in it, you have colleagues who've put in their time, and all of a sudden you realize 'We're never going to cross-examine this witness.' You've put in so much energy and you feel like going home and crying. But that's not your role. Your role is not to demonstrate your virtuosity in the courtroom. It is to get the result that is satisfactory for your client." As for criminal cases specifically, "if you can settle cases where your clients don't got jail," says Liman, "you're doing your clients a service."

Still, Liman's cases do not settle to the same degree as other lawyers'. "Often when I'm brought into a case, it's because the case could not be settled earlier," he explains. The same is true for most of the nation's top trial attorneys. When a case does come to Liman that he thinks he can settle, it's sometimes because the client just "needs the courage to make the decision." Liman is the one to provide it.

When the City of New York and the New York City Transit Authority sued Pullman Incorporated and Rockwell International Corporation in 1979 over the purchase of defective subway cars, it seemed that Liman and his plaintiff client wouldn't give up under any conditions. In their minds it was an all-or-nothing battle for $100 million, a salvation of taxpayer pride. The case ultimately became one of two important victories in which Liman represented the Big Apple.

Liman had effectively defended the city in an earlier fight in 1978, when contractors abandoned a multimillion-dollar water tunnel construction project, charging the city with breach of contract. When the contractors sued in what became the city's largest contract suit ever, they demanded damages of more than $270 million. The city government considered offering $40 million to settle the case, but when Liman joined the defense, he negotiated a much lower price—$18 million. Mayor Koch was ecstatic, and he didn't forget his satisfaction the next time a city agency needed legal help. While the city's corporation counsel represented it in the subway car case, the Transit Authority asked Liman to work on its behalf.

From the time of first use in early 1976, the 754 Pullman R-46 subway cars, costing over $200 million dollars, gave the Transit Authority plenty of trouble. The cars had a newly designed, lightweight undercarriage, called the truck, which carried each car on its tracks through the New York subway system. The R-46 trucks, manufactured by Rockwell as a subcontractor to Pullman, were touted as fuel-efficient, quieter than the traditional trucks, and more maintenance-free. The problem was that shortly after the cars were put in service the transom arms of the new undercarriages, or trucks, cracked and started breaking apart. In effect, the bottoms started falling away from the subway cars.

The city and the Transit Authority sued both the contractor, Pullman, and the subcontractor, Rockwell, because Pullman was the primary contractor, and because the Transit Authority was having difficulty with other aspects of the cars beside just the trucks. However, the non-truck-related complaints were severed off in a separate lawsuit. While Pullman remained a defendant in the truck suit, Pullman had indemnity, so Rockwell was, in effect, the party that would pay should the city and the Transit Authority successfully prove their claim. As a result, Rockwell's lawyers,

Chadbourne, Parke, Whiteside & Wolff of New York, handled the bulk of the defendants' suit, assisted by Pullman's attorneys, Davis, Polk & Wardwell, also of New York.

Rockwell never denied that the trucks were inadequately designed, that they were cracking, or that they would continue to crack. The company maintained, rather, that the Transit Authority was responsible for the design flaw, and that poorly maintained subway tracks caused the trucks to crack. Rockwell's settlement offer was to fix or "retrofit" the trucks, rather than replace them.

The case was an incredibly difficult one, explains Les Fagen, one Paul, Weiss lawyer who assisted Liman on the matter. For one, Rockwell had suggested the retrofit program. Because the company is a widely acknowledged aerospace giant—rife with scientists, engineers, and computer experts—it appeared that the city should trust Rockwell and give it the go-ahead to remedy its own manufacturing. But the Transit Authority had lost confidence in the company because all of its earlier efforts to cure the problem had failed. The Transit Authority, according to its lawyers, was obsessed with safety and would no longer settle for any trucks other than the traditional, tried-and-true ones. Second, the defendants blamed the Transit Authority, alleging that it had participated in the design and manufacture of the new trucks, and should therefore share in responsibility for the design judgments. The evidence showed that Transit Authority engineers had, indeed, been involved from time to time in the trucks' design. Lastly, one of the Transit Authority's own top executives, former Senior Executive Officer John De Roos, was on record as supporting Rockwell's trucks. De Roos had been ousted from the agency in 1979 during a coup d'état among the staff, and afterwards he remained opposed to the lawsuit.

And of course, the New York subway case, like many in today's litigation arena, involved a multitude of technical issues, with their own specialized vocabulary, that had to be made readily understandable to a jury of ordinary citizens. Attorneys for the two sides questioned over 160 witnesses during pretrial discovery, resulting in about 30,000 pages of deposition transcripts. They had over 1,000 documents ready as trial exhibits. The comprehension hurdle was sizable.

At the time of the trial New Yorkers' openly hostile attitudes toward the Transit Authority—it was the era of the city's fiscal crisis and widespread anticity bias—only added to the plaintiffs' challenge. There was a risk that these sentiments would poison a jury's mind in a case where the Transit Authority's competence was very much at issue.

The trial, beginning in mid-November 1980, lasted five and one-half weeks, ending just before Christmas. Presiding over the case was U.S. District Judge Edward Weinfeld, then known to be one of the best on the bench. A wizened Dickensian figure, he was directed and strict when managing a trial. Weinfeld was a no-nonsense judge, says Fagen, and without him the case could have gone on for three months.

The courtroom overflowed with lawyers, reporters, and court buffs, on hand to watch a cause célèbre involving the biggest transit system in the world. Liman played hardball, his witnesses ranging from corporate executives to engineers to transportation experts. The attorney went for a home run, asking the jurors to award New York and the Transit Authority its full claim. If Rockwell was wrong, he entreated them, then give us our due.

The Rockwell case is a study in Liman's ability to adapt, or modify, his cross-examination technique and style to meet the needs of the lawsuit at the time a witness takes the stand. The trial offers examples of different kinds of cross-examination, says Liman, including discrediting a witness, and turning a witness to the cross-examining lawyer's advantage.

The trial similarly underscores how Liman makes his points before a jury without being either aggressive or sarcastic. His questions are straightforward and seemingly objective, but with each subsequent query, the witness for the opposing side unravels, bit by bit. To the jury in the Rockwell trial, it appeared that

Liman was only pointing out the obvious; they steadily moved over to his side of the case.

Finally, the case of the cracked subway cars illustrates how well Liman can take a highly technical subject—subway machinery—and make it understandable. He can take his theory of a case and make it so simple that any alternative explanations seem unlikely.

About a month before the trial was to begin, Rockwell's attorneys made a motion that the case be heard without a jury, by the judge alone, because "the scientific and engineering testimony which must be presented is so technical and sophisticated that it will be beyond the capacity of the average juror to understand." The city and the Transit Authority lawyers responded that Rockwell was trying to deny plaintiffs their constitutional right to a jury trial. "We believe Rockwell's motion is based not on a fear that the jurors will fail to understand the retrofit issue," responded the Transit Authority's lawyers, "but that they will understand it all too well." The judge denied the motion, and Liman proved that prediction.

Before a trial Liman prepares his cases thoroughly to form a strategy for convincing the jury of his client's view. "I have the benefit of a superb law firm" to help prepare a case, admits Liman (about one-third of the lawyers at Paul, Weiss are litigators), "but I cannot examine a witness unless I have read all of the witness's prior testimony and all of the documents. By the time a trial is scheduled, it is total immersion for me for a month to two months." At the same time, Liman is receiving reports from other lawyers assisting him in his research and study. "I'm an open-door lawyer," he explains of his close working relationships with other attorneys. "Most people would consider me hands-on."

Liman's team approach carries over into the courtroom. Unlike some other successful attorneys who believe only they should speak in the courtroom, Liman allows other lawyers preparing the case with him to argue parts of it. "I understand you have to do enough so you have a rapport with the jury," explains Liman. "It just doesn't work if the only time the jury hears you speak is at opening and the summation. They would think of you as almost a carpetbagger. But there's no reason why you can't share responsibility with your associates. How will they become experienced trial lawyers if they don't get that experience with you?"

Liman brought to the Rockwell trial his team for that case, a small army of lawyers, either sitting at the counsel table or sprinkled around the courtroom. Bruce S. Kaplan and Anthony Z. Scher from the Corporation Counsel's office for the city joined the Paul, Weiss attorneys at the counsel table. At the opposing table—the defendants'—sat the Chadbourne, Parke and Davis, Polk lawyers. Glaring down from his high bench in the small but imposing federal courtroom, Judge Weinfeld proceeded, as is the case for federal trials, to voir dire the potential jurors. As he questioned those one-hundred-plus prospective jurors, Weinfeld read through a long list of people who had some connection to the case; jurors who knew any of these people were automatically disqualified from serving.

The resulting jury of six (plus six alternates) was an intelligent one—mostly college graduates. The selection process stumbled only once, ironically after the jury was in place. It turned out that one of the jurors, an auditor, worked for an accounting firm that had Rockwell as one of its clients. The juror, however, wasn't aware of this until after the voir dire, at which point he made his position clear to the court. Because the juror did none of the accounting work for Rockwell himself, the attorneys in the lawsuit agreed that he could remain.

Liman's opening statement was short and low-key. "I originally believed in a very spartan opening statement," explains the attorney when asked about the Rockwell case. "In complex cases I still believe the opening statement can, at most, leave the jury with the memory of an opening theme. If you try to cram too much in an opening statement the jury won't remember anything, and it's better that they remember something than nothing." Yet Liman says that recently he has decided opening statements can be too spartan: "I want to discuss the evidence in civil cases with the jury so they understand it is not rhetoric and that they will be getting evidence that will support what I tell them. So I have lengthened my opening statement," continues Liman, "partly out of a belief that the opening statement in a complex case can make a difference."

This change in trial technique has evolved over time, he says, just as attitudes of juries have evolved. "They're affected by the times, by television, by what's happening in the world around them. Jurors of 1987 are different from the jurors that existed in the 1920s, when great trial lawyers would wear boutonnieres," explains Liman. "The jury then expected trial lawyers to give them very flowery speeches. If such a trial lawyer lived today, they'd put him in a museum. He certainly wouldn't win cases." So, concludes Liman, the evolution of his opening statement derives partly from some form of "sixth sense" about changes in the world and attitudes around him, and partly from talking with jurors after a trial.

Liman says that his Rockwell opening was one of his more spartan ones. It lasted under an hour and was recorded on only thirty-three pages of trial transcript. But the opening is a masterpiece in setting forth for the jurors in simple words and clear sentences the parties in the lawsuit, the source of their controversy, and the requested remedy. To assist the jurors' understanding, Liman called on comparisons familiar to them, referring to television and refrigerator warranties, Rolls Royces and Edsels, and mounds of junkyard debris:

"May it please the court and ladies and gentlemen of the jury," Liman began.

"My name is Arthur Liman, and I and Mr. Felleman and Mr. Fagen and others represent the New York City Transit Authority, one of the plaintiffs in this action. The Transit Authority operates the largest urban mass transit system in the world.

"The other plaintiff, the City of New York, is represented by Mr. Kaplan and his colleagues, and the City of New York owns the transportation system which the Transit Authority operates. The city owns the subway cars and tracks.

"Now, this is a case, as the court indicated, of breach of contract and breach of warranty. The term 'warranty' is familiar to anyone who has ever bought a refrigerator or a television set. Here we are dealing with warranties on a different type of product and a different consumer. Here the consumer was the City of New York and the Transit Authority, and the product was subway cars.

"The case involves the purchase by the City of New York and the Transit Authority of a fleet of new subway cars, 754 cars in total, known as the R-46. These cars were bought from the defendant Pullman. Each car has as its undercarriage two undercarriages known as trucks, and the undercarriages have the frame, the axle, the wheels, the motor, some other equipment, and they are what supports the passenger car that you are all familiar with.

"The trucks for these R-46 cars were manufactured by the defendant Rockwell under a subcontract with Pullman. Pullman contracted to supply the R-46 in its totality. It bought the trucks from Rockwell, which manufactured them.

"To give you the case in a nutshell, the proof here will show that when the defendants were selling and promoting the R-46 to the city, they promoted it as if it were a Rolls Royce of the subway industry, fast, safe, quiet, and long-lasting.

"We will show you that they didn't deliver a Rolls Royce. They delivered an Edsel, a lemon, a car whose undercarriage is disintegrating, literally."

Liman explained to the jurors how the crossbeam that held together the frame of the truck and supported the motor above it began cracking and breaking apart. "Of the 1548 trucks that were manufactured and delivered by Rockwell, some 1054 have had cracks in these crossbeams, which are called transom arms," explained Liman. "The cracking is only part of the problem, because this truck was designed so badly that it vibrates violently and it's shaking the equipment that is attached to it, the various instruments, including safety instruments, off the truck.

"In fact, I could turn this courtroom into a junkyard by bringing in samples of what has fallen off this truck and has been found along the tracks of the City of New York.

"The only way that the city and the Transit Authority know of salvaging this fleet, for which they paid Pullman two hundred million dollars—two hundred million dollars—the only way that they know of salvaging this fleet is to replace these cracking and vibrating trucks with another truck, tested in service, a reliable truck, and we will prove to you that the cost of substituting this truck for the defective R-46 trucks, as well as the costs of repairing them and inspecting them to date, is in the neighborhood of one hundred million dollars, and those are the damages that we are seeking."

When attorney Donald Strauber rose to make his opening statement for Rockwell, he agreed that the R-46 trucks developed cracks in their transom arms, but he blamed the city and the Transit Authority for the problem. He particularly lambasted the plaintiffs for refusing to let Rockwell repair the cracks:

"Rockwell is a large company. It employs one hundred and fifteen thousand people. Fifteen thousand of them are engineers and scientists. The key to their business is research and development and manufacture of products for use in all forms of transportation, products which must perform properly and safely. When President Kennedy decided to put men on the moon in the 1960s and bring them back safely, it was Rockwell that designed and built the Apollo spacecraft which achieved that goal. . . . Because the problems of the R-46 involved stress and strain on metal, engineers were brought in from the space division. . . . The engineers that were put to work on this . . . are the Willie Mayses and the Mickey Mantles of the engineering profession. They are devoted, intelligent, honest engineers."

As a plaintiff, Liman called his witnesses first. One of his early and primary witnesses was Joe Sebastiano, a middle-aged, mid-level Transit Authority manager, who told the story of the subway car contract. But before he explained what had happened, Liman established for the jurors that Sebastiano was a man just like them, a person whom they could trust. "We had high-ranking professionals, and sophisticated professionals," recalls Fagen, "but the ball was carried to a large degree by real-life people." Liman "made it appear to the jury that it was a case of the Transit Authority engineer, on a civil service salary, trying to do his job." All he needed was equipment that would work.

Liman asked Sebastiano about his background.

Sebastiano: I graduated from Stuyvesant High School here in Manhattan in 1942. I immediately took a course in the Drake School in downtown Manhattan in technical engineering, drawing, and became employed by a firm in New Jersey called Robert Reiner, Inc. as a draftsman. They were manufacturers of textile machinery. There was a three-year lapse of service because I was inducted into the United States Army.

Liman: Where did you serve in the United States Army?

Sebastiano: I served in France during World War Two.

Liman: Did you receive any citations?

Sebastiano: Yes, I received two personal citations: the Purple Heart and the Bronze Star. [Sebastiano walked with a limp, although it was never mentioned in trial.]

Liman: What did you do after the war?

Sebastiano: Immediately after the war I joined the predecessor of the Transit Authority. It was Border Transportation at the time. I entered service as a draftsman.

Liman: After that, what positions did you hold until you attained your present office?

Sebastiano: During my thirty-four years of service, I was promoted from draftsman to assistant mechanical engineer, then to mechanical engineer and senior mechanical engineer, administrative engineer, into my present position as division engineer.

In keeping with the simplicity of his presentation, Liman called only two expert witnesses, Dr. Robert Scanlan, a Princeton engineering professor, and Dr. Arthur McEvily, from the University of Connecticut engineering faculty. Both had served as consultants to the mayor and the board of the Transit Authority as to whether the Transit Authority and the city could safely accept Rockwell's offer of a retrofit. Both scientists rejected the retrofit.

When questioning Scanlan, Liman again helped make the case comprehensible for the jury:

Liman: Are there generally accepted principles of stress analysis applicable to all structures?

Scanlan: Yes. The general principle to stress analysis is to find out what these internal stresses or pressures or tensions may be and compare those with certain criteria which are set up according to the type of material the structure is made of. Now, this can be any kind of a structure, from aircraft and spacecraft down through buildings and of course, including railway and other structures.

Liman: Including subway trucks?

Scanlan: Yes, most definitely.

When Liman asked Scanlan why he could not recommend Rockwell's proposed retrofit, the professor referred to a crude model that he had made for the trial:

Liman: Now, Professor Scanlan, as a result of your study of all of this material and your experience you bring from your profession to stress analysis, have you reached a conclusion as to why the Rockwell truck is cracking and vibrating so much?

Scanlan: Yes, I have.

Liman: Would you tell the court and jury what your conclusion is?

Scanlan: Well, in looking over the ensemble of events, and there are many, many individual failures connected with this truck, one looks for a central core of cause. I think this stems particularly from the design.

. . . There are two side frames to this truck, and I have made some very crude models, and I'll apologize for the crudeness of them, but I wanted to illustrate the character of it. There are two side frames which these simple pieces of wood illustrate. Again, this is not a model of the truck but a model of the principle. Then there are some transom arms which cross over and enter a ball joint. . . . In this case the outside frames were placed exactly that way, outside the wheels, which is a bit unusual with this type of design, rather than within the wheels as in other forms of the design. This meant that these long transom arms were indeed longer than normal. Furthermore, they were what I might simply call rather skinny. . . . They had to support the motor . . . [and] these motors were unusually heavy. So this combination of events just led right into a design which was fraught with difficulties from the very beginning and still is.

When Liman and the city's lawyers had finished calling all of their witnesses, the Rockwell and Pullman attorneys had a chance to put on their case. But their opportunity was also an opportunity for Liman. As he had demonstrated his ability to make a case understandable through direct examination, Liman also demonstrated, during cross-examination, his skill in turning defense witnesses to his own client's advantage.

"I believe that cross-examination depends on sizing up the witness, making a judgment as to what you can hope to get out of that witness," instructs Liman today. "The art of cross-examination, in essence, is the art of knowing what is possible.

"In some cases," continues Liman, "the object of the cross-examination is to discredit the witness. If you have the material to impeach the witness, you should go in and do the job quickly, cleanly, and end it before the jury develops sympathy for the witness on the stand. In other cases you want to turn the witness to your own advantage." Liman says that the Rockwell case offers "instances of application of every method of cross-examination."

But before Liman makes a judgment about his approach to cross-examining a particular witness, before the witness even takes the stand, he thinks ahead about what he may likely want to do. "Everyone has his own style" of preparation, says Liman. "Mine tends to be yellow sheets, where I indicate what the topics are [in the cross]. When I prepare for cross, I will have a yellow sheet that deals with each separate subject and which indicates or has stapled to it some document or statement that the witness may have made and that I may want to confront the witness with. The reason that I use that method is because it allows me to shuffle the papers so that I can try to get a thematic examination. Since I don't know until the witness finishes his direct examination precisely how to start the cross, and since I believe you have to be adaptable, I don't want to be tied down to even the written material that would not enable me to alter what I'm doing. So I tend to be very, very fluid and flexible in the way I manage the cross-examination that I've prepared."

With his planning and yellow-sheet notes, Liman essentially conducts a cross-examination in his own mind before the trial begins. "You may envision ahead of time three different cross-examinations," says the attorney. Planning is easier in most civil cases, he points out, where lawyers have an opportunity to examine witnesses before a trial. This enables them to predict how the witnesses might respond once on the stand. However, this is not true in criminal cases. In these cases, says Liman, "you have to say to yourself 'What is it that the witness is likely to say?' and 'If the witness says that, what will I do?' and 'If the witness changes prior testimony, how will I handle that?' "

Once a witness takes the stand to testify under direct examination, Liman listens intently and applies what he hears to his own preparation for cross. He uses a different-colored pen to write down on his yellow sheets "nuggets" of information that come out on direct that he hadn't expected. Such listening requires enormous powers of concentration, emphasizes Liman. And "if the witness's direct gives a different impression, has a different impact [than Liman expected], that cross-examination will change." If, continues Liman, a lawyer writes out a detailed cross-examination on paper ahead of time—and therefore what the witness says on direct is almost irrelevant for cross—then that lawyer is going to miss opportunities on cross-examination. "You may not join issue with the direct examination," concludes Liman.

Liman's adaptability carries over even after he's begun his cross-examination. He believes strongly that he must concentrate and listen to the witness's response to his every question. "Their answer might suggest the next question," instructs Liman, who believes that young trial lawyers' most fundamental mistake is not following up on witness answers. "The jury is sitting there, they're listening to the answer," explains Liman, "and in their minds the witness just said that, [and] the next question should be this. Without a follow-up pattern, your cross-examination is not going to be comprehensible." Sometimes a lawyer might want to alter the question-and-answer pattern, adds Liman, "but that ought at least to be a conscious decision, and not because you're so set in your ways with your examinations in concrete."

Courtroom aficionados generally recognize Liman for his genteel and courtly manner of questioning witnesses. He doesn't shout; he doesn't scream; he doesn't pound the table, act insulted, or sarcastically demean a witness. In sum, Liman is a gentleman. "It's natural," he responds with a small grin when asked whether his style is one he's cultivated over time. "I think juries don't like people who are too sarcastic," he says of one of the negative attributes listed, but then he also admits that he may be a little sarcastic, on occasion, with some witnesses. And sometimes he may seem more aggressive. "But it's not every case that you have the kind of material to be more overtly aggressive," observes Liman. "And I happen to be of the school that thinks you can score your points without your own anger."

In the Rockwell trial Liman did just that. One of Rockwell's early witnesses was Richard Bruggen, a program manager from the company's Atchison, Kansas, plant that produced the New York subway car undercarriages, or trucks. In this first cross-examination excerpt, Liman responded to Bruggen's direct testimony about other cracking problems Rockwell had encountered before it agreed to produce the New York subway undercarriages. Liman clearly showed in a direct but controlled way that Rockwell purposely underplayed the seriousness of the cracking defect:

Liman: I am going to start at the beginning, Mr. Bruggen. You testified that you had before 1972 [when the Transit Authority signed its contract for the subway cars] provided trucks for the Chicago Transit System, am I correct?

Bruggen: Yes, sir.

Liman: And you testified that you had some cracking in the Chicago system before you contracted to make the trucks for New York, is that correct?

Bruggen: Yes, it is.

Liman: And you testified that you proposed a fix for that cracking, am I correct?

Bruggen: Yes.

Liman: And that fix was adopted, am I correct?

Bruggen: Yes.

Liman: And you testified in answer to a question by Mr. Strauber that the Rockwell trucks are still operating in Chicago, am I correct?

Bruggen: Yes.

Liman: Did you neglect to mention that those trucks have continued to crack since your fix?

Bruggen: I didn't neglect to mention it. In '72, they had not cracked again. We have learned subsequent to that that they have cracked, yes.

Liman: In fact, did you learn from a Mr. Petersen who works for you in April of 1980 that since that fix, the Chicago Transit Authority has experienced continued cracks at the mount in approximately sixty percent of the frames? Did you learn that?

Bruggen: Yes, I did.

Liman: You testified that when Mr. Weidman went out to

Atchison before this contract was let, you didn't want to raise any red flags about cracking with him, is that right? That's what you said this morning: that you didn't want to raise red flags. I wrote it down.

Bruggen: Yes, I said we covered the problem completely with him. What I meant by that is, when he stepped off the plane, we didn't say, "Hey, Ed, we have this terrible problem in Chicago." When we got him back in the plant and reviewed the development of the truck, all the developments at that time, problems of the truck, we reviewed them with him and he already knew about them.

Liman: Mr. Bruggen, you didn't want to raise any red flags today about the fact that your truck was continuing to crack in Chicago, did you?

Bruggen: I don't think we were sure or anybody else is sure why that truck is cracking.

Later during the cross-examination Liman asked Bruggen about a Transit Authority specification that did not reach him before Rockwell signed its contract to produce the undercarriages. This second excerpt shows how Liman contains his own anger during cross-examination even when a witness's remarks might offend him personally:

Bruggen: My letter which confirmed the contract, with all the understandings we had, was dated December twenty-seventh. The meeting at the Transit Authority took place on December twentieth. I didn't even see the minutes of that meeting until after the holidays.

Liman: So that was just another failure of communication within Rockwell, is that what you are saying?

Bruggen: No. It has to do with the Christmas holidays—which we celebrate at Rockwell.

Liman is Jewish. Both of the top Transit Authority engineers who were pivotal in recommending rejection of the proposed Rockwell retrofit were also Jewish. Some thought Bruggen's tone of voice and words were clearly anti-Semitic. But instead of turning on the witness, and instead of asking more questions to drive home the response, which could have allowed Bruggen to soften his gaffe, Liman simply stepped back and stared at him with disbelief turning to disdain. For a full twenty seconds all eyes in the courtroom were focused on Liman's own shocked expression. "The words hung there like a foul odor," recalls the city's lawyer, Mr. Kaplan. "You could see the shock and disgust on the faces of the jury."

"It was a reflex," says Liman today of his stone-silent response. "I didn't expect it. [But] he said it, and he destroyed himself by saying it."

A third example, Liman's subsequent cross-examination of Rockwell expert witness and Massachusetts Institute of Technology professor Merton Flemings, illustrates Liman's ability to discredit an expert. On direct examination Flemings had supported Rockwell's quality control in the manufacture of its undercarriages. But when the company's lawyers prepared this expert for trial, they obviously didn't show him all the documents relevant to his testimony:

Liman: You testified that you reviewed manuals and paper at Rockwell and that you found that their procedures, quality control standards, were excellent. Is that your testimony?

Flemings: I thought so.

Liman: Were you there when the trucks were being made?

Flemings: No.

Liman: Do you know the extent to which Rockwell conformed to these manuals and written documents you saw?

Flemings: I have no way of testifying to that. I was not there.

Liman: Among the manuals and documents that you were shown, were you shown Plaintiffs' Exhibit 363 for identification? . . .

Flemings: I haven't seen this memo.

Liman: This wasn't in the quality control manuals or mass of documents they gave you?

Flemings: I don't remember seeing it.

Liman: Is it accepted foundry practice to "leave some things for New York inspection to find so that they do not continue to nitpick and make work when our volume was low"? Is that accepted foundry practice, to leave defects on surfaces for inspectors to play with?

Flemings: . . . I haven't really read every word of this, but I did catch that very clearly. I had to smile at that because it's such a common problem for a foundry producing castings where with these complex specifications and design requirements and with the competing goals of these different organizations, it's such a common thing for people to make work in any of these games. I have worked with several other foundries where just to get the inspectors off their backs, because the trouble is if you make things too good for an inspector, he doesn't have anything to do, he doesn't know what to tell his boss, so you leave a few little ones and you give him something to do and everything is happy.

The Court: "Leave a few little ones," what do you mean by that?

Flemings: Leave a few little defects that aren't going to hurt anything, maybe in some noncritical areas, and the inspector can find them and his boss is happy.

Liman: And the inspector doesn't have to keep looking and nitpicking and find something that he otherwise would discover?

Flemings: I don't recommend the practice, but you asked me if I have ever seen it. Sure I have seen it.

Liman: You came on the stand saying you only testify to your convictions. Is this practice something that you teach at MIT?

Flemings: No, we certainly don't teach that at MIT.

Liman: Is it in your book?

Flemings: No. I have never written about that in a book.

Liman: When you say that you have seen it done at other foundries, your intent was to make light of this and condone it?

Flemings: Well—

Liman: It doesn't bother your scruples, does it?

Finally, Liman's greatest stroke of cross-examination genius evidenced itself during his questioning of Robert Anderson, Rockwell International's chairman and chief executive. This was a cross-examination where Liman turned a witness to his own advantage. Anderson was a corporate role model—clean-cut, straightforward, and articulate, and highly reputable as a business executive. He made a great witness for the defendants.

Strauber first asked Anderson on direct examination when he learned about problems with the New York R-46 subway cars and how his company developed a solution:

Strauber: Do you have an opinion as to the technical soundness of the retrofit that Rockwell has proposed?

Anderson: My opinion on that would be based on the opinion of our top group of engineers, which I think are demonstrably as good as there is in the free world, and their judgment that this is an outstanding solution. . . .

Strauber: Was the proposal that Rockwell made ever implemented?

Anderson: It was approved, as I understand it, by a member, Mr. De Roos, I believe it is, one of the [Transit Authority] people we had been working with during the course of this correction. I was absolutely shocked when I learned that after all his work and all this effort on our part in working with the City of New York and, as I understand it, signed by their top representative in this area, Mr. De Roos, that . . . for some reason which I'm still not aware of, we have never been allowed to try it. It was summarily dismissed and we went back to square one.

Obviously, Strauber had put Anderson on the stand to lend credibility to Rockwell and to the company's rejected retrofit proposal. But here Liman took Anderson's credibility and turned it around to help the plaintiffs' case. "He had nothing in the way of firsthand knowledge about the case," explains Liman today. "He had not handled the cars and he was unfamiliar with the facts relating to the city's claims of defects. I therefore decided, after listening to his answers on the stand, to contrast his high standards with the performance of his company in this case. That was fair use and a rather dramatic way of presenting the City of New York's case.

"I confronted him with all sorts of facts that he was unaware of, didn't know, and said, 'The Rockwell of Robert Anderson wouldn't endorse that kind of practice!' "

Liman: Now, Mr. Anderson, Rockwell is the thirty-seventh largest company on the *Fortune* 500 list?

Anderson: Give or take a few.

Liman: And given the structure of management, you depend upon the people who report to you?

Anderson: That's true.

Liman: You have a lot of other businesses to be concerned with?

Anderson: Yes.

Liman: And you have a great deal of confidence in your staff?

Anderson: I certainly do.

Liman: And a great deal of confidence in these thousands of scientists and engineers who Rockwell has in its employ?

Anderson: Yes.

Liman: Is it fair to say that the Rockwell that you represent, you personally, Mr. Anderson, is not a company that would use the wrong instrument on a road test?

Anderson: I think that's a fair statement.

Liman: And it is not the company that would misread the data coming out of a road test, that's not what you would expect out of Rockwell?

Anderson: I have said it is not what I expect, but we have fifteen thousand engineers and some of them somewhere could make a mistake and might make a mistake. I don't know.

Liman: And it is not the company, you wouldn't expect it to be, a company which would produce castings replete with anomalies, would you?

Anderson: I think all castings have anomalies, so it is a matter of degree.

Liman: You wouldn't expect it to produce castings that people in your organization would be appalled at, would you?

Anderson: I don't know which people are appalled at what, so I can't answer that question. . . .

Liman: Now, is it also fair to say that the Rockwell that you, Robert Anderson, represent, is a company that you wouldn't expect to conceal things from customers?

Anderson: Well, that's a broad statement, but I, certainly, as a matter of policy, would not expect to conceal things from our good customers, no.

Liman: I showed you Plaintiffs' Exhibit 138 at your deposition . . . the Petersen [a Rockwell employee] memo, and you had never seen that before?

Anderson: The number doesn't mean anything. But I don't believe I saw it.

Liman: And no one showed you this memo, until [your] deposition, in which the words appear . . . "Troy [headquarters of the Rockwell division responsible for the contract] wants to keep failure [in the testing of the fixed truck] quiet until after their presentation to the TA board [to ask the Transit Authority to accept Rockwell's modification of the defective truck] which is now rescheduled for May first, '79." I was the first person to show you this document?

Anderson: That's correct.

Liman went on and on, questioning Anderson about the action of a company that a man of Anderson's high caliber would represent. "Is it fair to say, sir, that the Rockwell Robert Anderson represents is not a company that you would expect to tell a customer that it had a permanent solution to a problem when its own automotive and space division were saying that there was insufficient data available to predict reliability of redesign during the post-retrofit period?" asked Liman pointedly.

The Transit Authority's lawyer also made it clear to the jury that Rockwell's chairman had no direct knowledge or involvement in the contract to manufacture the subway trucks:

Liman: . . . did they tell you that the information was buried in reports that were being submitted on a routine basis by Rockwell?

Anderson: I have no knowledge of how the information was submitted. I was told it went to the City of New York.

Liman: And you have no knowledge of why Troy would want to keep the failure quiet until after their presentation to the TA board, do you?

Anderson: I have no knowledge of that. I'm relieved to know that it was not done [keeping the failure quiet] and it was presented to the City of New York.

Liman: Was it presented to the board of the TA?

Anderson: I have no knowledge of what the channels of communication are between our people and the City of New York.

Liman: Do you know in what kind of document it was presented?

Anderson: No, sir, I don't.

Liman: Do you know whether it was in a document that was likely to have been read within a week?

Anderson: I have no knowledge of that.

Liman: Mr. Anderson . . . have you spoken to Mr. Petersen, who wrote this?

Anderson: I do not know Mr. Petersen.

"His examination didn't last very long," concludes Liman of the Anderson cross, "but when he left the stand, everybody had to know there was a major departure from good standards." Rockwell had urged the Transit Authority to trust it to repair the undercarriages because Rockwell is a large, credible, first-class organization. But Liman showed when cross-examining Anderson that the company was engaging in behavior that betrayed trust. It was behavior of which top management was not even aware, and which it certainly did not condone.

Having shown his adaptability over the course of the Rockwell trial, Liman faced the time for his closing argument on December 22, 1980. Following the defendants' summations, Liman addressed the jury in his traditional, gentlemanly way, keeping his persuasion simple and direct. He first thanked the jurors for their patience, and then continued:

"My role at this stage of the case, and it is the last time I am going to be talking to you, is really to review the evidence and guide you through it. I do not intend to respond to a number of the rhetorical flourishes in my colleagues' arguments, though I appreciated them. I intend to stick to the issues, and for that reason you are not going to hear very much from me about finite element models or binning or even an SN curve, because the City of New York and the Transit Authority did not buy an SN curve here or a bin or a finite element model. What it bought was a fleet of modern subway cars which were supposed to have under them carriages, undercarriages, trucks that were proven in service, warranted as to workmanship and free from patent and latent defects. That is what this case is about."

Liman then walked over to an easel with a large pad of white paper, which he used as a visual aid to guide himself and the jury in a review of the evidence. He outlined what the defendants promised to deliver, and what they delivered. "You can see I didn't win any awards for handwriting," said Liman as he began writing. Then he started to list what the jurors had heard during their weeks in trial.

But partway through his closing, Liman started talking about rabbits and began drawing on his white-paper easel almost childlike depictions of bunnies. "Now I want to talk about rabbits," Liman began as he scribbled. "There is a sort of logical syllogism in a contract case. You prove the contract and then you prove whether or not they delivered something that conforms to it. And there is no dispute that what they delivered doesn't conform to the contract. So we come to their excuses.

"I call them rabbits because they remind me of the mechanical rabbits that they have in tracks where they have dog races, and the dogs are let loose and they chase after the mechanical rabbit and they expend a lot of energy, and of course, they never catch it, and they come away very, very confused. And they have set a lot of rabbits loose in this courtroom and I intend now to deal with them and show that they are nothing more than that. They are nothing but phony alibis." Liman then ran through Rockwell's defenses, discounting them one by one.

"Liman made the argument vivid," recalls his partner Fagen, enthusiastically describing the rabbit analogy. "When the jurors went into the jury room, I'm willing to bet they were thinking about rabbits. [They were hearing] be careful, because the rabbit [each Rockwell excuse] maybe a metal decoy that disappears."

As he concluded his summation, Liman took a chance. "I gambled in the summation in getting everything that I thought were our full damages," he recalls. "I urged the jury not to compromise. I thought I had the case won and the jury would respond to an appeal to principle."

"Ladies and gentlemen, I don't want you to compromise," said Liman as he began closing his summation. "I want you to vote your convictions. New York isn't here asking for mercy or charity or anything like that. . . .

"If you were to vote to compromise, and if the city wasn't to get what it was entitled to, then it's at the mercy of every purveyor of merchandise. If you think we are wrong, then vote against us, but please, the principle here of integrity of contract is too important to be bargained away. . . .

"We have been together a long time, and I only ask of you one thing, which is to let your verdict speak the truth for both sides. Truth is important here, principle is important. Thank you."

The verdict did not meet, but it approached, Liman's requested $100 million in damages. After a long day's deliberation, the jury awarded the city and the Transit Authority $72 million, which covered the cost of relacing the defective undercarriages. What the plaintiffs lost out on was approximately $28 million, the amount expended for an interim inspection and repair program while waiting for the Rockwell trucks to be removed. Having lost its courtroom battle over the largest transit procurement deal in U.S. history, but still refusing to admit responsibility, Pullman and Rockwell appealed the award. They lost again.

Today, an enlarged one-foot-by-three-foot copy of Rockwell's $72 million check to the City of New York hangs on Liman's office wall. It has a special place among the array of memorabilia Liman has gathered from his various cases and public service activities. Among Liman's souvenirs is a piece of weaponry from the Attica prison uprising. And the newest piece in this ever-growing collection is a huge gavel, a gift from Liman's staff in the Iran-contra investigation.

JAMES F. NEAL

Neal & Harwell, Nashville

The Tennessean

Criminal defense attorney James F. Neal says he never wins a trial. The point, emphasizes the native Tennessean, is that the other lawyer just loses.

"The defense counsel *can't* win cases," insists Neal in a southern drawl thicker than the smoke curling from his enormous cigar. "If the prosecutor has done his job, if he has analyzed his case properly, if he's done his homework—with all the massive resources prosecutors have—he should never lose a case.

"Or rarely, rarely, rarely lose a case."

Of course, the fifty-nine-year-old Neal creates exceptions to that rule. Prosecutors opposing him in court never seem to fare well.

Neal's clients are colorful and high-powered; adventure and

intrigue spice their case stories. And many of their trials are firsts of a kind.

In the early 1970s, Neal handled the nation's first air piracy case to be tried to verdict. The government charged Neal's client with hijacking, kidnapping, intimidating the crew of an aircraft, and going aboard an aircraft carrying a concealed weapon. "Because of the [serious] nature of the case, I offered to plead my client guilty of intimidating the crew of an aircraft—which didn't have a minimum punishment—and accept ten years," recalls Neal. "The government refused—and by gosh, he was acquitted on all counts."

Neal represented the Ford Motor Company, maker of the Pinto automobile, the first time an automobile manufacturer was indicted for homicide in connection with the design, manufacture, and sale of an automobile. The trial followed the fiery deaths in 1978 of three Indiana teenage girls whose Pinto exploded after a rear-end collision. If Ford had lost—which it didn't—the company could have been liable for millions of dollars in punitive damages in hundreds of pending civil suits.

The case of Elvis Presley's doctor—Dr. George "Nick" Nichopoulos—was another to catch the nation's eye. It wasn't the first time a doctor had been charged with criminal prescription of drugs, as had Dr. Nick in the case of Presley, but the patient and the circumstances were certainly unique. For years Presley had been consuming vast quantities of addictive drugs as part of his daily fare. It seemed that the government even wanted to link Elvis's white-haired physician, who prescribed those drugs, with the singer's death—and success looked all but assured. But Neal portrayed his client as a caring doctor who tried the best way he could to help Presley control his many addictions. Dr. Nick was acquitted.

Most recently, Neal convinced a Los Angeles jury after a ten-and-one-half-month trial to acquit his client John Landis in the first case charging a movie director with involuntary manslaughter in the making of a film. Actor Victor Morrow and two

Vietnamese child actors died when a helicopter crashed in the filming of *Twilight Zone: The Movie* under Landis's direction.

Neal did argue a couple of famous cases in which the prosecutor won—but Neal *was* the prosecutor in those trials. In 1964, while working for the U.S. Department of Justice as a special assistant to Attorney General Robert Kennedy, Neal became the first prosecutor to convict former Teamster boss James Hoffa, who was sentenced for jury fixing to eight years in prison. Neal says it was that case, tried when he was only thirty-five years old, that allowed him to step out in front of the pack of other lawyers. Kennedy was his patron, and many very capable lawyers, Neal says, aren't lucky enough to have someone like that give them the same kind of opportunity.

Neal attracted the most attention in his career when he was a prosecutor. Chief trial counsel for the Watergate Special Prosecution Force in 1974, he put John Mitchell, H. R. Haldeman, and John Ehrlichman behind bars. Watergate, says Neal, "represented the application of our system of criminal law enforcement functioning at its best in respect to crimes at the highest level of government. It was also high drama. The importance of demonstrating the effectiveness of our system both in the court, and to the country through the media, caused me to operate at the highest efficiency at all times."

Notwithstanding such eloquence, Neal is an earthy, down-home country boy—and he's proud of it. He was born in 1929 on a hundred-acre strawberry and tobacco farm in rural Sumner County, Tennessee, north of Nashville. His family was poor, but he never found himself to be wanting.

"Now that I've been around the world, I [know I] was poor," says Neal, who worked on the farm from four-thirty A.M. until it was time for school. "In that little community I didn't know I was poor because no one had anything." He worked again after school. "It convinced me I needed to be a lawyer," he jokes, not because he wanted more money, but because he thought he wouldn't have to work as hard as he did on a farm.

"I consider myself the great common man," says Neal. "I've never pretended to be anything but plain, simple folk. Came from it, always been it, and that happens to be a fact." (Lea D'Agostino, the Los Angeles prosecutor in the Landis case, is quoted in one newspaper article as saying of Neal: "He is able to manipulate people. He plays the country boy, just simple folk, when we all know he's anything but that.")

"I *am* a simple fellow; I am not a Renaissance man," stresses the ruggedly handsome Neal, who is invariably described by reporters as "steely-eyed," "jut-jawed," and "barrel-chested." "I do one thing okay. And I believe that I can develop rapport with a jury because I am simply like them. I don't try to sound superior, more intelligent. What I do try to do is to be understood. The most tragic thing that can happen to a lawyer is to lose a case because he wasn't understood."

Sometimes Neal's upbringing catches his opposition off guard. "They thought in Watergate they were really going to have fun," says Neal, a close friend of country singer stars such as Johnny Cash. "They said, 'Here's a southern boy coming up here with all the blacks in Washington.' Man, no problem. I've tried [cases] in New York, Chicago, Los Angeles, everywhere you can think of, and I've found jurors just alike all over the country. I think that's because I am what I simply am—and I don't pretend to be more."

After finishing high school, Neal captured a football scholarship to the University of Wyoming, where he played as a running back on the university's undefeated team. He says he wasn't much of a scholar and likes to tell the story that he scheduled all his classes in the morning so when he got up at noon, he'd be through for the day.

After college, the five foot eight inch, 170-pound Neal headed for the U.S. Marine Corps, and what he thought would be a tour of duty in Korea. Instead, he was sent to the Naval Justice School in Newport, Rhode Island.

When Neal went home, he enrolled in Vanderbilt Law

School, this time a very serious student. He graduated first in his class and moved on to a master's in law program at Georgetown University in Washington, D.C.

Despite repeated stints in Washington—first as special assistant to Robert Kennedy, then as Watergate prosecutor, and most recently as chief counsel to the Senate select committee to study undercover operations of the Department of Justice (following Abscam)—Neal has always returned to Nashville. Offers to leave steadily roll his way. Once the National Basketball Association asked Neal to be commissioner, but he cut off discussions, Neal quips, when the NBA wouldn't move to Nashville. While he hasn't tried a case at home in several years, Neal's partnership with Aubrey Harwell dates back to 1971, and Neal refuses to live anywhere else. Clients just keep coming to him.

Ensconced in his tastefully understated office overlooking the meandering Cumberland River, Neal relishes talk of law and Tennessee politics. A framed photograph of Neal and his young, glamorous, brunette wife, Victoria Jackson—president and CEO of Diesel Sales and Service, Inc.—faces him from across the room. (Neal's first marriage ended in divorce after twenty-four years. He has two grown children.) A longtime player in the local Democratic party, Neal was at one time considered a strong gubernatorial candidate. He says he considered it seriously, but now the job, in his mind, is no longer an option.

Coming off of the Landis trial, Neal agreed to slow the whirlwind of telephone calls and other interruptions to retell the story of Dr. Nichopoulos. The timing seemed appropriate in the summer of 1987, when Tennessee prepared to embark on a widely heralded commemoration of the tenth anniversary of Elvis Presley's death. Today, over ten years later, Neal's views on Nichopoulos's trial and the techniques he used to win it are still unshaken. Some say it was one of Neal's finest hours.

Elvis Presley died on August 16, 1977, while sitting on his toilet. Forty-two years old at the time, he had been consuming a shocking variety of uppers, downers, and painkillers for years, ever since he had been a young man in the Army. At the time Presley died, the drugs had made him desperately constipated.

The official cause of death was heart failure. Presley's family never made public the autopsy it requested, leading to widespread speculation that drugs had been involved. In 1979, the ABC television program "20/20" reported that Presley's death was in fact drug-related.

Dr. George Nichopoulos, had been Presley's personal physician for eleven years. He also cared for numerous other entertainers living in Memphis and frequently traveled with Presley and his entourage (nicknamed the Memphis Mafia) to be on hand for all their medical needs.

It's important to recognize that Dr. Nick, who was fifty-three at the time of his trial, was not charged with killing Presley. He was, rather, charged with illegally administering—or overprescribing—drugs to Presley, as well as to Jerry Lee Lewis and nine others. The charges against Nichopoulos followed an investigation of his medical practice by the Tennessee Board of Medical Examiners. The board suspended Nichopoulos from practicing medicine for three months and placed him on probation for three years. At about the same time, the media were raising questions about Presley's death, and any role drugs might have had in it.

The fourteen-count grand jury indictment—issued May 16, 1980, after Nichopoulos had resumed his practice—said specifically that "controlled substances were dispensed not in good faith to relieve pain and suffering and not to cure a physical infirmity or disease." Along with charges of overprescribing, the indictment said that Nichopoulos dispensed drugs to Presley and Lewis when he knew they were addicted, and that he did not attempt to help cure them. For each count Dr. Nick faced a possible prison sentence of two to ten years and/or a $20,000 fine.

Because of Presley's fame and notoriety as the king of rock 'n' roll, he overshadowed—even in death—the other patients named in the indictment. The case quickly became known as the case of Elvis Presley's doctor. The prosecution would attempt to prove during the trial that Dr. Nick had prescribed nineteen thousand doses of narcotics, sedatives, stimulants, and other drugs during the last approximately three years of Presley's life.

Neal was not the first attorney to handle Nichopoulos's case. The bushy-headed physician had originally retained four leading Memphis lawyers. But in January 1981, with a trial date set for May 4, Nichopoulos announced he wanted new counsel. Some press reports said that the lawyers had urged him to plea-bargain—to plead guilty to a lesser charge—but the attorneys vehemently denied that accusation. For whatever reason, Nichopoulos hired in early February just one lawyer to replace the others—James F. Neal of Nashville.

Nichopoulos knew that Neal would be expensive, and the doctor, despite rumors that he had received numerous gifts from Presley, was not a wealthy man. At $200 an hour, the legal bill would quickly add up. But Nichopoulos's friends and patients, many from the tightly knit Greek community in Memphis, gathered around one of their own and built a legal defense fund that guaranteed Neal $150,000. Although the total bill far exceeded this amount, Neal never received additional payment, nor has he taken action to get it.

For big cases today, Neal always demands an initial, variable nonrefundable retainer to reserve his time. Then he bills his hourly rate—now about $250—after beginning work on the case. The amount of the retainer depends on what the client can pay, and Neal does not bill against it. "Sometimes I don't charge anything," says Neal, who also returns portions of a retainer when a case settles earlier than he had expected.

Despite his last-minute involvement, Neal was ready for trial by spring, but Criminal Court Judge Bernie Weinman postponed it—because, ironically, the prosecution requested a later date to help schedule witnesses. Jury selection didn't actually begin until October 1, 1981.

"You work damn hard," says Neal when asked how to try lawsuits as challenging as Nichopoulos's. "It's mainly preparation.

"You try to identify and research all the legal issues involved, and you prepare to meet them with memoranda or motions in limine [before trial].

"You try to know everything there is to know about the facts in the case and try to use imagination in marshaling those facts and presenting them to juries," he continues, offering no shortcuts to relieve the tedium of studying reams of material before a trial. Prior to defending Louisiana Governor Edwin Edwards, for example, Neal read over "hundreds and hundreds of pages of grand jury testimony."

"And then you hope you're lucky," concludes Neal regarding preparation technique. "You wait for the prosecutor to make a mistake and hope that your total, thorough preparation will allow you to take advantage of that mistake. And they will make mistakes."

While Neal tries to take advantage of others' errors, his overriding rule is not to beat himself. "I never take the chance that will result in a bad error," he explains. "I try not to stretch what I'm doing into making a mistake—not to try to put on too much cross-examination, not to put a witness on who might [either] be a great witness or a disaster. If someone is going to win a case against me, they're going to beat me," says Neal. "But I don't beat myself."

He cites his college football coach's game maxim—"The team that makes the fewest mistakes wins"—and proceeds to tick off some of the cases the other side lost. In the Ford criminal case, the prosecution failed to determine all the facts leading up to the accident; in the hijacking case, the government lost critical pieces of evidence; and in the Landis case, the prosecutor put on too many witnesses. In all of these cases, says Neal, he deserved to win based on the merits, but his opponents' mistakes insured the favorable verdicts. It's as if Neal wants to credit the biggest victories in life to other people's carelessness and stupidity.

But few lawyers can jump on an opposing lawyer's mistakes the way Jim Neal does.

"The difference between a lawyer who gets verdicts *against* himself in more than his share of the cases, and a lawyer who gets verdicts *for* himself in more than his share of the cases," says Neal, "is the ability—by preparation—to take advantage of the mistakes his opponent makes."

Neal does agree that trial attorneys must have charisma, a "command presence" before the jury. He defines command presence as "the ability to have the eyes and ears of the fact finders [i.e., the jury] riveted to the lawyer." But here again, he harks back to preparation as the means for acquiring this attribute. "If you know more about the case than anyone else does in that courtroom, you can be a Mr. Peepers [the timid biology instructor played by Wally Cox on the 1950s NBC television comedy "Mr. Peepers"] and have more command presence than a more imposing figure who doesn't know what he's doing or hasn't adequately prepared," says Neal.

In contrast to the vastness of his preparation, Neal narrows the focus of his presentation in court. "Jurors will really understand fifty percent of what they hear—and remember fifty percent of what they understand," explains Neal. "That gives you about twenty-five percent of everything that goes on. What you've got to do is make sure that the jury understands—and remembers—that twenty-five percent that you want them to understand and remember."

He believes first and foremost in a clean-cut, straightforward, readily comprehensible defense. The reason Claus von Bulow—who was accused of attempting to murder his socialite wife Sunny—was convicted the first time and acquitted the second, speculates Neal, was that in the second case the attorney had a single, specific defense. "They stuck with that defense and didn't get deterred by anything else, and it won for them."

Consider the jury, says Neal. "We put impossible burdens on jurors," particularly in complex white-collar crime cases. "First we get jurors—hopefully—who have read little or nothing about the case. Number two, they can listen to the case during the day, they can't study the case at night, and they can't talk about the case during the trial. So they sit up there—they're not supposed to know anything about the case, they're not supposed to talk about the case or study the case at night, and they're not supposed to discuss the case with their colleagues during the trial—and then at the end, after months of hearing testimony of innumerable witnesses, and [looking at] these massive documents going through, then they're supposed to understand?

"They can't, they just can't," Neal answers. "You can take a bunch of PhDs [on a jury], and if you try to fight every issue, and you've got a multitude of issues in a complex case, nobody given those circumstances will comprehend them."

Some lawyers take the position that if a case isn't comprehensible, the defense ought to win because it's the prosecutor's burden to prove guilt beyond a reasonable doubt. "I fear too much," responds Neal, "that if it's incomprehensible, jurors tend to say, 'Well, okay, if there wasn't something there, he wouldn't have been indicted.' "

A case may offer more than one good defense, continues Neal. "You've got to pick and choose. That sounds like you're making up something—it's not. In most cases there are many different ways to appraoch" the jury. A lawyer has to pick out the one that will sell. And the lawyer should resist contesting every issue that comes up in a trial to avoid confusing the jury. Often issues raised by the opposition have nothing to do with the case. For example, in the *Twilight Zone* trial, Landis did not contest that he illegally hired the child actors. But that was beside the point; he wasn't on trial for doing that. He was on trial on charges of causing their deaths. "If your conception is that [an issue] is not critical to your defense," instructs Neal, "don't contest it. Unless," he adds, "you know they can't prove it." Then a lawyer may want to contest that issue just to make the opposition look bad.

"Now once you've [picked a defense], that can change," admits Neal. "Nothing is written in stone," and lawyers must keep in mind that they may have to change. "But you try not to. If a lawyer changes mid-trial, it's usually death."

Of course, Neal says, backing up a step, "the first thing you must do [in preparing a case] is determine whether you've [even] got a defense.

"The client comes in and you get involved in the case," he begins, moving in to a hypothetical situation. "It is very helpful if the client comes in early enough that you're involved in conducting an investigation parallel to the prosecutor's investigation," before a grand jury can issue an indictment. Better still, says Neal, is if the client comes in before the grand jury even convenes. Generally people are not formally notified that they are under investigation, but usually they find out from others who have been subpoenaed or questioned by investigators.

At least if the client comes in while the grand jury investigation is going on, says Neal, "you then have the opportunity to conduct your own, parallel to the prosecutor's.

"Then—the greatest coup of all—is to convince the prosecutor that he should not proceed," proclaims Neal.

How can a lawyer do that? Initially, "your client can give you some idea of what they're going into—the areas they're investigating and your client's involvement in those areas," explains Neal. He suggests having a young attorney sit outside the grand jury room (since the meetings are secret) and try to interview every witness coming out to get some idea of what is happening. Some of the witnesses may talk to the lawyer, although they aren't required to, depending on how they feel about the investigation.

"Then you try to figure out what information the prosecutor has, what information he doesn't have, and try to convince him that this is a case that, for whatever reason, should not be brought—either because it doesn't serve any good public policy, or it doesn't have sufficient admissible evidence to convict, or he's missed witnesses who will blow his case out of the water."

Particularly "in the white-collar-crime area, it's death for your client to be indicted, so that's what you really want to avoid," says Neal. In those cases, if the client comes to him while the investigation is ongoing, the first thing Neal does is call up the U.S. attorney or the prosecutor or the strike force and say, "Look, I represent John Jones. I know you're investigating his activities. I want to reach an agreement that you'll give me an opportunity to talk to you before you bring an indictment."

"And," says Neal, "almost invariably they'll agree. Then you start your own parallel investigation."

In the case of Louisiana's Governor Edwin W. Edwards, who faced federal charges of racketeering and fraud, Neal went a step further. He not only met with the prosecutor, he even went with the prosecutor to the U.S. Department of Justice to appeal the prosecutor's decision to indict Edwards. The Justice Department in Washington, D.C., has to approve indictments under the Racketeer Influenced and Corrupt Organizations Act (which was Edwards's situation), as well as criminal tax cases. In other federal criminal cases, says Neal, a lawyer frequently can get a hearing to appeal a prosecutor's decision. "It's not a matter of right. [But] they will [sometimes] grant you that privilege," he explains. "I've done that on many occasions.

"Part of that's good ol' boy school. If you're a good ol' boy, you've been a prosecutor yourself, they'll give you an opportunity—in most cases."

Of course, meeting with the Justice Department doesn't always work. In the case of Jake Butcher, the Knoxville, Tennessee, banker accused of making loans to nonexistent or shell companies, Neal called an official he knew at Justice to ask about appealing the impending indictment. "I said, 'I'm going to appeal the Butcher case.' He says, 'Be glad to see you. Come on up and have a cup of coffee. But I can tell you right now it won't do a bit of good.' I said, 'Okay. I can drink coffee in Nashville.' "

Neal's Washington efforts didn't help Governor Edwards either. He became only the sixth governor to be indicted while in office. "I sat up there with Department of Justice officials and said, 'No way you're going to win this case,' " recalls Neal, slapping the back of one hand in the palm of the other for emphasis. He was convinced that Edwards had not committed the offense, and that the government had no proof. Furthermore, says Neal, it's harder to convict a governor in the state of Louisiana than it is to convict most defendants. Edwards's first trial was a hung jury—eleven to one for acquittal. In the second trial, which Neal could not argue himself because he had to move on to the Landis case, Edwards was acquitted.

Basically, says Neal, the extent to which the Justice Department will heed a defense attorney before issuing an indictment "depends upon the strength of the U.S. attorney—the Department of Justice's regard for the U.S. attorney."

It's always worth the effort. Avoiding an indictment in the first place "is the most critical thing a white-collar criminal defense lawyer can do," says Neal. "The indictment itself is devastating—when you're indicted you're presumed guilty. When the media gets through with you, you're no longer the same kind of person." (Obviously Neal won't talk about his clients whose indictments he stopped midstream.)

If the client doesn't come in until after an indictment, continues Neal, picking back up with the Nichopoulos case, "then you've got to spend hours—bloody boring hours—going over what's been developed." In federal cases the actual transcript of a grand jury proceeding is not made available until after a witness takes the stand. The procedure in state cases varies depending on the state. But Neal finds out what witnesses testified by sending a member of his staff out to interview them, or by asking them to come in to his office where he interviews them personally.

Neal insists on having full control of his preparation. "I'm not satisfied with somebody summarizing an issue [for me]. I'll go through everything myself," says Neal of his process for reviewing documents for a trial, and information witnesses can provide when called to take the stand. Some [reviews of witness information] may be "a hurried, cursory run-through, simply to eliminate that person as a big player. Then once I've eliminated that person as a big player, or documents as being remotely relevant, I may have somebody else work on those, and I'll stick to the big players and the important documents. But I go through them all first."

After reviewing all available material "you've got to come to a conclusion," instructs Neal. "Do I have a rational defense? Not do I have a fifty-fifty chance. Jesus, do I have a thirty-seventy chance? That's pretty good. If I do, what is that defense?"

Developing and arguing a defense for a client in a multidefendant trial, as in the *Twilight Zone* case, is particularly difficult, notes Neal. When there are so many defendants, he explains, "you can't ever try a case the way you want to." A lawyer in these circumstances must always adjust to other defendant attorneys' tactics and strategies. Neal advises lawyers in multidefendant cases to "try to avoid killing each other off." Sometimes the prosecution can get started and then sit back and watch the defendants' lawyers fight. "Tell the other defense lawyer you know they have to represent their clients, but [say] 'Don't go out of your way to hurt me,' " suggests Neal. In the *Twilight Zone* trial Neal argued on John Landis's behalf that the death of the three actors involved no criminal negligence. It was, says Neal, simply a tragic accident, and accidents do happen.

If a lawyer concludes a client has no defense, continues Neal, then that lawyer has got to try to get the client to let the lawyer try to work out a plea bargain. In the Jake Butcher case "there came a time when there was absolutely no defense—none, zero. And he was indicted on some one hundred counts, in five different cases. So you've got to try to work out something. There is just no other alternative." Butcher pled guilty to bank fraud, conspiracy, and tax evasion, and he received a twenty-year prison term instead of one that could have been hundreds of years.

Neal has had rare cases where the only defense was obfuscation, but he says he doesn't like it. He opts for that route only when he can't find a rational, comprehensible defense—and the defendant won't let him plea bargain. "To put it in legal terms," says Neal of his least-favorite tactic, "you try to prevent the prosecution from proving his case beyond a reasonable doubt. To put it in street language, you confuse him." A lawyer can do this, for example, by making "apparent attacks" on testimony, that is, asking questions that seem to relate to the case but which in fact have no bearing on its outcome. A lawyer might ask an opponent's expert, "Do you mean to tell me that you met the plaintiff only today when you first walked into this courtroom?"

But if a lawyer has concluded there is a rational defense, "then you bend everything—your total will and mind and body—to developing and supporting that defense and destroying anything that tends to attack that defense," Neal explains.

"A case never stays the same: It either gets better or worse. If you don't work on it, it's going to get worse for you. If you do work on it—hard—once you've determined this defense, it's amazing the number of instances that case will get better and the possibilities [of success] will rise."

In the Dr. Nick case, the single, specific defense Neal chose was that of "the Good Samaritan," a character taken from the Bible. Here's how he developed it.

"The first thing I knew was that Dr. Nichopoulos had been found guilty of certain charges by the medical review board," says Neal. "While they had a lot of empathy for him because his patients were difficult, nonetheless, he was suspended from practice.

"I look at the same facts and say, 'Wait a minute. That ain't right.' What the doctors [on the board] looked at was the general rule in the *Physician's Desk Reference*—the *PDR*—for prescribing drugs, and he violated that law. He prescribed too much according to the *PDR*, he prescribed it too frequently, he prescribed over too long a period. And he potentially prescribed it when there were contraindications," says Neal.

The prosecution maintained that Nichopoulos knew Presley was hooked on drugs, but he continued to prescribe for him increasingly greater amounts of amphetamines, barbiturates, and narcotics until the time of Presley's death. According to the prosecution, many of Presley's other medical problems were caused by his drug dependency. The complaint against Dr. Nick said he similarly overprescribed drugs to other patients.

"But what were the real facts of why he was doing this?" asks Neal, remembering his strategy preparation. "He did it simply because the patients involved were addicted—and his philosophy was 'I will go ahead and treat these patients and try to keep them under my care rather than having them go out on the streets in an uncontrolled fashion and get the drugs. And I will continue to reduce the amounts of these drugs over the period of time in the hopes of weaning them off of them.' " Nichopoulos was successful with some of his patients, and the amount of medications he prescribed for them diminished over time.

Dr. Nick felt this way about all the addicted patients he treated, says Neal. But he was not particularly successful with Elvis's rehabilitation. "He quit Elvis Presley [as his physician] two or three times, only to find Elvis Presley [getting drugs on the street and then] coming back to him in worse shape," notes Neal. Given Presley's personality and schedules, committing him to a hospital rehabilitation program was not a viable option.

"All told what I said was, here was a doctor willing to sacrifice himself, to sacrifice even his medical profession if that was necessary—to violate those general rules in the *PDR*—in order to help his patients." Thus a man depicted as a professional pill pusher became the paradigm of a sympathetic figure, in fact, a persecuted figure who had been willing to help others, even to his own professional detriment.

Neal found that with careful analysis, the prescriptions over a long period of time "did show, overall, a consistent decline in the amount of drugs prescribed to his patients." For the trial, the attorney made large charts of the prescription lists to show the jury to prove this point. He called members of the "Memphis Mafia" (Elvis's entourage) to describe how Nichopoulos gave

Presley placebos and how he half-emptied injections on the rug before administering them to the singer.

Several witnesses testified that if it hadn't been for Dr. Nichopoulos, Elvis Presley would have been dead years earlier.

Neal talks less about a corollary to his defense—the destruction of the Elvis Presley myth. By portraying Nichopoulos in such a good light, he necessarily made Presley look pretty bad.

Yes, acknowledges Neal, "the story of Elvis Presley's life had to be handled very delicately." But, he explains today, "we didn't attack [Presley] as a human being. We attacked him as an individual who had the tragic misfortune of getting hung up on prescription drugs. He was a hypochrondriac.

"When Elvis Presley first started getting involved in drugs, it was a different world," says Neal of the sympathetic point of view he offered regarding the singer. "Many of these [drugs] were not considered bad back then.

"So we didn't attack Elvis Presley as anything but a guy who had a very difficult life," concludes Neal, describing Presley's unremitting stardom and total loss of privacy. In fact, "Dr. Nichopoulos was the one man who genuinely cared for Elvis Presley and who tried to control and reduce his drug dependency."

Once Neal selects the best approach, in this case the Good Samaritan defense, the second stage in trial preparation is to narrow the issues in his case. Here he includes both factual and legal issues. Limiting the issues, he believes, helps reduce or eliminate surprises in the courtroom. Neal does this in "any way I can," including pretrial conferences, or motions in limine [pretrial] to get advance rulings on the law. In the Ford criminal case, Neal filed enough pretrial motions to fill an eight-inch-thick binder.

One of the big issues in Nichopoulos's case was whether to allow into evidence the Presley autopsy report with information on the cause of the singer's death. "We filed motions [in limine saying] that we wanted to keep that out," says Neal, "and we were successful." He argued that the report was irrelevant, and even if it did have some slight relevancy, that that was outweighed by its prejudicial effect. Nichopoulos was charged with criminally prescribing drugs, reasoned Neal; he was not charged with causing Elvis Presley's death. "The prosecutor had intended to put [the report] in. He had intended to try this case like the murder of Elvis Presley," says Dr. Nick's lawyer.

"You can certainly say that Elvis Presley's ingestion of drugs over a period of time led to his death—just like overeating and overdrinking could lead to death over a period of time," explains Neal today. "And certainly the amount of drugs Elvis Presley ingested over time so weakened his system that it was a remote cause of his death. No doubt about it. But it wasn't the cause. And [Dr. Nichopoulos] wasn't charged with that." (Neal's victory over the autopsy report was not total, however. The judge did allow the prosecutor to prove how many different drugs were in Elvis Presley's body when he died.)

As another technique to reduce issues, although one he uses during trial, Neal stipulates uncontested facts. This reduces their importance, minimizes their impact on the jury, and eliminates surprises witnesses testifying about those facts might bring. "After all, if you know somebody can prove something, stipulate it—get it out of the way. Stipulations come and go quickly.

"Smart prosecutors won't stipulate," says Neal.

In the Presley case, he recalls, the prosecutor was going to bring on as witnesses several medical doctors to testify that Nichopoulos "was wildly wrong and grossly negligent in how he prescribed drugs. One doctor came on and so testified. We cross-examined him," recalls Neal.

"But then we jumped up and said 'We'll stipulate the other doctors called—A, B, and C—will testify the same on direct and cross.' For some reason the prosecutor agreed. So instead of two more days of this kind of stuff—it was over."

The prosecutors must have felt relieved that their other physician witnesses wouldn't have to suffer through Neal's cross-examination. But their relief was overshadowed by the error of their judgment.

"Now, they could say in summation, 'Look, defense counsel agreed that A, B, and C if called would testify like Dr. Jones did,' " explains Neal. But in such cases the jury will never feel the same impact as if all the doctors had actually taken the stand and repeated their views over and over again.

One big mistake for the prosecution, counts Neal.

After determining the Nichopoulos defense, interviewing witnesses, reviewing documents, preparing documents for introduction of evidence, and writing pretrial motions, Neal was ready to find out what kind of jury he might get. "In the Dr. Nichopoulos case I was terrified—not knowing anything except that Elvis Presley was and is an idol in Memphis, Tennessee." And Nichopoulos had been subjected to a flood of negative publicity following the singer's death.

Neal was convinced he would have to move the trial in order to get a fair hearing. But first, the lawyer needed to find out if he had grounds to request a change in venue. He hired some experts to help him—a Memphis market-research company called Yacoubian & Associates. He asked them to profile a potential jury.

"More than anything else," says Neal, "I wanted to know what the attitude of the community was about Elvis Presley, about Dr. Nichopoulos, about who was responsible for Elvis Presley's death."

Neal hired the National Jury Project to assist him in the Edwards and Landis cases, University of Chicago law professor Hans Zeisel in the Ford criminal case, and trial consultant Hale Starr of West Des Moines, Iowa, in a marijuana importation case in South Carolina. Asked whether he always uses trial consultants, Neal replies: "If I've done all my fact investigation, if I've researched and prepared all my motions, if I've got all my witnesses interviewed—and I've got money left—absolutely. But they're not as important as a thorough preparation of the facts and the law."

Neal doesn't remember how he came across Yacoubian & Associates. "But I met him, I liked him, I wanted to try him. I said, 'I'll take a chance on you and you give me a bargain basement price.' " Neal says that all he could afford from consultants in the Nichopoulos case was an attitudinal survey.

It turned out that that survey provided some very important answers, not just about possible prejudice against Nichopoulos but also about community attitudes toward Presley, his drug addiction, and his death. Neal worked with the Yacoubian group to prepare a questionnaire, and the consultants identified a valid sample of persons to complete it. That sample consisted of 519 registered voters in Shelby County, Tennessee, out of a universe of 410,000 voters. (As in most trials, Tennessee juries are selected from the voter registration rolls.) Yacoubian's interviewers, who were told neither the reason nor the sponsor of the survey, telephoned those identified for the sample during a weekend in late September 1981.

The survey began with some very broad questions, such as how the respondents felt about the seriousness of different types of crimes in Memphis and Shelby County, and how they viewed different professions such as doctors, lawyers, and musicians.

The survey also included questions about how the respondents felt about Presley's music, how they felt about him personally, how many times they had visited Graceland Mansion where Presley lived, and whether they thought he died of drug-related or heart-related problems. But the answers to two questions in particular hit home for Neal.

In response to the question—"Suppose Elvis really died of a drug overdose. In your opinion who, if anyone, should be blamed?"—the survey showed the following answers:

His father	1.0 percent
His doctor	19.9 percent

His manager	1.0 percent
Elvis himself	67.1 percent
Don't know	3.3 percent

It appeared that two-thirds of any jury Neal might get would think that Presley himself was responsible for his addiction problems. Neal was surprised.

He also noted with keen interest responses to this question: Suppose Elvis went to his doctor for drug treatment. Do you think his doctor should have:

	% Yes	% No
Refused treating him and turned him over to the police	12.3	83.6
Refused treating him and referred him to drug treatment	61.7	34.3
Agreed to treat him in order to reduce Elvis's dependence on drugs	70.3	25.0

The survey, says Neal, told him "Hell, no, try the case in Memphis. Memphis doesn't blame Dr. Nichopoulos. If Elvis Presley took too many drugs and that ultimately led to his death, he's responsible." Many community attitude surveys are not clear in their results, but this one was.

And the responses to these two questions told Neal something about his defense. "The doctor shouldn't turn him away. Be a Good Samaritan," the respondents were saying. Neal insists that his defense did not depend on the market survey—his defense depended on the facts—but as long as he was conducting a general community attitudinal survey to decide whether to request a change in venue, he decided to find out if the defense he had already planned "would fly in Memphis, Tennessee." It appeared that it would.

With the survey Neal gathered information about specific categories of people who might be on his jury. Yacoubian broke down responses to questions about the cause of Elvis's death, who should be blamed, and whether the doctor should have treated him, among other questions, by age, education, occupation, income, race, and sex. For example, Neal saw that white males were most likely to believe that Nichopoulos was right to treat Presley's addiction. Females (both black and white) were least likely to believe this.

Neal is, however, guarded in relying on this kind of information about jurors. "First," he says, "the differences [between categories] frequently aren't great. Second, even if you got an indication that this [certain] group has an adverse attitude toward your defense, that doesn't mean that that living human being in the box there has the attitude applicable to this group." But Neal does admit that the responses to the Yacoubian survey convinced him in the Presley case to avoid at all costs one category of jurors: elderly white women.

Jury consultants in other cases have helped Neal via another effective preparation technique—mock trials. "They will get a long written statement on the prosecution's case; they will get a long written statement on the defense. They will then select a fair cross section of seven to ten people, and they will present the prosecution's case and the defendant's case to this mock jury," explains Neal.

"Then they will put this mock jury in a room with one-way mirrors. And they will videotape their discussions and deliberations." Even though this way of presenting the trial to a mock jury is greatly simplified, Neal thinks it works and is particularly suited for a case with tight time constraints.

What's important is the result of the mock trial—what these jurors picked up. What issues did they think were important, and in what order? "Then," says Neal, "you can look back and you may say, 'Jesus, I didn't think that was important.' To a lawyer [an issue] may not be legally that significant. But to a lay person it's very significant." After one mock trial Neal rewrites his defense, emphasizing issues the mock jury talked about most.

Neal did not run a mock trial in the Nichopoulos case. "It's all a matter of money," he stresses with a pained look on his face. "If I got indicted, I couldn't afford—and I'm not a pauper—the kind of first-rate defense that's doable in this country." But he has staged mock trials in about four cases, including Governor Edwards's.

Remember, Neal adds on the subject of trial consultants, "we're talking about cases that are unusual" and that merit the expense of a jury consultant. "Everybody hates a rapist," he says. "You don't have to go out and get a survey about a rapist." It has to be something about which there might be some controversy in the community.

On the first day in October 1981, fifty prospective jurors walked into Judge Weinman's Memphis courtroom. He told them that the trial would be lengthy—about a month—and that jurors would be isolated from outsiders for the duration. Then he dismissed those who said the trial would prove too much of a hardship.

A frenzy of excitement and anticipation wrapped the courthouse. The shockingly long list of 135 potential prosecution witnesses, released the same day that jury selection began, included, among others, Presley's manager, Colonel Tom Parker, Jerry Lee Lewis, former Presley girlfriends, and pathologists who undertook the Presley autopsy. Despite protests from the press, Judge Weinman prohibited cameras and sound equipment from the courtroom and even from entryways leading to it. Undeterred, a flock of reporters covered the trial fully, shadowed in their vigilance by Presley fans and the simply curious. Some fans in the visitors gallery sported T-shirts with their idol's image painted on the front.

Early in the trial Neal arranged with the reporters to make a few comments for them every day as he left court, describing very carefully what had transpired that day. He views this agreement as a particular service for the electronic media, which depend on interviews for their visuals. In return, Neal asked the reporters at the trial, "Please don't follow me around." In California during the Landis trial, however, Neal found that he had to break with this traditional mode of handling courtroom reporters. "I found it very traditional out there for everybody to go out and talk about everything," says Neal. "The prosecution went out and talked, and we had to respond. We had to fight fire with fire, but that's not my usual approach."

As the Nichopoulos trial began, Neal and assistant district attorneys Jewett Miller and James Wilson began voir dire, questioning the potential jurors in groups of twelve. Miller, who has since died, was a gruff, chain-smoking, very southern career prosecutor, who always seemed angry during the Nichopoulos trial. Wilson, younger than Miller by about twenty years, was somewhat more subdued. The two prosecutors asked the jurors for their views on drugs, doctors, and Elvis Presley's death. Wilson tried to make points by talking to the jurors about physician responsibility. He asked them if a doctor should allow a patient to have drugs when the patient did not need them.

When Neal's turn came for questioning, he immediately zeroed in on his own theory of the case. Neal asked the jurors how they felt a doctor should treat a patient who has problems with drugs. He told them that they would have to decide whether Nichopoulos's heart was "in the right place" when he provided Presley with prescriptions for addictive drugs.

"Proof will probably show he didn't do absolutely right and he didn't do absolutely wrong. The question is," said Neal to the prospective jurors, "did he do the best he could?"

Among the jurors Neal rejected were a couple of older white women. Neal's attitudinal survey had indicated that older white women generally would not look favorably on Dr. Nichopoulos.

After five days of intense voir dire questioning, Neal and the prosecutors agreed to a five-man, seven-women jury. It included a housewife, a grocery store cashier, a nursing home aide, a hospital nurses' aide, a retired hospital maintenance worker, an auto parts handyman, a waitress, an interior designer, a player piano repairman, a hardware store supervisor, a musician and composer, and a secretary. (Several days into the trial, the nurses' aide would be excused because she couldn't find anyone to care for her young children; she was replaced by a bus driver.)

In his opening statement Assistant DA Miller described Nichopoulos as a doctor eager to gain favors from his famous patient, and a man who just liked to hobnob with the stars. He told the jury that Nichopoulos prescribed for Presley "staggering" amounts of drugs—even though the doctor knew that Presley was addicted—and the amounts prescribed multiplied over time. The prosecutor also talked about drug prescriptions Nichopoulos had written for Jerry Lee Lewis and for other patients listed in the government's indictment.

Neal painted a far different picture of Nichopoulos, relying on his defense that Nichopoulos was the Good Samaritan helping desperate and difficult patients. Neal told the jury that Nichopoulos jeopardized his medical license to help all his addicted patients diminish their supply of drugs and cure their addictions. He did this when many other doctors turned these people away, explained Neal. Nichopoulos was the man who would take a chance and even practiced in what other doctors would see as an unorthodox way if he believed it would help—rather than turning his back and passing on, leaving these victims to the mercy of the street peddlers.

"You want to make a clear, concise, opening statement where you lay out what you're going to prove, and you do it in a narrative. But you never overstate; if anything you understate," says Neal, who speaks only from notes and never unbuttons his suit coat when speaking before a jury. It's important that lawyers never risk saying anything in an opening that they can't prove during the trial.

"When you step in the courtroom to try a case," he continues, "you ought to know how you're going to set up the case." In fact, "before you cross-examine the first witness, you ought to know what your summation is probably going to be. There will always be surprises, but to the extent of ninety percent you ought to be able to give your summation before you cross-examine the first witness.

"I think the way to try a case is to be able to visualize the case from the beginning to end. You can't do that perfectly. But you do try, like Jack Nicklaus playing golf. Coming up to a hole, he knows where he wants to hit the drive, he knows if he hits the drive there, he knows where he wants to hit his second shot to the green, and he knows how he wants to putt—before he ever tees up the ball on the first tee. And that's the way you've got to try a lawsuit. You've got to be thinking about that summation all the time.

"With every witness you cross-examine, ask 'Why am I asking this question—or line of questions?' Number one, for the impact it will immediately have on the jury, or two, to elicit information for use in summation. If it doesn't do one of those things, then you don't ask that line of questioning."

The prosecution's first witness was a handwriting expert. Among the favors Nichopoulos curried from Presley, the government alleged, were large loans of money. Robert J. Muehlberger, a U.S. Post Office Crime Lab document analyst, testified that Nichopoulos had completed parts of a $25,000 check paid him by Presley. He said that Nichopoulos had written out his name as the recipient on the check and the words for "$25,000"; Presley had written the rest. Muehlberger could not say whether Nichopoulos or Presley had written on the check first.

With Muehlberger on the stand as a handwriting expert, the

prosecutor also entered into evidence prescriptions allegedly signed by Nichopoulos. Although the total number of prescriptions with Nichopoulos's signature was not clear, the state board of medical examiners said that the doctor had written them for thousands of pills during the last months of Presley's life. (Many of these prescriptions, the defense would later prove, were actually written for the entire Presley tour, so Nichopoulos could have them available should they be needed.)

In cross-examining Muehlberger, Neal was able to get him to testify that at least one of Nichopoulos's patients (not Presley) had altered the prescriptions as to their amounts, raising doubts about calculations of total drugs prescribed. By questioning some of Muehlberger's testimony, explains Neal today, he was able, by implication, to attack the accuracy of anything that expert said.

"To reduce the effect of testimony of a witness on direct," says Neal, "you attack the credibility of the witness—or you act as if you assume the witness is credible and attack the accuracy of his testimony."

The prosecution's second witness, a Memphis pharmacist, actually turned out to be a boon for Neal's case. Earlier, druggist Jack Kirsch had pleaded no contest to charges that he had filled prescriptions for large quantities of pills for Presley. (The jury, of course, was not told about this plea.) The prosecution called Kirsch to the stand to prove that Nichopoulos had ordered vast numbers of prescriptions for Presley and others, and that those prescriptions had actually been filled.

But on cross-examination Neal shed some light on Nichopoulos's approach to treatment. Neal was reported to have asked Kirsch about his conversations with Nichopoulos, a longtime friend:

"I want to take you back to the life of Elvis Presley," said Neal. "Do you agree that you had conversations with Dr. Nichopoulos in which Dr. Nichopoulos referred to Elvis Presley as a problem patient?"

"On several occasions," replied Kirsch.

"Did he mention that Mr. Presley was getting drugs from everywhere under the sun?"

"Absolutely," replied Kirsch.

Kirsch also said that Nichopoulos told him several times that he tried to substitute harmless pills for drugs he prescribed to Presley to help control the singer's addiction. Nichopoulos asked the druggist how he could get other possible placebos to put in place of the addictive medications.

"Didn't he ask you to help him by asking manufacturers about placebos?" asked Neal.

"Yes," replied Kirsch.

"He's getting nothing but a saline or water solution [in the placebos]?"

"That is true."

"Didn't [Dr. Nichopoulos] tell you about drugs being shipped to Elvis Presley [that the doctor had intercepted], and didn't he bring them to you and ask you what they were?"

"That's right. Some of them—I had no idea what they were. Some of them were injectable. Some of them were tabs, and some I was fairly familiar with."

In the end, Neal had, in effect, turned Kirsch into a defense witness.

Similarly, Neal was able to remold on cross-examination testimony from Jerry Lee Lewis's drug treatment specialist. Dr. David Knott stated that Nichopoulos incorrectly continued prescribing amphetamines for the entertainer, who was addicted to them. When Neal took over questioning, he asked Knott who his physician was. Of course, Neal already knew the answer.

"Dr. Nichopoulos," replied Knott.

And, asked Neal, was Dr. Nichopoulos doing the best he could in treating Lewis, who was a very uncooperative patient?

Yes again, the psychiatrist responded.

Testimony from Marty Lacker, a former member of Presley's entourage, and from his wife, Patsy Lacker, was not, however, as helpful to Neal's case. For one, the prosecution said that Nichopoulos indiscriminately prescribed for Lacker large numbers of painkillers. Also, Mrs. Lacker testified that she feared for her husband because he was taking sleeping pills, both regularly and in considerable quantities.

When Mrs. Lacker told Nichopoulos about her concerns—and asked him not to prescribe any more pills—"he didn't answer me," she was reported to have said. "He just turned and walked away." Mr. Lacker ultimately withdrew from the pills without medical supervision.

The prosecution switched back to its theme of Nichopoulos's indebtedness to Presley and introduced documents showing that Presley loaned the doctor $200,000 to finance building his home. Later Presley increased that by another $55,000 and arranged for Nichopoulos to pay him back in monthly mortgage payments over a twenty-five-year period. Subsequently, Presley loaned Nichopoulos another $25,000 with the check he and Nichopoulos had written together, bringing the doctor's total debt to the singer to $280,000.

An attorney who represented the Presley estate testified that Nichopoulos had paid back a substantial portion of the debt, and on schedule.

More damaging testimony came from the pathologist who lead the eight-doctor team that performed the Presley autopsy. Dr. Eric Muirhead told the jury that they found thirteen different drugs in Presley's body at the time of death. Neal fought strenuously to keep Muirhead's testimony out of the trial. "We were concerned about anything that might make it look like Dr. Nichopoulos had a hand in his death," explains Neal today. But Judge Weinman overruled Neal's objections as long as the prosecution did not attempt to tie the drugs to the cause of Presley's death.

In all, the pathologist's testimony still didn't turn out too badly for the defense. Of the thirteen drugs identified in Presley's body, "we could prove that only one of them could possibly have been prescribed by Dr. Nichopoulos," says Neal.

Neal made the greatest progress in the trial when he cross-examined a physician who testified as an expert for the prosecution. This physician was called to criticize Nichopoulos's method of treating addicted patients by giving them more drugs.

"The witness was asked 'And of course you've written many scholarly articles for publication,' " recalls Neal.

"Yes," the doctor responded.

Neal had known ahead of time that this doctor was to be an expert witness. "We had gone out to [the medical school at] Vanderbilt and done a computer check [with the MEDLINE data base]," explains Neal, "to find every publication written by every person we thought might be a witness for the prosecution. And we did a check on this man. [We could] not [find] one publication. Not one."

Another big mistake by the prosecution, stresses Neal.

"So I asked to take [the witness] over on qualification," he continues, referring to the procedure by which an attorney can question an expert witness for the opposing side about his or her qualifications to testify before that person's direct examination begins. "Once a person makes a mistake, never take your foot off his neck," says Neal.

Peering at the doctor from over his glasses, Neal took him through "every major medical periodical I could find, asking him if it was in there, in this one, in that one [that he had published his articles]. I went through them one by one by one—and he'd have to say no, no, no for over an hour. I made a monkey out of him," recalls Neal today.

"Finally I said, 'Isn't it a fact that you haven't written one article for any publication?' "

When the doctor insisted that he had published one article but said he could not remember in which publication, Neal asked him to determine the publication's name over the lunch break. But even after the doctor returned, he still had no answer.

"And this was on qualification," says Neal. "By the time he started his substantive case, no one was paying any attention to him. The prosecutor never recovered from that mistake. Never. I made sure everybody in Memphis, Tennessee, knew he had made that big blunder."

If he hadn't been prepared to take advantage of this mistake, stresses Neal, he would have missed the opportunity, and today he maintains that the cross-examination of that particular witness on qualification was one of the most important developments in the Nichopoulos trial.

"I did the same thing in the Ford criminal case," adds Neal. A witness "was going to testify for the prosecutor. I had reams of material [about this witness]. And so I took him over on voir dire [i.e., on qualification]. By the time we got through examining him on voir dire, I didn't care what he testified to. He was so bad thereafter that the prosecutor told him to get out of town and not come back."

When his turn came to present Nichopoulos's defense, Neal called among his witnesses one of Nichopoulos's medical partners. He testified that Nichopoulos had spent time counseling patients when it was not economically beneficial to their practice. A bookkeeper also testified that Nichopoulos practically lost money while treating most of the patients named in the indictment.

A nurse who lived at Graceland with her husband and child also testified to the great quantity of pharmaceuticals Presley consumed and supported descriptions of Nichopoulos's approach to treatment. One of Presley's employees told the jury how Nichopoulos had given Presley placebos and saline injections when the singer thought he was getting the drugs to which he was addicted.

To support Nichopoulos's claim that he was following the best path of medical treatment for his addicted patients, and to counter the prosecution's experts, Neal brought on his own medical expert, Dr. Forest Tennant, Jr., a drug researcher from the University of California. "We needed an expert to testify not only that Dr. Nichopoulos had this theory of how to treat people—gradually keeping them on, prescribing to them well beyond

[what] the general rules would prescribe—but [also] we wanted to find an expert who would give validity to that," recalls Neal, explaining his choice. "We talked to any number of experts around the country" before finding Tennant. "We spent hours and hours preparing him to testify."

Tennant did testify that Nichopoulos may have been following the path of treatment best suited for Presley and other patients under his care. In cases where patients absolutely cannot function without the drugs to which they are addicted, a doctor can only provide them with these drugs and monitor them closely so they don't seek sources on the street, he said.

Neal let his young assisting attorney in the case, Thomas H. Dundon, question their medical expert on the stand. "To put on an expert is not that difficult once he's prepared right," says Neal. "You put him on, put on his qualifications, and ask about his opinions and the basis for those opinions." Neal also allowed Dundon, who is now a partner at Neal & Harwell, to handle the direct examination of some other minor witnesses.

The California expert "was a big hit," says Neal. "He was well prepared to testify, and [the prosecution] could make no progress on him whatsoever." Tennant is now the drug adviser to the National Football League.

Finally, Nichopoulos himself testified over the course of several days. "We spent weeks preparing Dr. Nichopoulos," says Neal, explaining that he never decides whether to put a defendant on until after the prosecution has completed presenting its entire case. He may tentatively decide this issue, "but you can never resolve that until you've got the entire [prosecution] picture," he explains.

This decision comes once you determine "you're not likely to win unless you do," says Neal. "Is it necessary? If it's not necessary—of course you don't. Or the question can go, 'Do I have to do it in order to get a hung jury?' The defendant wins if he doesn't lose. The prosecutor loses if he doesn't win. Big difference."

The reason a lawyer prepares a defendant for weeks and weeks in advance is so the option is always there. "If you wait until the night before," says Neal, "you're dead."

Neal's witness preparation is not only long and tedious, but also potentially stressful.

All lawyers know to prepare their witnesses for cross-examination, says Neal. "But there is a real skill that many people overlook—and that is how you prepare your direct examination of a witness. How you get a rapport going between the witness and yourself. How you help him develop a selling personality, number one, and then, number two, how you help him project that selling personality."

The first thing a lawyer should do is get every document and all the prior testimony (if the person has already testified in some forum), and everything about the case that pertains to that witness's testimony, says Neal. The rules for preparing less important witnesses are comparable, he adds, but the time commitment is generally less—everything from preparation almost as intensive as that for the defendant to simply reviewing a witness's testimony and pointing out some questions he may be asked on cross-examination. "You give the defendant all the testimony that concerns him, specifically his previous statements (which you get as soon as the grand jury returns the indictment), and all the relevant documents." Neal also had a transcript of Nichopoulos's hearing before the board of medical examiners, and he had notes from his follow-up interviews with the hearing witnesses.

"I emphasize pretty strongly that [the client] is going to have an examination period and this is his homework," Neal explains. "Except that in this case, the examination is not a grade—A, B, C, or D. Pass and you stay out of prison, fail and you go to prison." Neal tells his clients to learn all the material in great detail, material that may total thousands of pages.

It's amazing, he notes, how many times a client won't want to study his assignment. "You have to be careful. They try to get away from the idea. They don't like to face this jury of their peers and a hostile prosecutor. I scream at them, curse at them, and finally they do it."

Then Neal starts "gently" going through all the information with his client in his office. He may work through subject by subject, or document by document. For example, in the Landis case, Neal spent half a day with the director just going over how he got involved in making the movie *Twilight Zone.* With Nichopoulos, Neal talked about individual patients, how he treated them, and why. "Why did you do this?" Neal would repeatedly ask Nichopoulos about various patients' treatment. Then he would work with Nichopoulos, going back through the medical charts and various prescriptions he had ordered. "There were many explanations as to why the prescriptions were coming so frequently," says Neal, recalling the trial preparation exercise.

But one time through is not enough for Neal. "You go through it again. You go through it again. And again. You're talking about events that happened a long time ago, sometimes years," he explains. "So there's a recall problem." And, adds Neal, "you're talking about people who really don't want to go back and face things. It's painful for them. Sometimes you're screaming at them" to get them to remember.

Once a client does recall events in question and can talk about them, Neal begins to worry about how the client actually relates those events. At that point Neal thinks about a defendant's style as well as the content of his testimony. Neal checks to see if the client has a nervous giggle, continually looks down when he talks, or twitches in his chair. He'll talk about mannerisms and style with a client. Sometimes Neal will even videotape a client, although he didn't videotape Nichopoulos because, he says, "I had about all I could do to get Dr. Nichopoulos prepared with the substance of his testimony, without worrying about the manner."

But Neal couldn't overlook Nichopoulos's natural tendency, like many doctors, to mumble when he explained things. Neal had to help him develop a stronger delivery. He recalls shouting at Dr. Nick "If you've got something to say, you may hate me when this is over, but you're going to say it so somebody can understand."

Neal also felt compelled to alter Nichopoulos's dress. Originally the doctor favored Las Vegas–type suits with green or blue shoes. Neal changed that attire to one of a businessman, with a conservative blue suit and black shoes appropriate for a serious occasion. He relied mostly on the doctor's wife to help him. (Neal didn't suggest touching Nichopoulos's long curly white hair—it would have been too noticeable, he says, because too many people already knew what Nichopoulos looked like.)

With Nichopoulos prepared for direct examination, Neal was ready to test him on cross. "Then you really have at it," says Neal. As the client's attorney, he likes to go first. "I give him brutal treatment, mean as can be." Afterward he brings in his partners, and even other lawyers in the community, to take a round of practice cross-examination. "The defendant is the number one pivotal witness," Neal reiterates when talking about preparing his client to take the stand. "There is nobody else who comes close in importance. A defendant who is a good witness can carry the day, even if most everything else has gone against you."

In the trial Neal thought he'd get a hung jury if he didn't put the doctor on the stand. "But we wanted to win," explains Neal today. "We made that decision—let's win it." In the last analysis, says Neal, Nichopoulos "had to explain our defense. We had supported him all the way along, we could hint at it by cross-examination. But he had to get up there and say 'I prescribed all these drugs over these years to Elvis Presley because . . .'

"It's very difficult to win cases without putting the defendant on the stand," Neal concludes, and more times than not, he has his client testify. When he doesn't, it's usually because he's been able "to articulate his rational defense accurately without having the defendant do it." For Nichopoulos, all the objective proof—in the sense of how many drugs had been prescribed for his patients over a certain period of time—was against him. "The state of mind of why he did that was so important," explains Neal, and only Nichopoulos could share what he was thinking.

When that time came, Nichopoulos admitted prescribing most of the drugs the prosecution listed. But he also said that he threw many away and gave Presley placebos in their place. He said that he had to purchase the real drugs because Presley—a self-taught drug expert who kept a copy of the *PDR* next to his bed—would have otherwise grown suspicious. Nichopoulos told the jury exactly how and why he had been trying to help Presley and other patients with drug problems. He was very convincing.

In his closing argument Neal hit hard again on his Good Samaritan defense. "I can't think of anything that fits Dr. Nichopoulos better," said Neal to the jurors. "Dr. George Nichopoulos is the one who stopped and looked at these people and then offered to help. You are judging the Samaritan."

The Good Samaritan was not harshly judged. On November 5, 1981, five weeks to the day after his trial had begun, the jury deliberated only briefly before acquitting Dr. Nick of all charges. Several of the jurors told reporters that they were convinced that the doctor had acted in good faith in prescribing drugs to Presley and others. They did decide that, given the circumstances, he was doing the best he could.

The trauma over, Nichopoulos shook hands with well-wishers and returned to his medical practice, a free but marked man. He cared deeply about Presley and some say, even loved him like a son. That love may or may not have clouded his judgment as Presley's doctor. But in the end it did bring him a position as a pallbearer at Presley's funeral, and the indelible, lifelong, and sometimes dubious distinction of having served as Elvis Presley's doctor. For the medical profession Nichopoulos's trial only added to already intense debate over addiction treatment: physicians around the country continued to argue about the best course to follow.

As for Neal, he quickly learned that his carefully articulated defense, his intense preparation, and his oratorical skill convinced everyone but the prosecution that Dr. George Nichopoulos had chosen the best treatment possible for the king of rock 'n' roll. In the courtroom hubbub the crowd gathered around with congratulations and pats on the back. Nichopoulos was free, but Neal was the victor. Even the jurors hugged him.

PHILIP H. CORBOY

Corboy & Demetrio, P. C., Chicago

Photo Ideas, Inc.

On a cold November Monday in 1986, Philip H. Corboy enjoyed a pleasure that seldom comes his way. He relaxed. Casually attired in plaid wool slacks and a black jersey, Corboy seemed somewhat out of place in his highly formal office with its 1848 four-sided partners desk and other exquisite antique furnishings. But that day Corboy was a man without a schedule: he had been set to try the case of a badly burned coal-yard worker in a small Wisconsin town, but after days on site the preceding week, during which Corboy made his final trial preparations, the case settled for more than $2 million, a new record in that part of Wisconsin. Juiced up and raring for one more plaintiff's courtroom victory, Corboy instead returned home to Chicago where he hoped his bottled-up energy would dissipate into the familiar surroundings.

Exactly thirty-six years ago that very morning, Corboy had begun his first trial. At that time the premier personal injury lawyer in Chicago, sole practitioner James A. Dooley, had taken Corboy under the wing of his law practice. The two men had met through the activities of the law school fraternity, Phi Alpha Delta, at Loyola University in Chicago, where both Dooley and Corboy had graduated first in their respective law school classes. The first case the twenty-six-year-old Corboy tried, in November 1950, involved two young men, Pedro Espinoza and Esteban Martinez, who had grown up as childhood buddies and who eventually worked for the same company. One night Espinoza and Martinez got drunk together, and each shot the other dead. The men's wives claimed the deaths were accidental and sued for double indemnity under the terms of an insurance policy provided by their husbands' employer. Corboy, as the women's lawyer, argued in court that both men were so drunk they didn't know what they were doing. He argued that, indeed, the two good friends couldn't possibly have intended to kill each other, so the deaths were an accident. Corboy was able to convince the jurors, but an appellate judge overruled their decision. The judge said the shootings were not accidental, and because murder is a felony, and the insurance policy did not cover death caused by participation in the commission of a felony, the women were not entitled to double payment.

Thirty-six years later in 1986, despite a string of jury trials and victories too long to remember, the fair-haired and fair-skinned Corboy still hung no diplomas, awards, or certificates on his office walls. As a newcomer to the profession, he hadn't wanted clients to know exactly how inexperienced he was. "When trying cases, no one likes to brag about how young they are," he explains. Corboy's rationale is a different one today. "If they don't believe I'm a lawyer," they shouldn't be in my office, he says. Only once in nearly two decades has Corboy failed to emerge victorious from a jury trial, and his loss in that case was subsequently overturned on appeal.

Something else about the sixty-four-year-old Corboy has changed little—his belief in the mentor system. But today, Corboy himself has become the mentor, having nurtured enough young lawyers in the skills of trial advocacy that his office earned a reputation as the "Philip H. Corboy School of Law." In 1983 about forty-five clerks and associates from Corboy's office gathered to honor their tough taskmaster with a "roast" and a football inscribed with "Corboy U." Corboy has done "an unparalleled job of educating and training trial lawyers," says Al Hofeld, fifty, who left Corboy's firm in 1968 to set up his own Chicago practice. "A completely disproportionate number of plaintiff's lawyers in Chicago today have come from his office." Corboy, who follows the Socratic method of teaching by asking young lawyers questions to help them determine their own trial strategies and tactics, was the sole leader in his firm until 1982 when he formed a partnership with Thomas A. Demetrio, thirty-nine, a decision Corboy celebrates to this day. Currently a total of twelve lawyers work at Corboy & Demetrio, including Corboy's son Philip, Jr. (Flip). Corboy, who always works on a contingent-fee basis, maintains his preference for a small law firm, one which, despite its size, files about 250 lawsuits a year and regularly turns down that many again. Of cases the firm handles, Corboy takes between five and seven percent as favors for friends—many of them Chicago notables—but he often assigns those to other attorneys in the office.

Perhaps most enduring over Corboy's years in practice are the hallmarks of his personality. Corboy has a piercing blue-eyed gaze, and a rich, emphatic manner of speaking. He often repeats the same idea three or four different ways to make a point, and he has an unabashed eagerness to share his trial experiences. Of the forty speaking invitations he receives annually, Corboy accepts fifteen to twenty. He has on file one of the most complete sets of newspaper and magazine clippings ever compiled by an attorney anywhere in the country, clippings readily provided by Corboy's two personal secretaries to anyone who should inquire about the famous plaintiff's lawyer's cases.

Corboy's commitment to the practice of personal injury law has only intensified. When trial lawyers are very young, he explains, they are most "concerned about developing their skills, a repertoire of resources and methods. Most young lawyers' waking hours are spent on their own development as a lawyer, and the medium they use is the courtroom with their cases." As Corboy matured, he says, he began to focus more on his clients. "I understand and accept that all the people I represent have gone through something so terrible that they are expected to be emotionally lacking, drained," he explains. Personal injury lawyers "have to accept the fact that their clients are not normal. If they can't handle the horror and the devastation, they should get out." Once personal injury lawyers can understand and accept their clients, says Corboy, they can recognize that these people are entitled to the finest legal representation. "Why?" he asks rhetorically. "Because the odds against them are so high."

Corboy sat back in his chair, looking out his glass-walled office across the Richard J. Daley Plaza, home of the Cook County courthouse and Chicago's City Hall, and considered his rise to the pinnacle of his profession. Pushed to name his most successful trial, he turned to the story of Danny Schaffner.

In September 1976, fifteen-year-old Danny was riding bikes with a couple of pals down the streets of his community, Highland Park, Illinois. The three boys had been to an evening movie and were heading for the local Baskin-Robbins ice cream shop. But when they pedaled over a bumpy railroad crossing—one they had passed over often before—Danny's front wheel came off, causing him to fly from his bike and hit the pavement. Brain-damaged from the fall, in a coma for two and a half months, Danny became physically and mentally crippled, never able to enjoy a normal life again. With Corboy's help, Danny's parents sued the Schwinn Bicycle Company and the railroad, the Chicago and North Western Transportation Company, which maintained the crossing. Two months before the trial began, the defendants offered to settle the case for $1.3 million; before the trial was over they had upped that to $3 million. Corboy and the Schaffners rejected both offers, and by the end of the ordeal, in October 1985, the jury had found the railroad fully liable for Danny's injury. The jury awarded Danny Schaffner more than $8 million.

One reason Corboy got more than $8 million for Danny was because he developed for the trial—as in every case—a plan. "You have to have an overall plan," says Corboy. "You cannot try a lawsuit without a strategy." In contrast to case strategy, Corboy refers to day-to-day trial activity as his tactics, which "are provided on an ad hoc basis as the trial progresses."

Explaining the difference between strategy and tactics, Corboy cited the fictional case of "a young man who may not be desirable cosmetically, intellectually, ethnically, and educationally to everybody in the world. My strategy," says Corboy, "will be to get the jury to like this man despite their antipathy toward him. My tactic will be to decide whether he should or should not wear a black jacket in court."

Corboy explains: "If this kid is a black-jacket kid, he's going to wear a black jacket. He's not going to wear a dark blue suit." Trying to fool the jury will backfire, says Corboy, who won't have a widow dress in black six years after her husband died in an accident, or wear the same dress every day to trial to impress her hardship on the jury. "You cannot fool twelve people on a long-term basis," says Corboy, noting that "even poor people have more than one dress." Corboy recalls that some jurors may have thought he was trying to fool them in a 1954 case when, in his opening statement, he said that his client had difficulty picking things up because he had left-sided brain damage. Corboy used a quarter to illustrate himself how his client, who was sitting in the courtroom behind the lawyer, could not pick up coins with his right hand. Unfortunately, Corboy later dropped a pencil on the floor, and without Corboy's knowing it, the client picked it up. "We didn't say he couldn't pick up a pencil," emphasized Corboy. "It was a pencil, not a coin. I talked to the jurors afterward [they gave Corboy's client a $50,000 verdict, a lot of money in those days] and I asked them what they thought. They said, 'If that had been a coin [you dropped], you'd have been in trouble.' "

Corboy's strategy to maximize the damages awarded in the Schaffner case required, first, that he convey "the pathos of this boy," and second, that he eliminate any other complicating issues such as the relative fault of the parties. Corboy did not want the jury placing any blame for the accident on Danny himself.

It wasn't hard for Corboy to portray pathos. Testimony at the trial showed that Danny's brain damage caused him to be partially paralyzed, to fall on his face when he walked, to drool, to talk with a speech impediment, and to see very poorly. James Fiocchi, one of the two friends riding bikes with Danny the day of his accident, poignantly described for the jury during the trial nine years later what his friend, at that time twenty-four years old, was like both before and after his fall:

Fiocchi: . . . [Today] people that haven't seen him before, you may think, well, I would think, I would think he was retarded in the true sense in that his facial features, mainly the left side of his face and body, he doesn't have very good muscle control at this time, and he'll have a tendency to—well, the left side of his face doesn't do anything. It just sits there.

He'll drool from the left side, and when he walks, he won't walk normally, he'll hobble, he'll drag his left side. His arm is up a little like this (indicating), and it's a very sad and unpleasant thing to have to look at really. So it's hard for me to go out with him on a regular basis and have a friendship with him like I used to.

Corboy: How does he get along with other men?

Fiocchi: He doesn't have any other friends really. . . .

Corboy: How does he get along with women?

Fiocchi: I don't think he has ever dated, if that's what you mean.

Corboy: With reference to his personality, would you give the jury your opinion as to somebody who knows him, if, in your opinion, he is or is not a lonely man?

Fiocchi: In my opinion in the truest sense of the word, he is a very lonely person.

Danny's brain damage also resulted in a condition that causes him to tell nonstop jokes. "Now, a joke is good and it's funny once in a while, and it has its place," explained Fiocchi on the stand, "but in Danny's case, he does this continuously and it doesn't stop, and he thinks it's funny, and some of the jokes he tells are truly funny, but if I sat you down and told you sixty or seventy jokes in a row, they wouldn't be funny anymore, and it isn't."

If the Illinois jury had found Danny at fault for his accident in any way, the jury's monetary award would have been reduced by the same percentage as Danny's negligence. That is, if the jury had decided that the accident was twenty percent Danny's fault, his compensatory damages award would have been reduced by one-fifth. But Corboy cast aside the issue of comparative, or contributory, fault—the idea that Danny could have been partly to blame—through some clever and skillful maneuvering. Before the trial began, Corboy filed an amended complaint seeking punitive, in addition to compensatory, damages from both defendants. Punitive damages serve to punish the wrongdoer, while compensatory damages simply compensate the wronged party for financial loss and for pain and suffering. Corboy said in his amended complaint that Danny deserved punitive damages because the Chicago and North Western knew the track was in poor condition and therefore, should have repaired it as required by Illinois law. He also said that Schwinn knew Danny's ten-speed bicycle model was dangerous because the company had received more than eighty complaints about that particular model's quick-release mechanism, a device that enables the bike's user to remove the front wheel easily. The complaints to Schwinn said the mechanism caused the front wheel to separate from the bike when in motion.

Despite his request for punitive damages, Corboy says he does not like to seek them because they often interfere with jurys' awarding appropriate compensatory damages; because punitive damages are taxable (while compensatory damages are not); and because courts often later set aside punitive damages awards. Seeking punitive damages can make a client look greedy, adds Corboy, which affects the plaintiff's credibility. "If you talk about compensation, and seek punishment, you're wearing two hats," he explains. Corboy says he generally refuses cases motivated by vindication or revenge.

So, after about three weeks into the month-long Schaffner trial, after Corboy felt confident he had hammered home for the jury the Chicago and North Western's negligence in maintaining its crossing, and the unreasonably dangerous condition of Danny's Schwinn bike, and when the pathos of Danny's accident was coming across loud and clear, Corboy asked the two defendants' lawyers if they would make a trade. As Danny's lawyer, he would withdraw his request for punitive damages if the railroad and the bike company would give up their defense of comparative negligence or fault, that is, if they would not try to argue that Danny was at least partially to blame. (Definitions of contributory negligence, or comparative fault, their use in personal injury suits, and their effect on jury awards vary widely from state to state.)

The plan worked. "Your Honor," said Corboy in Judge Anthony J. Bosco's chambers, "I have discussed this matter of amending my client's complaint at this time with counsel for North Western Railroad and counsel for the Schwinn Bicycle Company. . . . I have informed counsel as to both defendants that it is my intention at this time to file an amended complaint restricted to three counts [minus an allegation of willful violation] upon the following condition . . . that Mr. Brant will not raise the defense of contributory negligence or comparative negligence. . . . Have I stated it properly?"

George Brant [counsel for the railroad]: I believe you have, sir.

Corboy: And is that our agreement?

Brant: This is an agreement that we have reached in order to help both counsel and the Court narrow issues [to make it easier for the jury to reach a verdict].

Corboy: And there will be no such instruction of any kind tendered by you with reference to comparative negligence or contributory negligence?

Brant: Quite correct.

Schwinn counsel Michael Murtaugh also agreed with Corboy that the jury would be given only three verdict forms from which to choose: one would find in favor of Danny and against both defendants; one would find against the railroad only; and a third would find against the bike company only. None of the forms provided the jury with the possibility of holding Danny himself responsible for his accident because the two defendants had agreed that they would not argue comparative or contributory negligence in their defense. That is, they promised in exchange for Corboy's not requesting punitive damages that they would not say that the accident occurred in any way because Danny was careless.

Corboy: Am I correct that you're agreeing those are the only three verdict forms which go to the jury?

Brant: That is a conversation I recall. That is a conversation I recall, and I do so agree.

Corboy: You agree that those are the three verdict forms that should go to the jury?

Brant: Yes, sir.

Corboy: Mr. Murtaugh, I ask you the same question. Are you agreeing that those are the three verdict forms that should go to the jury?

Murtaugh: Yes.

Judge Bosco: I got them.

Corboy speculates that the railroad and Schwinn agreed to the trade because "they didn't have a legitimate basis for comparative fault" and because a request for punitive damages allows the plaintiff to bring into court the defendants' net worth, something neither party wanted divulged. "We maneuvered the case so they were in a box," says Corboy, his excitement and determination still evident. "They could have argued that Daniel Schaffner knew the crossing was rough," and they could have asked "why didn't he go on the sidewalk and get off" his bike. Instead, they were left pointing their fingers at each other, blaming the other for Danny's condition, instead of trying to blame Danny himself.

Murtaugh, Schwinn's lawyer, disagrees with Corboy as to the rationale behind the decision to drop the punitive damages charge. Murtaugh says Corboy dismissed the punitive damages count "so that he could prevent Schwinn from producing evidence of the state of the art. It was our intention to introduce testimony that there was no manufacturer of bicycles which incorporated a positive retention clip [a safety device] on their quick release mechanisms prior to Schwinn introducing its own positive retention device in 1977," says Schwinn's attorney today.

In one of Corboy's earlier cases, in 1982, he developed a very different strategy from that of the Schaffner trial: This strategy took contributory negligence into full account. In that case, Corboy represented a high-school Spanish teacher who had gone swimming at a Lake Michigan beach that had "no swimming" and "no diving" notices widely posted—in both English and Spanish. The man was hit by a motorboat and lost both of his legs. Corboy admitted to the jury in his suit against the Chicago Park District, which managed the beach, that his client was wrong to swim in the area, but he pointed out that the Park District had been ignoring swimmers there for years. He also showed photographs to prove how inviting the area was, and he called in a recreation expert who said the posted "no swimming" signs were inadequate to keep people away. "I had to convince the jury that they would do the same thing," says Corboy.

"My client was careless. My client was negligent," Corboy says he told that jury. "But then I asked them to forgive him, to have charity, to have tolerance of the peccadillos of human nature.

"If the law will forgive, will you not forgive?" Corboy asked the jurors. They did—and found the teacher only fifty percent negligent. That meant that out of the $4.4 million the jury awarded the teacher, he received half, $2.2 million.

Before the Schaffner trial began, Corboy readied himself by following his standard, intense, two- to four-week preparation ritual. Corboy secludes himself in his elegantly decorated Water Tower forty-sixth-floor condominium (among his neighbors is talk show host Oprah Winfrey), where he turns off his phone. He orders all meals delivered from a restaurant in the Hotel Ritz Carlton, which occupies the first thirty-two floors of the building. Associates, paralegals, secretaries, and messengers continuously fetch and deliver materials for him. Corboy and his staff prepared for the Schaffner case for six years, and his pretrial seclusion had the intensity of a final examination cram session.

In his rite of preparation Corboy first reads the thick correspondence section of a case file—"that which flows between the client and us, and people who may or may not be witnesses, or people who have some contact with the file which is not covered by any other section of the case materials," Corboy explains. The correspondence refreshes the lawyer's memory about all the persons involved in the case, and all the events surrounding it. The plethora of information it holds gives him "the opportunity to sit down and start deciding the overall strategy and the overall complexion that I would like to see presented—the color the case is going to be.

"I can tell by looking at the correspondence section if there's been any friction during the preparation," says Corboy. "Let's assume there's been a urinating contest between one of the lawyers in our office and one of the lawyers on the other side, and it's been recorded. I get the flavor of what's going on. Or let's assume the client has a complaint. It's going to show up in that file."

The file's correspondence section, which covers years of material, also includes all communication between the client and the attorney who referred the case to Corboy. Corboy will share up to one-third of his standard fee—which is one-third of the gross amount of money recovered—with the referring lawyer, but only if the client agrees and if the referring attorney will continue to share responsibility for the case. Some referring lawyers, says Corboy, don't want this responsibility. In the Schaffner case Corboy agreed to give the referring attorney twenty-five percent of the jury award.

When reviewing the correspondence section of the Schaffner file, Corboy recalled "that the client [Danny's mother and father]—rightly so—was concerned about the time it was taking [the] case to reach trial." Corboy also learned what communication the referring lawyer had had with insurance companies involved in the case. While the referring lawyer had originally filed the Schaffners' lawsuit in 1977 in Lake County where Highland Park is located, twenty-five miles north of Chicago, Corboy had dismissed that case and refiled the suit in 1979 in Cook County, where Chicago is located. "Verdicts are reasonable here," he explains, and Chicago "is where I practice law." Corboy dropped Highland Park as a defendant when he refiled the suit; the accident wasn't the city's fault, he said.

The correspondence section of the Schaffner file reminded Corboy that Danny's mother had cancer and had undergone two operations for it. That had nothing to do with the lawsuit, he explains, but it renewed his concern that this information never be brought up during the trial. Later, during the pretrial discussion, Corboy warned the opposing lawyers that if they claimed Mrs. Schaffner could be Danny's caretaker (thus reducing the amount of a potential award), Corboy would introduce testimony that she had a cancerous condition. Actually, Corboy wanted to keep Mrs. Schaffner's cancer from the jury not only because it was irrelevant to Danny's liability case, but also, he says, because he did not want to add to Mrs. Schaffner's anguish about Danny's future. And on top of that, he did not want the jury thinking he was looking for additional sympathy, a development that could have backfired on him. "It's very easy to make a jury cry," says Corboy, and that is something a lawyer should not do—at least not excessively. Why? Because they go into the jury room, they're embarrassed and resentful of the lawyer for making them cry, and they want to make up for it in some way. "You have to be very careful that you don't overplay sympathy. You want empathy, not sympathy," stresses Corboy.

The Schaffner file's correspondence section summarized for

Corboy what was happening to Danny all those years since his accident—including information such as how many schools he'd attended and how many doctors he'd gone to. It "tells me about a lot of pathos available," he explains, and "reinforced my impression that this family did everything they could to find medical attention for this boy. They went all over the country," a fact Corboy stressed during the trial. "These people are interested only in the welfare of their son," he emphasizes. Danny's medical expenses by the time of the trial totaled over $235,000.

The correspondence records also reminded Corboy about the history of Danny's bike from the time of his accident—where it had gone and whom he had asked to examine it. (The broken bike, as the first of Corboy's sixty exhibits, sat in the courtroom during the entire trial. Today, the bike still resides in Corboy's offices.) Corboy reviews documentation reminding him that he had sent associate Bruce Pfaff, who assisted Corboy with the Schaffner case, to the Schwinn company specifically to examine their complaint records.

And the correspondence file reminded Corboy of all the other people in his office who had worked on Danny's case, including a lawyer with nursing credentials, and what outsiders he had hired to help out, such as a photographer. (Corboy opted to use still photographs for the trial, and not the typical personal-injury-case movie, which would have shown a day in Danny's life after the accident.) In all, Corboy's office spent more than $72,500 preparing for Danny's lawsuit.

After reviewing all the correspondence relating to the Schaffner case and totally immersing himself in the details that documentation revealed, Corboy read the file's computer printout, which listed chronologically Danny's medical expenses, all the pleadings filed in the case, witnesses deposed during discovery, and expert opinions regarding Danny's future. The expert opinions discussed Danny's prospects for employment and living away from his family; his need for therapy and medical care for the rest of his life just to keep him from backsliding; and his life expectancy. Corboy's law firm devised its own software written in computer language RPGII to produce these printouts, helping the firm's lawyers manage their case work and document their expenses. It's a way, says Corboy, to chronicle and refer back to the many developments in all the cases the office handles, a valuable tool most lawyers don't have. Corboy & Demetrio relies on an IBM Systems 36 computer, with IBM or ITT personal computers serving as terminals on each lawyer's desk. However, to prevent errors, only the secretaries, bookkeepers, and computer docketing staff type information into the firm's computerized case files.

On the Schaffner file printout Corboy saw that since Danny's accident, he had been billed for medical care by more than twenty different doctors, therapists, psychologists, and orthopedic surgeons. He saw that Dr. Bruce M. Gans, a Boston psychiatrist, or rehabilitation expert, who had treated Danny, said that his inappropriate, and annoying, use of humor resulted from his organic brain injury. Gans noted that Danny understands this humor is inappropriate, but can't stop and finds the predicament frustrating. Corboy read that Dan wants to live alone, but would require daily supportive guidance, that he has a normal life expectancy, and that he will need speech and physical therapy indefinitely.

Corboy also reviewed his opposition's case against compensating Danny. He read that Arthur Frederick DeLong, a seventy-year-old, long-standing bicycle expert, testified in his deposition that the only reason Danny's wheel broke off was the roughness of the railroad crossing. Corboy also read that Glen Krebs, a Chicago and North Western engineer, recalled no problems with the crossing where Danny fell, a crossing that Krebs himself had inspected twelve to twenty times before the accident. Corboy stores away for jury selection information about the opposing expert witnesses because, he believes, some types of jurors may be more favorably inclined toward some types of experts. If, for example, an opposing expert speaks with an accent, Corboy may not want a juror who also speaks with an accent because that person may identify with the expert. Of if an opposing expert wears a toupee, Corboy probably won't want a juror who wears a toupee.

Finally, Corboy reread every pleading filed in the Schaffner case. "In preparation for trial, during that two- to four-week period before the trial starts, I fill the bathtub up," explains Corboy, describing his absorption of all the information relevant to his case. "I get surfeited with everything that's important about this case from the personalities of the parties to the intricate medical aspects of the case. I diminish as much as I can outside activities and outside interferences [he tries to avoid all social invitations] so that the only thing in my mind is this lawsuit." For Danny's trial Corboy became thoroughly versed on bicycles (especially Schwinn bicycles), on railroad crossing cases, and on closed-head injuries. Shortly after a case is over, however, Corboy empties "that bathtub," thus enabling him to move on to his next trial. "What distinguishes him is his methodology," says Al Hofeld of his former mentor. Corboy is of the "no stone left unturned" school. "There's a tremendous amount of digging involved in these cases," explains Hofeld. "Nobody gives you anything, particularly a major corporation or a health-care provider." Corboy often has to begin by requesting subpoenas for records and files, and then interviewing people whose names appear in those files. "Corboy's methodology is that you just dig and dig and dig," says Hofeld. "It's a total thing—where he's going to know more about that case than anyone in the world."

To help him meet such strenuous mental demands time after time, Corboy, at age fifty-three, quit drinking. "I just found out that the stamina I had was being lessened, not that it ever interfered, but I didn't want it to interfere," he explains. "It was a matter of ego. I did not want to end up the way I had seen other lawyers end up who drink too much.

"Drinking was a great way to relax," he continues, "but I don't relax that way anymore." Corboy does try to exercise two or three times a week, swimming or specialized aerobics through a cardio-fitness club, but no longer tennis or jogging because of a bad knee. But when he's getting ready for trial, "even that suffers," says Corboy.

In fact, he hardly reads a newspaper when preparing for trial. "If I have any forte, it's discipline," says the attorney, whose efficiency and impatience for excellence are viewed by some as mere arrogance. Corboy—who says he constantly looks for new ways to hone his skills—maintains he has failed if he's not thoroughly exhausted after a trial. He refuses cases that don't merit this kind of preparation. "I don't believe being a great lawyer, and certainly not a good lawyer, requires being a genius," he says of the need for hard work.

"You have to be street smart, and you have to understand people and human nature and you have to have gone through a lot yourself. You have to have been the beneficiary of some type of hardship, whatever it might be. That doesn't mean you have to be poor. It means you have to have gone through some things in your life that give you the ability to understand the needs of other people, the ability to empathize with them—and to persuade other people of that. You've got to know what it is to suffer."

The son of a Chicago policeman, Corboy maintains that he did not himself come from a deprived childhood. But his life has not been without tragedy. In 1976 the youngest of his five children, Bobby, then twelve years old, was killed by a car that hit him as he stood on a Chicago sidewalk. And in 1980, Corboy separated from his wife of thirty years, Dorie. They were divorced in 1985.

After studying the Schaffner file, and after asking staff to find answers to remaining questions, Corboy was ready in September 1985 to face the first challenge of trial—selecting the jury. In Illinois courts each lawyer has five challenges against potential jurors for a trial. But for every additional party in a case, each side has an additional three challenges. Thus in the Schaffner trial,

Corboy had eight challenges, and codefendants Schwinn and the Chicago and North Western each had four. "You never use your last challenge" because you don't know what kinds of jurors lie ahead, says Corboy, "unless," he jokes, "it's the president of Allstate Insurance Company.

"I do not know how to select juries," insists Corboy, despite his reputed skill for doing just this. It's impossible to select a jury fully to his liking, he explains, because the opposing counsel also has a part in the process and may eliminate jurors Corboy wants. "All I do know how to do is deselect jurors," Corboy says. "I can remove from the jury corpus supplied me those that I think will [find it] most difficult to agree with our version of what the truth is, and our version of what the results will be." To assess jurors, Corboy—who calls the process jury "acquisition" rather than "selection"—relies on several techniques: his own inquiries based on jury lists provided before trial, visual analysis of jurors (including body movements), knowledge of general background characteristics that provide certain proclivities, and the jurors' answers to questions. Open-ended questions are best, says Corboy, because they allow potential jurors to reveal more information about themselves. Because he knows his case file thoroughly, Corboy can predict by different jurors' characteristics how they will react to the case as it unfolds.

In the Illinois court system lawyers can photostat the questionnaires completed by each potential juror before the jury selection process begins. Included on the questionnaires are basic facts, such as name, address, occupation, and home and office phone numbers. For his case in Wisconsin, Corboy had the jury list two months ahead of time, but in the Schaffner case, in the much larger Chicago court system, he received the list for the first time the morning of the day the trial was to begin. Corboy immediately took copies of the questionnaires back to his office, where he met with a very special person on whom he had been relying for seven years—a cabdriver.

"He's a guy who's been driving a cab for thirty-five years, he knows the community, he knows when you look at that name" the ethnicity of the person, says Corboy. "He knows neighborhoods" and can talk about the kinds of people who live in them. He can look at the juror's employer and offer even more information. "Let's assume one of these people works for the John Doe Pharmacy," suggests Corboy. "John Doe Pharmacy may be a hangout for kids who are buying drugs. He knows it and he tells me."

Corboy met his friend the cabbie one day while riding in the man's taxi. Because Corboy had spent his entire life in Chicago, the two men started talking about Chicago neighborhoods. Now "I bring him in on every case," says Corboy, who pays the cabbie one hundred dollars a day just to tell him about jurors based on their questionnaires. "It gives me one more layer of information; it's one more resource. By the time I come back and the first jurors are about to go into the box, I know something [more] about them."

An attorney must be present for the jury acquisition, says Corboy, "to watch how those jurors walk in, to see if they have argyle socks and a plaid shirt on, to see if they limp, use a cane, wear glasses, what reading material they have in their hands, whether they are spending their time idly, whether they're dressed up or dressed down."

Although Corboy won't make definitive generalizations based on juror ethnicity or other characteristics, he does depend on "certain general principles" to eliminate a type of person who might vote against his client. "We know, for instance, that Irishmen are supposed to be very sympathetic and very aware of the downtrodden, and very concerned with injustice," explains Corboy, an Irishman himself. But "what if your plaintiff's name is Albritton III? Would I want an Irishman on that jury?" (Watch out for the effects of intermarriage, warns Corboy. Just because a woman's name is Mrs. Sweeney doesn't mean she's Irish.)

"We also know that blacks—like whites—can have certain preconceived ideas about things," Corboy continues, and "that certain blacks live in neighborhoods where there are nothing but poor people. If my client is a well-to-do black person, do I want that type of black on the jury" who will resent the wealthy black client? However, adds Corboy, the jury may have six blacks on it and you have to be very careful if you knock one off because the others might take offense. Or that same black juror may have the potential to become wealthy and would thus be inclined to favor your plaintiff.

One of Corboy's favorite juror questions is "What organizations do you belong to?" One man explained how active he was in the National Rifle Association. Another named the National Association of Manufacturers. Those answers, says Corboy, "told me a lot right there." Jurors' leisure time activities are important in a personal injury case, adds Corboy. "The sports enthusiast can appreciate damage to a body" more than someone who reads a lot. Questions about occupations provide critical information. Airline pilots are terrible jurors, says Corboy, because they are "all archconservatives who go by the book and are very company oriented. They're well paid and think no one should get more than they do at seventy-five thousand dollars a year." Nor does Corboy like government employees or professional military people on a jury because they, too, are "all too conservative so they don't adequately compensate the plaintiff." The lady who works in the complaint department of Marshall Fields is a bad juror, Corboy continues, because every day she sees people complaining. But then, he adds in the next breath, all these generic rules can fold. "What if I represent a lady who works in a complaint department?"

Corboy says that he isn't afraid to try cases in jurisdictions where only the judge, and not the lawyers, asks the jurors questions. "If you give the judge the right questions, you can learn a lot about the jurors," he explains. Judges can also ask questions that lawyers can't or don't want to ask—such as "How many times have you been married?" In the Schaffner trial Corboy gave Judge Anthony J. Bosco a list of eighteen questions inquiring, for example, about juror work history, accident history, leisure activities, friends and relatives who are lawyers or doctors, and ties with the Chicago and North Western Transportation Company or Schwinn Bicycle Company.

Whether the jurors are answering the lawyers' or judge's questions, Corboy—whose daughter, Joan M. Corboy, is a Cook County circuit court judge—never takes notes. "I'm not a scrivener. I'm not a customs official. I'm not a clerk in the American Airlines lost-luggage department," he says with typical Corboy hyperbole, explaining that a lawyer who is writing is not watching. "I watch the jurors, I eyeball them," Corboy insists. "You'd be surprised at the lawyers who are scriveners. The court reporter is taking down the information; I don't know why they're writing, too."

In looking at all the variables, summarizes Corboy, "what you're really doing is playing chess. Ideally you get a jury which will understand your position, and accept it." After almost two days of jury selection for the Schaffner trial, Corboy had "deselected," among others, a man who in college had majored in economics because, as an expert, he could unduly sway the jury in calculating damages, possibly to Danny's detriment; a man who owned three ten-speed bikes because he could pose as a bike expert during the jury's deliberations and confuse the testimony of the lawyers' experts; an older woman with a disabled son because she was caring for this son unassisted and probably would not be able to empathize with the Schaffners' needs; and a younger man with a slightly retarded brother because he might have experienced some sibling rivalry or ill will at some point in his childhood, and by extension, might feel negatively toward Danny. The final jury consisted of six women and six men, ranging from a twenty-one-year-old secretary to a thirty-five-year-old systems analyst to a sixty-two-year-old assembly line worker.

Unlike some lawyers, Corboy is not a stickler about appearing alone in court, although he did have this steadfast rule when he was younger. "Things have changed," says Corboy now.

"Number one, I've matured, I've become more secure, and I'm not afraid to admit that I need assistance. Secondly, the kind of cases I'm trying are much more complex than they were twenty-five years ago. There's much more paper involved." Thirdly, says Corboy, a competent lawyer must keep the proof moving, something impossible to do alone in cases with many witnesses and many pieces of evidence. "If it takes two lawyers to appear competent," he demands, "is there something wrong?"

Bruce Pfaff, who assisted Corboy in the Schaffner trial, explains that Corboy keeps the proof moving by making sure his witnesses are in court on time, that his exhibits are labeled and ready ahead of time, that he doesn't call witnesses who offer the same information as previous witnesses and bore the jury, and that he avoids private side-bar conferences with the judge that interrupt the trial. "Tempo is very important with Phil," says Pfaff.

Corboy, a past president of the Chicago Bar Association and of the Illinois Trial Lawyers Association, always takes into court a worn, black, three-ring notebook, a gift from his former mentor, Jim Dooley. That notebook, compiled by Dooley and updated regularly by Corboy, is a homemade encyclopedia of trial law. "It contains everything I know about trial law," says Corboy, who has court cases categorized in the notebook by subject (such as "ice cases").

Corboy never finishes preparing his opening statement until after the jury is picked. "I have devised," says Corboy, "what I think is a better way of giving opening statements than most lawyers." He settled on his technique during a trial in Louisville, Kentucky, when he found out that the judge restricted final argument to five minutes for every day of trial. With the time stricture, Corboy decided he had better get his case over to the jury in his opening statement. So, rather than following the traditional route of telling the jury that an opening statement is not evidence, and that he, as the plaintiff's attorney, would paint only a picture of what the evidence would be, Corboy took a more definitive tack. He decided to make an opening statement that was devoid of traditional rhetoric—one that got right to the point. "I've learned," explains Corboy, "that if you tell the jury 'this is not evidence,' they're likely to believe it. The judge is going to tell them, the other lawyer is going to tell them, so why should I tell them?" Instead, Corboy "started giving opening statements in a story fashion. The trial of a lawsuit is the telling of a story," he says.

After introducing to the Chicago jury Danny's parents, Perry and Jean Schaffner, Corboy began his hour-and-a-half-long opening statement:

"This is the story of a typical family, had its ups and had its downs, had its heartbreaks, it's had its good times, and had its bad times. But it was a normal everyday American, mid-American type of family.

"Perry and Jean Schaffner met sometime before 1953 where they both lived in Chicago, both attended high school in Chicago. They fell in love, got married in 1953, and they started to raise a family. They moved in 1960 out to a far north suburb, as a matter of fact, even into a different county called Lake County where they began to raise their children in Highland Park, Illinois.

"There were three children born of that marriage. Terry was born in 1956. James was born in 1958. And Daniel, the boy who has been injured, was born in 1961, approximately a year after they moved out into the suburb.

"Danny was a—I was going to say he was a typical baby, but I don't think you can call him quite typical because he was eight pounds two ounces when he was born, so he was a typical big baby, but he was a typical big healthy baby."

And so Corboy continued, chronicling Danny's ordinary childhood diseases, his broken arm, a few broken fingers, and the time Danny was hit in the head playing basketball about a year before the bike accident. The Schaffners, to be on the safe side, had Danny undergo a complete neurological examination at that time, "and that examination showed he was completely normal," related Corboy.

Corboy made a point of not glorifying Danny, but of telling the truth about the kind of child he was—slightly overweight, an average student, someone with buddies, but someone who hadn't started to date yet. "Don't hide the warts," says Corboy when instructing on opening statements. "If there is anything in the background the jury would like to know, you have to tell them—particularly if it's contrary to your case."

Standing before his own lecturn, which he carries to every trial, Corboy described in minute detail what Danny and his friends were doing on Saturday, September 4, 1976, "a typical Saturday in the fall, sort of like it is out today, summer was waning, summer was disappearing, summer was going away." Danny and his friends were eating pizza at the Schaffners' house, Corboy explained to the jury, and then they decided to go to a movie. In his description Corboy followed the boys on their bikes across town, down every street and through every intersection, indicating north, south, east, and west in the courtroom so the jurors almost felt as if they were watching a reenactment of the event. "As Danny got on to these tracks," related Corboy after describing the crossing's location, "he started bouncing and his bike went out of control. All of a sudden he was bouncing and he eventually got to the other side of the tracks, and he was completely off the tracks when his bike disassembled and his bike came apart and he fell to the ground. When he fell to the ground it was immediately apparent to his pals who came up to him that he was hurt, and his pals asked him what had happened, and he does not respond as to what occurred on the crossing because he does not know. But he did say, 'My shoulder hurts,' and he said it loudly, and he was crying, and then he said 'My shoulder hurts,' and it was lighter, and then he didn't talk anymore. He went into a coma."

When Danny got to the hospital, the surgeon thought he was dead. Corboy, never looking at his notes, went on to describe the brain injury, Danny's operations, and his tortuous path of treatment since the accident. By then, he later explains, hopefully the jury is saying *"What caused this?"* By then, he says, the jury should be wide open to the idea of finding liability.

Continuing his opening statement, Corboy talked about the legal responsibility of the railroad to maintain its crossings "in such a manner that the surface of the roadway shall be substantially flush with the top of the rails." He explained that in February 1971, long before Danny's accident, the Chicago and North Western approved the repair of the crossing where Danny fell. But adds Corboy, that repair work was never done. And Corboy explained that Danny's bicycle's quick-release mechanism was defective: On that particular bicycle model the mechanism opened too easily, causing the wheel to come off on any rough terrain. While recalling his remarks to the jury, Corboy stresses that "liability is determined in your opening statement."

For his conclusion, Corboy returned to his theme of the destruction of the Schaffner family. He told how the Schaffners had arranged private tutoring for Danny so he could graduate from high school and how they had enrolled him in a small college hoping that he could cope. But Danny flunked out; and then he flunked out of two local college-level courses. "Despite everything [the Schaffners] have done, Danny is not a normal human being," concluded Corboy. "Danny has intelligence. He has an IQ of one ten, one twenty, one twenty-five. Danny is not retarded." If he were, Corboy finished dramatically, he'd be better off. Then Danny would not know the tragedy his life has become.

George H. Brant, the Chicago and North Western staff attorney in the Schaffner case, followed Corboy. He divided his opening statement between a defense that the crossing was reasonably safe and an explanation of how Danny's ten-speed bike would have worked if he had known how to operate it properly. Representing Schwinn, Michael Murtaugh of Baker & McKenzie in Chicago said that any previous problems with the Schwinn bike model Danny rode were due to the young ages of the users, that is, riders who did not know how to secure the quick-release mechanism properly. In his opening statement Murtaugh pointed a finger at the railroad, saying that the only reason the wheel came off of Danny's bike was that the crossing was rough.

In both of their opening statements, Brant and Murtaugh referred to Corboy's eloquence:

"I've stressed in my opening—and in my questions to you as jurors during the selection process," said Murtaugh, "that I was concerned that you would be able to keep an open mind.

"And I think even in this first day of trial, you have a good idea of why I was concerned.

"Because if the case were to be decided by opening statements, at this point the case would be over . . ."

Corboy says he knew he was going to win the case when he made his opening statement. "I never had any doubt I was going to win this case," he states emphatically. "It was just a question of how we were going to structure it for the maximum value.

"The trial lawyer's job is to structure the proof and deploy the evidence in such a way that the jury has an opportunity to find maximum damages on behalf of your client," Corboy concludes. One way Corboy structured his case was to get out of the evidence any opportunity to diminish the damages, as comparative negligence or comparative fault would have done. With all of his witnesses, and even with some of the defendants' witnesses, Corboy showed that there was nothing unusual about Danny's activity the night of the accident—that he did nothing wrong—and that the accident could have been prevented by the railroad and the bike company. During the trial, Danny's two accompanying friends, James Fiocchi and Brian Richard Coxon, testified that Danny had ridden his bike over the same crossing hundreds of times before. On that September night in 1976 he pedaled over the crossing right along with the two other boys.

Corboy found many of his witnesses' names on documents he had subpoenaed from the defendants. For example, in the case of the railroad, Corboy requested all the company's documents addressing the construction, maintenance, and repair of the Highland Park railroad crossing where Danny fell. Corboy's first witness, and his key witness against the railroad, was James L. Simons, a former Chicago and North Western employee. Simons testified after being subpoenaed that in 1971 he had signed a request for the crossing to be repaired. But he added, in 1973 he signed another form canceling the work order. The reason for cancellation typed onto that second form: "Work not carried out." If the railroad had argued that Danny was negligent in riding over the track because it was rough, argued Corboy, wouldn't the railroad have been negligent for not repairing it? The repair initially proposed in 1971 was ultimately undertaken after Danny's accident, in 1977, when the railroad rebuilt the entire crossing. Corboy's own railroad crossing expert, Illinois Department of Transportation employee Joseph J. Kostur, Jr., said that the crossing where Danny fell needed repair years before the accident.

Philip Henry Dittman, city engineer for the city of Highland Park, testified that he had written to the Chicago and North Western before the occurrence to complain about the rough condition of the crossing. In fact, the Highland Park police officer who investigated the accident—who said on behalf of the railroad that the crossing was safe—testified on cross-examination that he telephoned the railroad the very morning after Danny fell. The jury could thus conclude, Corboy later explained, that he was suggesting with his phone call that the railroad should fix the track.

Michael J. Fritz, a young engineer with Schwinn had testified during his deposition six years earlier that if Danny's bicycle had been equipped with positive retention clips to safeguard the quick-release mechanism—as Schwinn bicycles subsequently were equipped—Danny's front wheel would not have come off. Later Fritz contradicted himself when Murtaugh questioned him in court, saying he didn't know of any way the positive retention clips would have prevented the accident. But under Corboy's cross-examination, Fritz made still another about-face: "Had Dan Schaffner's bicycle been equipped with positive retention clips, he would not have been injured," Fritz finally testified.

"My whole strategy throughout the entire deployment of proof was to get [the defendants] in the mood where they were scared to death of punitive damages," says Corboy. "They didn't know *my* attitude toward punitive damages." If the jury awarded punitive damages—which are typically high—in addition to compensatory damages, the defendants' liability would increase significantly.

Rulings along the way helped Corboy with his strategy to limit any focus on Danny's role in the accident. For example, Danny was riding his bike the wrong way down a one-way street when he went over the crossing. "So what," responded Corboy. "What difference does it make which way he was going? They thought they were going to get that into evidence that he was going the wrong way. We kept that out: the court agreed with us that it would be unduly prejudicial. The railroad and Schwinn were aware that they couldn't muddy up the waters with that. So there was one more nail in the coffin of the burial of the defense of comparative fault, or comparative negligence."

Eventually both the Chicago and North Western and Schwinn took the bait. The two companies agreed that they would not ask the jury to blame Danny, that they would forgo their comparative negligence defense if Corboy would in turn not ask for punitive damages. "Their backs were up against the wall. They'd been pushed there by the way the proof went in," stresses Corboy. "The marshaling of sufficient evidence to convince your opponents that it's not worthwhile to go ahead with the defense of comparative negligence is no easy task. I [was] persuading the enemy."

Corboy named the railroad as the first defendant in his case because "they were our target." He believed that of the two defendants, the railroad was the weaker. "However, our structure was to get them both pointing at each other," said Corboy. "My job is to let that jury know there's only one thing they're there for—to have them think which of these defendants is, or are they both, responsible." As a result, the railroad and the bike company were constantly nicking at each other. When Schwinn's lawyer, Murtaugh, cross-examined Simons from the railroad, he hit hard on the canceled repair order:

Murtaugh: Turning to Exhibit Nineteen sir, the reason for cancellation, if you can explain this for me, I'm not sure I understand that's a reason for cancellation, and I don't mean to argue with you; but is that a standard phrase? Again, does that mean something in the nomenclature of the railroad that "work cannot carry out" has some special meaning?

Simons: No. No. It does not have a special meaning. The A.F.E. cancellation is a more or less of an accounting type document in order to transfer any charges that have been made to the authority into a proper account or ledger.

Murtaugh: So a decision had been made no longer to keep those funds frozen for the purpose of fixing this crossing; isn't that correct?

Simons: That's correct.

Murtaugh: This document itself implies in no way that the crossing no longer needed the repair, does it?

Simons: No.

Murtaugh: Thank you. No further questions.

When Brant, on behalf of the railroad, cross-examined James Fiocchi, he pointed his finger at Danny's bike:

Brant: You stated that as you went across the tracks you were going, I think you used the expression, I wasn't sure if you said "fairly fast" or "very fast" or just what expression you used. Could you help me out on that?

Fiocchi: I was going fast.

Brant: Would you be able to give me an approximation of how fast you went over the crossing?

Fiocchi: I'm not sure how fast I can ride a bicycle, but I was going to say I was going almost as fast as I could ride.

Brant: Full bore?

Fiocchi: Full bore.

Brant: Have you ever clocked yourself, ever had a bike that had any type of a—

Fiocchi: Yes, I did. It's hard to go past twenty-five, so it's probably around twenty or twenty-five on a flat surface. It's hard to go faster than that, so I was probably up there.

Brant: Your bike was also equipped with a quick-release device?

Fiocchi: Yes, sir, it was.

Brant: And in going across that crossing at that speed, you didn't obviously lose your front wheel?

As well as poking at each other, the railroad and the bike company put on their own defenses, after Corboy had completed calling his witnesses. One witness for the railroad, track foreman Peter Connena, said that he never thought the crossing was in bad shape, and that he never thought it needed repair. An engineering consultant who was formerly employed by the Illinois Department of Transportation also testified that photographs of the crossing showed it to be reasonably safe, with the rails and supporting timbers substantially flush with the road.

Schwinn's expert witness, DeLong, testified in support of the design of Danny's bike and said that Danny's quick-release mechanism was adequately secured when he went over the crossing. DeLong testified that it would not be possible to build a bike hub that would be able to hold on reliably under the circumstances. He said that the only reason the wheel came out of the bike was because of the forces placed on it when going across the rough tracks.

In attempting to prove that the railroad was negligent and Danny's bike was unreasonably dangerous—and in attempting to prove that this negligence and the condition of Danny's bike were what led to his accident—Corboy never lessened his campaign to show how very extensive Danny's injury was. Throughout the trial Corboy wove in testimony on damages that was provided by a steady stream of witnesses: Danny's pediatrician, the surgeon who first operated on Danny, the Boston psychiatrist who had been treating Danny for the previous two years, the nurse who vividly recalled the pain and agony Danny went through awakening from his coma, a speech pathologist, a neuropsychologist who saw Danny weekly, an economist who testified on the cost of Danny's medical needs as well as on lost income, Danny's two bike-riding pals, Danny himself, and lastly, Danny's mother. "Every morning and every afternoon," says Corboy, "we tried to have at least one witness talking about damages so the jury is simply reminded what they're there for. You have to keep doing something on a continuing basis to keep the jury reminded of their function" to reach a verdict.

Thus, while Corboy worked to keep his two defendants pointing their fingers at each other, he also kept "the jury aware that this finger-pointing can only result in a large damage award against one or both defendants." This, said Corboy, is where "the real pathos" is involved in getting before the jury "what this disability means."

One of the many reasons Corboy wanted Fiocchi and Coxon

present at the trial was to show the kind of person Danny might have been if he hadn't been hurt. "Here's Danny's alter ego, not quite his clone, but certainly his alter ego, this nice young man, Fiocchi," says Corboy describing that witness.

Dr. Bruce M. Gans, the Boston psychiatrist, and Dr. Joseph Tarkington, Danny's neurosurgeon, provided key medical evidence. Gans, a specialist in head-injury rehabilitation and chairman of the department of rehabilitation medicine at Tufts University School of Medicine, described at length Danny's condition. "When I first examined Daniel, the first thing that was apparent was that he had a dysarthric speech problem, which means that his speech was only partially intelligible," related Gans. "I could understand some of what he said. I knew he knew what he was saying, but the words were so pronounced unclearly with occasionally such poor breath support that I couldn't understand all of what he said and he had to repeat things for me.

"Just from appearance, Daniel shows some asymmetry. He looks kind of crooked. He stands listening to one side. He holds his head slightly tilted. His left body doesn't move very much or very smoothly compared to the right side." Gans went on, listing problem after problem. "Another striking observation was that his eyes didn't both point in the same direction when he was looking at you. His left eye tended to point out to a very significant degree."

After finishing his physical description, Gans told the jury about Danny's mental condition and his behavior. He noted that Danny understood, and could explain, what had happened to him and what he was doing at the present time. "But what was also striking," said Gans, "was that he was very quick to have quite inappropriate jokes and humor."

Later in his testimony Gans described, with the help of a skull model and X rays of Danny's skull, the extent of Danny's damage and its biologic results. He described Danny's inability to establish social relationships and his inability to organize and manage his own life. Most importantly, he testified that Danny needed a guardian for the rest of his life.

"I think if Dan were living totally on his own with nobody looking out for him, caring for him, watching what happened," Gans told the court, "I think that he would very likely have the quality of his lifestyle, his activities, deteriorate to the point where he could easily become a street person, the type of person living from hand-to-mouth out of a shopping bag, wandering relatively aimlessly without a great degree of purpose."

Because Danny's surgeon, Dr. Tarkington, could not take the stand, Corboy showed the jury Tarkington's videotaped deposition. For one and a half hours, the gray-haired, bespectacled Tarkington described how he was first called to the hospital shortly after midnight on the night of Danny's accident. He told of Danny's condition in the emergency room. Tarkington told how he at first decided not to operate because Danny's couldn't breathe on his own, and Tarkington thought he was dead; but how after a few spontaneous gasps from Danny, Tarkington operated, removing a portion of Danny's skull to relieve the pressure that had built up from internal bleeding. Tarkington described Danny's condition after the operation, and a second operation he performed when he relieved additional pressure by removing the dead portion of Danny's brain. Tarkington gave his prognosis that Danny's current physical and mental status would never improve.

In a trial with thirty-two witnesses, Corboy never put Danny's father on the stand. "We made a tactical decision," he says, "that his emotional involvement with his son and his propensity to—he was a mixture of anger, legitimate anger, and legitimate emotional response—that he could not go through testifying without crying, without breaking down. We do not put witnesses on the stand if we don't have to who will have that type of exposure. The juries will say that we will do anything to tug at their heartstrings. That's not helping your case.

"Mr. Schaffner was very much involved in the repair of his

son," explains Corboy. "He had borrowed one hundred thousand dollars, or more, to assist in his rejuvenation. He had acquired a persona of haplessness whenever his son's question ever came up." Furthermore, adds Corboy, Mr. Schaffner's anger, although it was legitimate, would have made cross-examination difficult for him, and he would not have come across well. "His reaction would not have served the child well," summarizes Corboy.

On the other hand, Mrs. Schaffner, Corboy says, is a very maternal but handsome woman who "came across as Florence Nightingale." A school teacher who took time off to take care of Danny after the accident, Mrs. Schaffner was Corboy's last and star witness, taking the stand right after Danny himself. "Jean Schaffner is a very, very nice fifty-nine-year-old woman," says Corboy. "She's everybody's mother; she's everybody's sweetheart; she's everybody's daughter; she's everybody's grandmother. Why was she such a good witness? Because she's so credible." Without duplicating what the other witnesses had said, Mrs. Schaffner "wrapped it all up." She told of Danny's life before and after the accident, and she told what happened on that very night, after James Fiocchi called the Schaffner home and Danny's parents had rushed to the hospital, arriving even before the ambulance:

Mrs. Schaffner: They brought him in on a stretcher and I went up to him and he didn't answer me. And they took him in the emergency room and I didn't see him again.

Corboy: All right. Did you eventually see a Dr. Tarkington?

Mrs. Schaffner: Yes. While we were waiting in the emergency waiting room there somebody came out. I guess it must have been a doctor. He came out and told us they had called for a neurosurgeon, and I was kind of surprised, and it wasn't very long, I guess, shortly thereafter this person came out and called us and told us he was the neurosurgeon and he took us into a little side room.

Corboy: Pardon?

Mrs. Schaffner: He took us into a little side room to talk.

Corboy: What information were you given?

Mrs. Schaffner: He told us that our son was dead and he had been without oxygen for eight minutes, and I don't remember much beyond that that he said except that he left us and went back into the emergency room. And my husband and I—I think we were standing in the entryway at the emergency room trying to get some air. It was hard to breathe. And a nurse came up and asked us to sign a release form, and it turned out that Dr. Tarkington had seen Danny struggling to breathe and evidently he took him up to surgery, and that was the first we had known that he was still living. And then they took us up to the waiting room, the surgery waiting room, and we waited.

Telling Mr. Schaffner that he could not testify was no easy task, given how much he wanted to vent his anger and show how his family's life had changed. "I used my persuasive abilities to convince him he should not take the stand," says Corboy, who viewed this decision as part of his lawyerly responsibility. It was a decision that took some courage, Corboy says, "knowing full well that if anything had backfired, [Mr. Schaffner] could have come back and said, 'It wouldn't have happened if I had taken the stand.' "

Both opponents, Brant and Murtaugh, were skittish about contesting damages, that is, the fact that Danny was so terribly, permanently hurt, says Corboy, because "when they're in a finger-pointing contest, the one who talks about damages indicates that's he's not so sure of himself. If I'm saying 'It's your fault, not mine—but—he really wasn't hurt, was he?' " it weakens the finger-pointing and shows that the defendant is concerned about his own liability, explains Corboy. "Our overall plan was to keep them talking about the liability of the other party and the absence of their liability. Our overall strategy was to keep them talking about liability *as between themselves.*"

Schwinn and the railroad should have sat down together and decided to contest damages, suggests Corboy, Monday-morning quarterbacking for the two defendants. "But because they were so concerned with their intramural skirmishes about liability, they never got around to sitting down and agreeing that they would cross-examine on damages," that they would contest the severity of Danny's condition. Corboy notes that Brant did go partway out on the damages limb for the railroad when cross-examining Gans about Danny's medical condition. But Murtaugh did not do the same.

Corboy was "outstanding in presenting the damages," comments Murtaugh when asked about the trial, "and that's where the case was outstanding—partly because neither defendant challenged the damages issue because they each thought they had a chance of getting out" on liability. Corboy "gets inside the family he's representing and brings the jury inside so they know the pain the family is feeling," adds Murtaugh. "It's a tactic he uses extremely effectively." Corboy's job would have been harder, agrees Schwinn's lawyer, "if we had not taken shots at each other, or if we had agreed to a judgment-sharing deal." Of the final settlement offer, Schwinn had kicked in $2 million and had asked the Chicago and North Western to match that amount, but the railroad held firm at $1 million.

The part Corboy likes best in any trial is closing argument. "I consider my strength to be wrapping everything up," he notes, a comment supported by the spectators he perennially draws for this event. (Corboy's potential weakness, he adds, is appearing angry in court and coming on too strong, especially during cross-examination.) In Danny's case, Corboy—knowing that at least one of the defendants would be found liable—pushed hard on damages. "You know," Corboy told the jurors early in his closing argument, "it's over nine years ago—and that's no fault of these lawyers. It's no fault of the Schaffner family. But it's over nine years ago that this occurrence took place. This man/boy was a boy/boy at that time. He was fifteen years of age. If any one of us were to go back nine years, you'd know how much our lives have changed during that period of time.

"It's probably fortunate, however, in this case that nine years have elapsed. Why? Because now there is absolutely no doubt—there's absolutely no doubt that this young boy's injuries are permanent."

Later in his closing, Corboy told the jurors he felt uneasy asking them to give his client money in compensation for a tragedy. "Sure," said Corboy, "he's earned it the hard way. Of course you'll fix damages. But how gross can this Corboy be when he says damages in compensation?

"Gross it might be, but it's the best the law can do. It's the only thing the law can do. You can't give this family's boy back his brain. You can't give him the ability to talk. You can only compensate by way of damages."

Nina S. Appel, Loyola's law school dean, who went to hear Corboy's closing argument in the Schaffner case, observes that "he didn't patronize the jury in any way. He seemed to speak directly to them and very logically proceeded to explain how the damages should be calculated." In his closing argument, Appel says Corboy avoided overplaying the pathos of the case; he kept his professional distance to maintain his effectiveness as an advocate for Danny's compensation. "The jury was following him very clearly," she says. "They were following him as jurors, not as in a soap opera."

Ultimately, after Brant and Murtaugh made their closing arguments, the jury decided that Danny's bike was not unreasonably dangerous, and that therefore Schwinn was not liable for the accident. The final result let Schwinn completely off the hook. The jury did find the Chicago and North Western Transportation negligent, and that negligence the source of Danny's injury, and held the railroad liable for $8,235,000 in damages. More than half of that award was allotted, as Corboy suggested with an itemized verdict request totaling $10,535,000, to the disability resulting from Danny's injury ($3,200,000 awarded) and to his past and future pain and suffering ($2,000,000 awarded). The rest was allocated among disfigurement due to the injury ($1,000,000), lost earnings ($1,428,000), past medical expenses and caretaking services ($235,000), and future expenses and services ($372,000). The jury had reduced Corboy's verdict request by $1,800,000 for the disability, and $500,000 for disfigurement, hence the $2,300,000 difference between Corboy's $10,535,000 request and the final $8,235,000 award.

Corboy thinks that he lost against Schwinn because the bike company beat him to the punch by bringing onto their team Fred DeLong, the best bicycle expert in the country—"a lovable person all juries like and trust," says Corboy. Corboy did have testimony from Schwinn's own employee Fritz that positive retention clips on Danny's bike would have prevented his accident. And Corboy's own bike expert, Irving Hazard, a consulting engineer brought into the case earlier by the referring attorney, testified that Danny's bike was defective without some kind of safety device such as a positive retention clip. However—during cross-examination by Murtaugh—Hazard waffled on this earlier testimony by saying that perhaps the accident was due to the rough railroad crossing rather than to the bicycle. Hazard admitted to the bike company's lawyer that Danny's quick-release mechanism must not have been tightened fully. It could have been tightened enough for normal usage, Hazard said, but not enough for a rough railroad crossing. Murtaugh's cross-examination, Corboy says, provided "the Achilles' heel" in the Schaffners' case against Schwinn because Hazard lost all credibility as a bike expert when he changed his opinion mid-trial about the cause of the accident.

Corboy says that he could have chosen not to put Hazard on the stand, even though Hazard's report on the case had already been supplied to the defendants' lawyers. Instead, Corboy could have just gone with Fritz's testimony. "But this is all hindsight," he adds. Murtaugh said that he thought Corboy's mistake was being overly aggressive in his own cross-examination of Schwinn's bike expert, Fred DeLong. Because DeLong was seventy years old, the jury felt very protective of him.

After the October 16, 1985, jury decision, the Chicago and North Western appealed the jury's $8.235 million verdict. Corboy, in response, appealed the jury's finding in favor of Schwinn—maintaining that Danny got an unfair trial and that the jury decided in favor of Schwinn against the "manifest weight of the evidence." On September 23, 1987, the appellate court upheld the jury verdict in favor of Schwinn and against the Chicago and North Western.

The railroad then appealed to the Illinois Supreme Court, which against Corboy's protestations agreed to review the Schaffner decision. That court's ruling is still pending.

In August 1987, Danny's father, Perry Schaffner, died suddenly of a heart attack. Because Danny's case is still under appeal, he and his mother have yet to receive any compensation for Danny's injury. Corboy continues his fight on their behalf.

"If we go back to the trial court," says Corboy, "I want both defendants. I'm going to reallege punitive damages. If we do [go back to the trial court], we'll start the whole ball over again. "If," he adds, "that's what they want."

JULIUS L. CHAMBERS

NAACP Legal Defense and Educational Fund, Inc., New York

Copper Cunningham

When Julius L. Chambers traveled twelve miles daily to attend the all-black Peabody High School in rural North Carolina, his school bus drove straight past an all-white high school just a mile from his home. Chambers knew that the nearby white school was far better equipped than his own, more-distant black school. Nonetheless, as he progressed in his education and approached adulthood, Chambers determinedly pursued an impressive course of achievement. Ultimately he changed not only his school system, but all school systems in North Carolina, and even those throughout the United States.

In 1958, Chambers graduated from predominately black North Carolina Central University in Durham; the next year he earned a master's degree in history from the University of Michigan. He then moved on to the University of North Carolina's law school. At the end of his second year there, Chambers was first in his class. Subsequently he became the first black to earn the prestigious position of editor-in-chief of the UNC law review.

Dedication to his studies paid off in other ways. Civil rights leaders read in the newspapers about Chambers's ongoing law school success and wrote to him encouragingly. Chambers later met Thurgood Marshall and Jack Greenberg, the first two director-counsels of the NAACP Legal Defense and Educational Fund, Inc., an organization dedicated to erasing inequities resulting from racial discrimination. (The National Association for the Advancement of Colored People founded the NAACP Legal Defense and Educational Fund in 1940, but the Legal Defense Fund, as it is known for short, has been a separate, unaffiliated organization with its own staff and budget for over thirty years.) After Chambers received a master of law degree in 1963 from Columbia University School of Law, he went to work as the first legal intern with the Legal Defense Fund in New York.

But Chambers knew he wanted to go home, and the next year he returned to Charlotte, where, with about $17,000 backing from the Legal Defense Fund, he set up a solo law practice. As part of that practice, Chambers agreed to help the LDF with any North Carolina lawsuits it wanted to bring. The financial support was an opportunity for Chambers that no longer exists for young lawyers today; since the early 1970s, the Legal Defense Fund's limited budget has prohibited its continuation of this lawyer assistance program. Ultimately, Chambers became the lead partner in his own firm, Chambers, Ferguson, Watt, Wallas, Adkins & Fuller, P.A.

Today, almost a quarter of a century after the LDF gave him his start, the fifty-two-year-old Chambers is himself the Legal Defense Fund's director-counsel. Since taking that job and moving to New York in 1984, he has overseen an in-house staff of more than twenty attorneys, plus about four hundred volunteer lawyers across the nation. These attorneys handle at any one time about twelve hundred civil rights cases in areas such as education, voting, capital punishment, employment, prisons, housing, and health care.

Chambers, whose wife teaches elementary school in Harlem and whose children are now twenty-two and eighteen years old, teaches civil rights litigation at the University of Pennsylvania and at Columbia University Law School. He is a strong advocate of law school trial courses such as those he teaches because they give budding young lawyers opportunities to work on actual cases while they are still in law school. Chambers also sits on the board of visitors at Columbia and at Harvard University.

In his rise from solo law practice to civil rights leader, the handsome and solidly built Chambers handled almost every possible kind of lawsuit in the fight for blacks' civil rights, including public accommodation suits where restaurant owners refused to admit blacks, suits alleging discriminatory zoning and housing practices, and police brutality cases. Chambers has argued over two hundred school desegregation cases alone.

"I juggled a lot of things while preparing to become a civil rights lawyer full-time," says Chambers, "because civil rights litigation is not the most lucrative field. You have to do something to make a living." Chambers says that although he handled a variety of legal matters in his office, civil rights was always a major part of his work agenda, demanding on average about sixty percent of his time. Other lawyers in his firm, he explains, specialized in non–civil rights matters in order to support those lawyers in the firm working in the lower-paying civil rights field.

Chambers's frenetic pace and long hours of hard work won him many admirers, but also a number of enemies. In 1965, while he was speaking before a black church group, Chambers's car was dynamited. A year later his home was also hit, and then someone firebombed his office. Chambers's calm and stoic responses to each of these situations are now legendary. He didn't seem surprised by the hostility—nor was he deterred.

In spite of this violence, Chambers kept his goals firmly in mind. Ultimately, this small-town, southern, black civil rights lawyer, with his dignified and determined manner, argued and won some of the most important civil rights cases to pass through the U.S. court system. Among Chambers's key Supreme Court cases was *Griggs v. Duke Power Co.,* where the Court held in 1971 that employers cannot rely on job requirements, such as educational or test requirements, that disqualify blacks at a much higher rate than whites if those requirements are not "significantly related" to the needs of the job. In another Chambers landmark case, *Albemarle Paper Co. v. Moody,* the Court decided in 1975 that back pay can be mandated for victims of job discrimination even if it could not be proven that the employer had acted in bad faith in violating civil rights law.

Chambers is most proud, however, of his victory in *Swann v. Charlotte-Mecklenburg Board of Education,* a case decided by the Supreme Court in 1971, but begun seven years earlier. This lawsuit—against a combined city-county North Carolina school board—tested Chambers's resourcefulness, stamina, and tolerance for adversity even more than his other courtroom challenges. It ultimately led to the first historic decision in which the U.S. Supreme Court sanctioned busing to desegregate schools. Thus *Swann* changed the course of public education in America. For the first time, civil rights leaders and public officials had a court-sanctioned tool that enabled them to initiate massive integration of the public schools to improve educational opportunities for black children across the nation.

"The *Swann* case really started in 1964," relates Chambers, "with an effort to challenge the failure of the [Charlotte-Mecklenburg school] board to desegregate all the schools of [that] system." In 1964, as a result of a request from what was then the Department of Health, Education and Welfare to eliminate all discriminatory features in the school system, the Charlotte-Mecklenburg school board had closed all of the black schools in the county and had said it would assign those students to schools of other geographic districts. The board assigned students in the city to neighborhood districts. But at the same time, the school board adopted a transfer policy that permitted white students in black schools to transfer out to white schools, and black students to transfer from integrated schools back to black schools. So the board still ended up with seventy or more percent of the black students in traditionally all-black schools, and seventy or eighty percent of the white students in traditionally white schools. "They also failed to desegregate teachers," adds Chambers. "In effect, they went from about zero percent integration to probably twenty or thirty percent racial mixing of students."

A group of black parents in the school system wanted to challenge the closing of the black schools. The black community in general was concerned about the failure of the system to desegregate the schools, relates Chambers.

"I met with representatives of the NAACP and of local organizations," says Chambers, who at the time was assistant legal counsel for the state of North Carolina for the NAACP, as well as a cooperating attorney with the NAACP Legal Defense Fund. The black parents and community groups decided they wanted to force the school board to desegregate all the schools, their teachers, and all extracurricular activities. "So we brought this lawsuit," says Chambers.

The trial, which began on January 19, 1965, ran about three weeks. Judge J. Braxton Craven heard the case; as in most civil rights suits, there was no jury. "The court came down with an order in 1965," says Chambers, "to the effect that what the [school] board had done was sufficient to comply" with *Brown v. Board of Education,* which held that racially segregated schools were unconstitutional. Judge Craven told the disappointed plaintiffs and civil rights groups that the school board had no affirmative duty to promote desegregation; it simply needed to eliminate policies that compelled segregation of students. The judge did order the board to desegregate teachers and school personnel, but not extracurricular activities, says Chambers.

However, in 1968 the U.S. Supreme Court held in *Green v. New Kent County Board of Education* that school districts had *an affirmative duty* to remove all remaining vestiges of discrimination. And in 1969, the Supreme Court also said that school districts had to desegregate their schools immediately, not just with "all deliberate speed," as stipulated in the *Brown* case. Chambers saw his first window of opportunity in the *Swann* case since Judge Craven's 1965 order. Because the federal district courts retain jurisdiction in school desegregation cases and permit the parties to come back to ask for modifications of court orders as might be required by new judicial decisions, new laws, or changing circumstances, Chambers again approached the North Carolina district court that originally ruled in the *Swann* case. In 1969, he filed under *Swann* a "motion for further relief."

By then, Judge Craven had been elevated to the higher Fourth Circuit Court of Appeals (covering Maryland, West Virginia, Virginia, North Carolina, and South Carolina), and a new judge, fifty-one-year-old James B. McMillan, had been appointed to his place on the district court bench. Chambers was guardedly optimistic despite McMillan's popularity and prominence in the tradition-bound North Carolina legal community. The civil rights lawyer thought that if he could make his case to McMillan—if the judge could understand fully what was happening to the black children in the Charlotte-Mecklenburg school system—McMillan would prove to be fair and strong enough to pursue his convictions.

Chambers's hunch proved more than right. McMillan was so fair, so concerned with enforcing what he became convinced was the law, that in the process he became a martyr, an outcast in his own hometown. During a series of hearings lasting almost a year, from March 1969 through February 1970, Judge McMillan repeatedly rejected ineffective desegregation plans submitted to him by the school board. In search of an effective solution for desegregating the schools, he finally hired a consultant, Dr. John A. Finger, Jr., from Rhode Island College, to design a plan for the school board. Finger's plan provided for the full and immediate desegregation of all 105 public schools in Charlotte and Mecklenburg County by using district-wide racial percentages as a guidepost for individual school desegregation efforts. To reach those percentages, the Finger plan paired or grouped black schools in the city with white schools in the county. It then provided that some black children be bused to a corresponding white school, and that white children be bused to a corresponding black school. On February 5, 1970, Judge McMillan issued his order accepting the Finger plan. The school board appealed all the way up to the U.S. Supreme Court, but on August 7, 1970, that court upheld all parts of Judge McMillan's order.

A couple of years later, a citizens advisory group of white and black parents met together to devise still new approaches to deal with remaining inequities in the Charlotte-Mecklenburg schools. In 1974, when the school board adopted these last modifications, including equalizing the amount of busing for the youngest white and black children, the district court approved those additional changes. And in 1975, Judge McMillan issued his final order in the case, which he labeled "Swann Song." In that order, McMillan removed the case from his active docket and closed the file.

Throughout his years in private practice, Chambers was continually aware that he operated in the courtroom not only as lawyer, but as a black lawyer, and one generally representing black people. He knew that sometimes his race influenced the judges and juries who listened to his cases. And this awareness affected the way Chambers prepared his cases for trial.

"It depended on where I was," Chambers explains. If he was in district court of some North Carolina jurisdictions, where he knew that race was a factor for a particular judge who would be hearing his case, Chambers "would prepare a case to get everything I could that was appropriate in the record—because I knew I would have to appeal." While all good lawyers follow this tactic should they lose a case and need to appeal, it was particularly critical for Chambers where he knew that an appeal was certain. However, when he knew that a judge was reasonably fair, Chambers prepared more to argue for the type of relief or remedy he wanted, rather than to demonstrate a constitutional violation as the legal premise for his suit.

The same approach held true for jury trials. "Juries in North Carolina were pretty racist for a while," recalls Chambers. "They were," he explains diplomatically, "representatives of communities—and communities had not become as tolerant as they have more recently. If I was defending a black person accused of murdering a white person, I would expect a jury to be unable to fairly evaluate the evidence," concludes Chambers, his placid demeanor masking any abhorrence of such situations. But "I would do everything I could to appeal to the reasonable minds of the jury and to appeal to their consciences about being fair in weighing the evidence." Chambers's only hope in these jury trials, albeit a slim one, was to offer such convincing evidence in favor of his client that the jurors would listen to rational arguments rather than to their irrational emotional biases.

Of course, prejudice in court still exists today. Sometimes in personal injury cases, notes Chambers, a jury won't award the same amount of compensation to a black person as they would to a white person. "But there's been a tremendous improvement in juries generally," he quickly adds. Discrimination is "not completely eliminated, but it's not as bad as it was.

"I look on the American people," concludes Chambers, "as basically fair and wanting to do what is right. That doesn't say that *everybody* wants to be fair."

During the *Swann* case, Chambers demonstrated his ability to deal with racial discrimination in a court setting and in a community. Throughout the turmoil of this school desegregation case, with its many hearings and intense public feeling, Chambers fought discrimination—both against him and against black school children—by staying calm. He says he had to stay calm to keep his mind on his daily concern of whether he was introducing enough evidence "to sustain the type of relief that we were seeking. I think any trial requires a certain kind of temperament," says Chambers, "that one maintain his or her ability to reason and to keep one's thought process together. If one becomes overly involved, there is the probability of failing to introduce certain evidence, of not examining a witness properly, of making some comment or taking some position that will be detrimental to the outcome of the case."

One of the school board's attorneys for the *Swann* case, William J. Waggoner, then with Weinstein, Waggoner, Sturges, Odom & Bigger, says that Chambers knew how to make a point without getting emotional. Early in the *Swann* hearings, recalls Waggoner, one attorney repeatedly used the word "nigras" in his remarks before the judge. Rather than objecting openly, and drawing more attention to the problem, Chambers simply slipped Waggoner a note saying that the plaintiffs would prefer the term "blacks." Waggoner was able to convince the offending attorney to change his ways. "Julius was very low-key," says Waggoner, who calls his former opponent "one of the finer lawyers around."

"Julius has a very quiet style," agrees James M. Nabrit II, an attorney who has been with the Legal Defense Fund since 1959, and who assisted Chambers with the *Swann* case. "There are different ways of communicating and making points to people. His style is particularly advantageous in a tense and inflamed situation. It enables people to stay calm and to think rationally and not get overwrought."

"He is studied and thoughtful and hence credible, and hence effective," agrees another of the *Swann* school attorneys, Benjamin S. Horack, then of Ervin, Horack & McCartha.

"I think that it requires some concentration in order to make sure one remains calm," says Chambers, whether a case involves school desegregation or personal injury claims or criminal charges. "I've done some criminal cases and gotten concerned about the client, and the way the client was treated in court," he explains. "I've done some other civil cases and felt that the court and the jury were simply unfair to the client. Whether it was because the client was black or because the client was represented by a black lawyer, there were problems." And Chambers says he has watched other lawyers defending clients in capital punishment cases where "many of them become very concerned about their clients." So, summarizes Chambers, *Swann* was not necessarily a unique trial where the attorney was likely to become overly involved. For every lawyer, he says, "it depends on the situation, and on the experience one has in litigating these cases."

In *Swann,* Chambers relied on tactics he had learned during past experience, ranging from thorough research on the judge presiding over his case to comprehensive documentation of his claim. Today, when asked to describe his winning trial technique in *Swann,* Chambers likes first to offer some general guidelines for courtroom success.

Chambers begins with controversial advice: concentrate on a particular area of trial practice. This contradicts the usual trend in many large law firms, where litigation departments are staffed by lawyers who are trial generalists, on the theory that trying a case requires skills that can be applied universally. "I just happen to think that nobody is going to know all of the law, and it's far better to develop some specialty in a given area," counters Chambers. Lawyers should at least "identify the particular emphasis that might be required in the different areas of litigation they might want to get involved in," he adds. "Develop some appreciation of what courts look for in various areas" of the law—the kinds of testimony and data requested—before going into a case. In school cases, for example, many of the same issues, such as freedom of choice, arise repeatedly, and courts ask the same kinds of questions, such as whether busing requirements are too onerous for children and whether the government has an obligation to desegregate public education. Thus an attorney trying a school case for the first time would be at a distinct disadvantage opposing an experienced school desegregation lawyer who is familiar with these arguments. Attorneys new to a field of law can gather the kind of knowledge they need from other trial lawyers who have already tried cases in the particular substantive area, suggests Chambers.

Trial lawyers should build their communication skills early and learn how to relate to other people, continues Chambers. Improving communication skills can be done simply, beginning with practicing speaking before a mirror. Of course, Chambers spoke publicly so much, so early in his career that he never had to resort to a mirror for practice opportunities. When he was in North Carolina, Chambers traveled throughout the state, taking every opportunity available to talk with individuals and groups about their civil rights. He recommends that other lawyers "get out and try to communicate through public speaking" and that they think about their communication skills when they speak before audiences and talk with their colleagues. Today, Chambers's speech is direct, articulate, and carefully modulated. He still gives six to seven talks a month, primarily to raise funds for the Legal Defense Fund's approximately $7 million annual budget.

After deciding on a specialization and developing communication skills, a trial attorney should concentrate on thorough preparation, says the LDF director-counsel. Chambers has always worked more than sixty hours a week. When preparing a case, he attempts to take witness depositions himself "to have some feeling for what they're going to say and how." How witnesses respond depends on how the questions are put to them, as well as on what they know about the subject, instructs Chambers. "The interrogator is extremely important," he says of his desire to play that role himself. Chambers also uses the various discovery devices available to attorneys—such as interrogatories, records inspections, and depositions—"to gain an appreciation of the facts. I don't know if it's necessary for the trial lawyer to do all of the discovery," he says, "but it's important to do enough to have an appreciation of the case, the documents, and the witnesses."

Similarly, Chambers studies the judge and the juries in the

assigned community of an impending trial to predict how they will react to his case and how he might best be able to convince them of his client's position. Today he can refer to computerized data bases; for example, West Publishing offers a data base from which case printouts can be grouped by judge. Newspapers and specialty publications such as *The New York Law Journal* also give summaries of what juries decide in certain areas, says Chambers. He wraps up his study of how judges and juries respond to particular kinds of cases in particular locations by talking with lawyers who practice in the area. "Know your environment as well as your case," summarizes Chambers when instructing other lawyers on preparing for trial in different locales. The history of past cases in a given area often reveals community values that continue to influence future court decisions.

After researching past trials in the community where his case will be heard, Chambers prepares his witnesses. "The witness," he warns, "should be as prepared as the lawyer." Chambers says that he wants his witnesses "to understand the whole theory of the case and why [that witness's] testimony is important." He also prepares his witnesses for cross-examination by telling them "what to expect from the other side in terms of efforts to challenge" the plaintiffs. In summary, instructs Chambers, "know what each witness is going to say, how the witness is going to say it, and how the witness will respond to cross-examination or to questions by the court." At the same time, also put in proper order supporting exhibits and documentary evidence, he adds. Make sure they are understandable.

Finally, says Chambers, prepare a trial outline and a brief that "map out everything to do along the way, with ready reference to evidence on legal questions that may come up and will demonstrate your entitlement to relief once you've done everything on the outline." In some cases, says Chambers, you need more than one lawyer, "especially if there are a lot of witnesses and a lot of evidence." But you can make use of paralegals, he urges, in preparing witnesses and exhibits, for example.

Moving on to speak specifically about his success in the historic school desegregation area, Chambers explains that school cases differ from typical tort cases, that is, cases alleging specific damages resulting from willfulness, negligence, or strict liability. Typically there is no jury in civil rights cases, although juries do hear civil rights cases when the plaintiff requests monetary damages, as in police brutality suits.

A lawyer arguing a case before a judge would expect to approach that trial differently than if there were a jury, says Chambers. "You don't need some of the stringent evidentiary rules because a trial judge is presumed to know what is relevant."

But there are occasions when convincing a judge of your argument might require some of the techniques used for convincing a jury, Chambers adds. For example, when Albemarle, North Carolina, closed its black schools as part of a desegregation plan, the superintendent reassigned the black principal of a high school as assistant principal at an elementary school. The man objected because he felt that the reassignment was demeaning. Chambers took his case.

The district court judge who heard the case said that the principal had to accept the assistant's job because the principal was obligated under the desegregation plan to reduce his losses, that is, to accept a position that would provide him as much of his previous salary as possible. The court also refused the principal back pay. Still the man rejected the lower position.

A three-judge panel of the U.S. Court of Appeals for the Fourth Circuit upheld the district court opinion, but Chambers requested a hearing en banc, or by the entire appeals court. Here he approached the row of judges as he would a jury and appealed to their equitable discretion and ability to empathize with the plaintiff.

"I argued that [the decision] set up a bad example," says Chambers. "One doesn't need to demean oneself to reduce one's losses. The court had to look at the effect [on the principal] of what the principal had to do." The appeals court agreed with

Chambers and reversed the lower court's earlier decision. "This is an example of doing a little more than articulating the legal principles," says Chambers today. It means talking to the judges as human beings about "something a court can look at other than just the cold facts."

When compared to a tort case, continues Chambers, a school case is generally more protracted because of the potential for numerous hearings. "In a personal injury trial, you prove that you were negligently injured and you demonstrate at the same time how much you lost as a result of it," notes Chambers. "And the jury goes away and comes back with a monetary judgment. In a school case it's the same approach—you prove that you were injured by a wrong, and then you try to demonstrate what type of relief you're entitled to receive. It's just that [seeking] the relief in this instance—because it's equitable and involves a large number of people—is much more protracted than in a personal injury case."

Yet in some sense civil rights and tort cases have much in common, says Chambers, because "the burden is still on the plaintiff [in the school case] to demonstrate what is constitutionally required as a remedy. [In school cases] the court likes to defer to a governmental agency in terms of what it can or should do in order to correct this violation. It receives whatever the defendant has to offer, and it receives whatever the plaintiffs want to say about it. And the court makes a determination of what is appropriate."

There are similarities among school cases, and knowing about these helps a lawyer better prepare and argue successfully. Chambers has found, for example, that he hears "frequently the same response from the other side. And many of the questions are somewhat the same." School boards often maintain, for example, that they are already working to desegregate the schools. "You anticipate what they're going to say," continues Chambers, "and that enables you to concentrate a bit more on what you need to do to prepare and present the case." This experience in civil rights cases, and knowledge about what to expect, particularly helps a lawyer focus and argue the facts and the law in a potentially emotional situation, reiterates Chambers. Young lawyers should work to gain experience even if they must begin by watching other civil rights attorneys as they argue in court.

In the early 1960s, six-year-old James Swann was denied the right to attend a predominately white school near his home. But James and his parents, Vera and Darius Swann, were just one of many families who helped initiate the lawsuit against the Charlotte-Mecklenburg school board. Similarly, Chambers and the other civil rights leaders who filed the lawsuit did so not only on behalf of this one black boy, or even on behalf of a small handful of black children. Chambers sued the school board to protest ineffective desegregation throughout the Charlotte-Mecklenburg school system. As time went on, the suit became "part of an effort nationwide led by civil rights advocates to impose an affirmative obligation on large school districts in metropolitan areas to completely disestablish racially segregated schools," says Chambers.

To file their North Carolina lawsuit, the civil rights lawyers needed to list plaintiffs who had standing, or who had a cause for registering their complaint with the court. Some say that the Swann family's name was chosen as the first and most visible name in the string of twenty-seven parents and children listed as plaintiffs—causing his name to be the one by which the case is known—because the father, Darius Swann, was employed by a university and was more secure financially in the face of impending reaction from the white community. Chambers agrees in part: "There wasn't any big reason that Swann was chosen over Reginald Hawkins or the Reverend Ezra Moore. It was just that in looking at the list of plaintiffs, we wanted to make sure that we had people who had children in school, people who were interested in the type of relief we were trying to obtain, and people who would be able to pursue the litigation over an extended period of time." Chambers knew that staying power would be critical.

Throughout the next six years, while the plaintiffs' lawyers and the school board negotiated over possible new school desegregation plans, Chambers would work hard to keep all the plaintiffs informed and to talk with them about the type of relief they were trying to obtain. "Some blacks in the community were concerned about whether the desegregation we were seeking was the best thing for black children in the system," says Chambers, who served as a mediator among the various black factions. "Working with them was a daily problem." At the same time, Chambers faced even greater concern, and anger, from the larger community. "There was hostility expressed in the community toward the plaintiffs and toward the lawyers," he notes with some understatement. "We didn't have the most favorable press."

But none of this deterred Chambers. In 1968, when his opportunity to reopen the *Swann* case arose, he began to research the new judge assigned to it. Chambers gathered information about Judge McMillan by talking with the judge's personal contacts in the Charlotte community. Plus "I knew him personally from having served on some boards and committees with him," says Chambers. While Chambers was on the local Legal Services Corporation board, McMillan had worked on a board committee. McMillan also served on a state-wide committee of the North Carolina bar that recommended state court reforms, and Chambers knew about that work. McMillan was a leader in the North Carolina bar and "a very intelligent person," says Chambers. *Swann* was to be the new judge's first big case.

"McMillan initially felt that the system was doing what it needed to do to provide an educational opportunity for the black children," says Chambers. "Part of the objective was to try to convince him that there was not only a problem with the intentional segregation but that the black children in the system were suffering because of it." Chambers thought that McMillan could be won over. "I felt, and I think most people felt, that he was sincere in what he was doing, that he was fair, that he would listen, and that he was a person of his convictions. Once he listened to the various interests and made a decision that something needs to be done, he was strong enough to pursue his convictions."

In order to convince McMillan "we had to demonstrate a number of things," Chambers explains. He lists four categories of evidence he presented to prove his case, all woven throughout the testimony of the witnesses he called to the stand.

One category was "that the schools in the system had been segregated by state action. We had the state constitutional and statutory provisions requiring segregation of students. We had evidence about practices the board had followed since *Brown* which perpetuated segregation. We had evidence about new school construction, about the assignment of teachers, the establishment of geographic districts, the placement of mobile units to accommodate overcrowding of students rather than reassigning them to schools that might promote some racial mixing. We had a completely segregated extracurricular program. So we attempted to demonstrate all of the practices that the board had followed in perpetuating and causing segregation of students and teachers and personnel," explains Chambers.

As part of this first category of evidence, he also presented information about other local practices that caused segregation in the schools, including city zoning and housing practices, discriminatory practices by private realtors, and practices of the federal Department of Housing and Urban Development.

Second, "we presented evidence demonstrating that the change that the board implemented in 1964 didn't eliminate segregation that the board had caused," says Chambers. Of the 24,000 black students in the system in the 1968–69 school year, 14,000 were in schools that were at least ninety-nine percent black. And most of the desegregated schools in the city of Charlotte were actually in transition from all-white schools to all-black.

Chambers showed the judge how the school district lines were drawn and how they could have been drawn; how new school facilities had been built and staffed after 1964 in ways that perpetuated segregation; and how teachers had continued to be assigned on a discriminatory basis, in the classroom and in relation to extracurricular activities. Of 900 black teachers, most were in black schools. Each black elementary school averaged less than one white teacher.

Third, Chambers presented evidence to demonstrate how black children were being harmed in their performance in schools as a result of the segregation because "the system didn't provide them the same facilities and resources that the system provided white kids," asserts the civil rights advocate. "We used test scores, college enrollment, and other indicia to indicate the disparity in performance of students."

Finally, Chambers presented evidence to show that the system, one of about 84,000 students total—twenty-nine percent black and seventy-one percent white—could be completely desegregated "in a reasonable manner without enormous burden to anyone."

Because different witnesses often provided testimony relating to more than one category of evidence, Chambers made a point of explaining to the judge why each witness's testimony was important. Relying on his outline of the case, Chambers worked to "keep the court apprised throughout the trial about the relevance of the evidence to particular issues" he was addressing. Chambers felt that by presenting all this evidence, thus convincing the court that the plaintiffs had a legitimate claim, he would establish the [legal and factual] basis for justifying court-ordered relief, or a remedy, for the segregated schools. Judge McMillan "was not a person who would be swayed by emotions, who would be swayed by public pressure, but [one who] would discharge his responsibility as a judge fairly as he perceived the law to require," says Chambers.

Even with his assessment of Judge McMillan, Chambers

didn't expect an easy time. "When we went into this case," he explains, "there was no court decision holding that an urban area like Charlotte had responsibility to effect the greatest possible degree of desegregation. While we felt that we could establish a constitutional violation, it was uncertain what degree of relief the court would be prepared to order."

Chambers and other civil rights leaders knew that the degree of relief provided in the *Swann* decision would reach black children far beyond Charlotte, North Carolina. "I thought we were working with a case that could have broad implications," says Chambers. "We were trying to convince the court to use whatever means—including transportation—were appropriate to effect desegregation in the schools." Chambers also knew that the *Swann* case would have implications for other conditions and practices affecting blacks in Charlotte.

To produce his four categories of evidence, Chambers amassed an encyclopedic collection of witnesses, depositions, and exhibits. "We had the problem of collecting and preparing the witnesses and of getting the exhibits together," he recalls.

At the first hearing before McMillan on March 10, 1969, Chambers began with a lengthy list of his supporting exhibits. He first included defendant answers to interrogatories, and about twenty depositions he had prepared. Then he followed with a map showing the racial housing pattern in the city of Charlotte, a census tract map of Mecklenburg county for 1960, and a census tract map with a racial breakdown for the city of Charlotte in 1960. Census and zoning maps, says Chambers, "are like photographs of damage in a personal injury case." Particularly when one is overlaid with the other, they show the effects of city policy on where people live.

"As Plaintiff's Exhibit Seven we have an overlay of that census tract map showing the racial composition as of October thirty-first, 1968," Chambers continued in his presentation to the court. "As Plaintiff's Exhibit Eight we have a map showing the income for family in the various tracts of Mecklenburg County as of the 1960 census. As Plaintiff's Exhibit Nine we have a zoning map for the City of Charlotte for 1947. . . . Plaintiff's Collective Exhibit Ten, zoning ordinance for the City of Charlotte 1968 and the zoning maps with index for the City of Charlotte 1968. Plaintiff's Exhibit Eleven, copy of zoning ordinance for the County of Mecklenburg. . . .

"Plaintiff's Exhibit Twelve, a publication of the Charlotte-Mecklenburg Planning Commission entitled 'The Next Ten Years' with the map showing the recommended residential zoning and industrial zoning for the next twenty years for the City of Charlotte. Plaintiff's Exhibit Thirteen, a map showing the major thoroughfares of the City of Charlotte dated June first, 1968. Plaintiff's Exhibit Fourteen, a map showing the urban renewal areas for the City of Charlotte dated November 1968. Plaintiff's Exhibit Fifteen, a publication of the Charlotte-Mecklenburg Planning Commission entitled 'Residential Blight in Charlotte' dated September 1962. Plaintiff's Exhibit Sixteen, a copy of a publication of the Charlotte-Mecklenburg Planning Commission entitled 'Review of Community Facilities' dated 1964. Plaintiff's Exhibit Seventeen, a copy of a publication by the Charlotte-Mecklenburg Planning Commission entitled 'A Statistical Summary of Population and Economic Data' dated March 1968. . . ."

Chambers continued until he had listed twenty-six exhibits, concluding with maps of the city's elementary, junior high, and high school districts.

He also called numerous witnesses at each of four hearings from March 1969 until February 1970. True to form, Chambers knew before each witness appeared exactly what he or she would say to support the plaintiffs' argument. "There are lawyers," says Judge McMillan today, "who come to court and who put witnesses on the stand without knowing what they are going to say. Julius spends all the necessary time learning what [the witnesses know], then he asks simple questions—and gets simple answers."

Of all Chambers's traits, the judge today still praises the

most Chambers's simplicity of presentation. Chambers, says McMillan, doesn't try to create a case where one doesn't exist, or to advocate a viewpoint that is not based on fact. As a trial lawyer, Chambers is an educator, not a debater, emphasizes the judge.

"The earmarks of a good trial lawyer" such as Chambers, concludes McMillan, are "thoroughness, promptness, honesty, and brevity. You don't have to be thorough by taking up a lot of time. You just go the shortest possible distance to get where you want to go." Although Chambers was thorough in *Swann,* he was, as McMillan says, direct. And such directness kept his presentation simple.

For example, during the 1969 hearings before McMillan, Chambers used the testimony of witnesses drawn from the school staff and various exhibits to show disparities in school facilities provided for black students as compared with those provided white students. He documented the number of library books, the number of typewriters, and other tangible facilities. "We had some reference, though slight, to the disparities in degrees held by the teachers assigned to the black schools," Chambers adds. He also talked about differences in the school buildings themselves.

Nobody, says Chambers, could dispute the data about the school facilities and equipment available for the white children versus that for the black children. "That data was produced by the staff and the board in discovery," he notes.

In effect, Chambers used his witnesses and his evidence to take the judge on a sightseeing trip through the city schools. The judge, "being familiar with the area [of Charlotte and Mecklenburg], and many of the facilities, could see the physical differences—and as we carried him into the classroom through testimony and through documentary evidence, with discussion about the number of books and lab equipment, and then carried him outside to the grounds with the extracurricular activities, he could see the difference."

The school superintendent, Dr. William C. Self, proved

most helpful in describing the school facilities and equipment available, as illustrated in this exchange:

Chambers: Dr. Self, do you charge fees in the school system?

Self: Yes.

Chambers: What are they for?

Self: For instructional supplies at the elementary level; for the rental of textbooks at the secondary level.

Chambers: How much are the fees for elementary students?

Self: I believe it's a dollar fifty . . . one dollar, Mr. Philips corrected me on that.

Chambers: One dollar for elementary students?

Self: That's correct.

Chambers: How much for the high school students?

Self: These will vary. I'm sorry, I can't recall that figure.

Chambers: Are they five dollars, twenty dollars?

Self: It's seven dollars and fifty cents, if I'm not mistaken.

Chambers: Does anyone know the facts?

Self: Dr. Hanes would know, I believe.

Chambers: Dr. Self, what is the percentage of the collection of these fees of the schools in the inner city?

Self: I would estimate fifty percent.

Chambers: What is the percentage of the collection of these fees of the schools in the outer city?

Self: Near one hundred percent.

Chambers: So your white or predominantly white schools would collect nearly one hundred percent of the fees and your Negro schools or predominantly Negro schools would collect fifty percent?

Self: That's correct.

Chambers: Does that reduce, Dr. Self, the instructional supplies for the Negro schools?

Self: It does.

After this kind of testimony, says Chambers, all the judge had to do was to look at the difference in the results for black and white children. Over the months of hearings, Chambers feels that what most affected the judge "was the testimony about the performance of the black and white students in the schools." Again using school staff as his witnesses, Chambers brought out the students' performance on the standardized tests used in the schools and on the College Board SAT examinations, proving "that blacks were far behind white students.

"We used staff people in the school system [as witnesses] to talk about the causal connection between the lack of facilities and performance by the student."

Chambers: Dr. Self, we have received some test results in answer to interrogatories showing that students in grade three in some schools are reading at a level or achieving at a level of a student in grade one or grade two. That situation exists in the system, does it?

Self: Yes, it does.

Chambers: I believe, Dr. Self, that the State of North Carolina supplies the basic curriculum textbook.

Self: That's true.

Chambers: What happens when a student in grade three, or take other examples, a student in grade six is reading at a level of grade three and gets a sixth-grade textbook, can he read it?

Self: He cannot. You try to put in his hands a book that he can read.

Chambers: Now, how does he get it?

Self: From the supplementary reader collection. . . .

Chambers: Who supplies the supplementary material?

Self: The school purchases its supplementary material.

Chambers: The individual school?

Self: Yes.

Chambers: The individual school would have to take some of the money which it could do something else with and buy supplementary material for the students in these schools?

Self: That's true.

Chambers: And thereby reduces its average per pupil expenditure even more, does it not?

Self: It reduces it, the amount of money available, yes.

Chambers: So not only would the schools in the more affluent areas collect their fees one hundred percent, they would also have students reading at a higher level and could use the textbooks actually furnished free by the state, could they not?

Self: Would you mind repeating that?

Chambers: The schools in the more affluent areas would collect the school fees?

Self: Yes.

Chambers: They would also have, according to your test results, students reading at the grade level and would therefore be able to read the textbooks furnished free by the state.

Self: Yes.

Chambers: Your schools in the inner city collect only fifty percent of the school fees.

Self: And their students read lower than the grade in which they are enrolled.

Self: Yes.

Chambers: And they cannot use the free textbooks furnished by the state.

Self: To a lesser degree, yes.

Chambers: And they have to use what funds they do have to purchase supplementary material.

Self: That's right.

To emphasize that the board of education was directly responsible for this kind of situation—for the segregation of the schools and the inferior quality of the black schools—Chambers called witnesses to talk about "the location of schools, the way school zone lines were drawn and perpetuated, how the board had acted affirmatively to insure that black kids stayed where they were and white kids went to other schools, how teachers were assigned, how the residential patterns were developed, and how the city worked in concert with the board to produce racially segregated neighborhoods for the board to then locate schools to accommodate the residents" of those particular neighborhoods.

Chambers called to testify educators, demographers, and city zoning experts. He questioned housing experts about public and private housing practices that affected school attendance, real estate agents who described the way real estate practices were carried out in Charlotte, and school staff who talked about the way the system located schools and mobile units, "and the results of those practices."

Daniel O. Hennigan, a Presbyterian minister and a real estate broker, spoke about discrimination in the sale or rental of houses, which in turn inhibited school desegregation:

Chambers: Mr. Hennigan, do you know of any instances where Negroes have been denied the right to purchase houses in white or predominantly white areas in the city of Charlotte?

Hennigan: I know of, yes, some instances where this has been true. I was not the collaborating broker, however, in instances where Negroes have actually gone to see houses and have offered to buy, and did not have the opportunity to do so. I have had personal experience where Negroes—and I have been a part of three groups where we have sought to buy land that we could develop housing for our people or for all people—and for various reasons, even though signs have been on these properties, either the selling broker would come back and say either we have a contract or I'm sorry, the price has suddenly gone up, and in other instances the property was suddenly taken off the market and reappeared three and four months later. . . .

Chambers: Mr. Hennigan, let me ask this: Have you followed the *Charlotte News & Observer* in its advertisement of housing in the city of Charlotte?

Hennigan: I have. . . .

Chambers: Prior to 1968, Mr. Hennigan, would you state whether they advertised housing for colored and housing for white?

Hennigan: This has been the pattern of advertising as long as I can remember. . . .

Chambers: Now, Mr. Hennigan, would you tell us further some of the specific instances you know of where Negroes have been unable to purchase houses in white or predominantly white areas?

Hennigan: I was involved, I was the broker in one instance where I had a house for sale in a white community, and of course, I had a purchaser. In this instance it was not a case of a noncooperative owner, the owner was perfectly willing to sell the house to any qualified buyer. However, upon the submission of an application for a mortgage loan, the lending institution refused to get involved on the grounds that it might cause some reprisals on the part of their patronizing clientele if they should make a loan in this particular area.

Chambers says he then showed the judge that it was "reasonably possible to eliminate segregated [school] conditions through redrawing of attendance zones, restructuring of grades in the system, and the use of the existing transportation system where necessary to move kids from one location to another; that it was possible and reasonable to eliminate the segregation in the teaching and the administrative staffs and simply to reassign teachers so as to achieve that objective; that with a system that eliminated race as a factor in assignment and employment, we could effect a better, freer system for all people."

To prove the possibility of full desegregation, Chambers put on the stand educators with expertise in pupil and teacher assignment policies who could talk about establishing attendance zones and locating schools in order to desegregate the students. The Legal Defense Fund helped him find the professional educators who helped him argue this point. "We had worked with a number of educators" through the LDF on school cases around the country, "so we used the contact [there] to get some of the educators to come in and look at the system" in Charlotte and to help develop a desegregation plan, explains Chambers.

Chambers also brought in parents (only black, no white parents would support Chambers's clients) who expressed their support for strong desegregation proposals. He additionally called school staff members, including the superintendent, to talk about what could be done.

"Since you have to desegregate," Chambers asked them in front of Judge McMillan, "what is the best way to do it?"

Chambers never let up in his questioning or his argument for desegregation. "Julius is really diligent and he perseveres," says James Nabrit, the Legal Defense Fund attorney who assisted Chambers with the *Swann* case. This is "a good characteristic for someone trying to present facts. He examines and cross-examines witnesses in a patient, methodical way that builds a record that is a foundation for an opinion." Many of the facts and details to which Judge McMillan refers in his opinions are drawn from Chambers's "painstaking work," says Nabrit.

Some also compliment the effective organization that helped Chambers reach his goal. Unlike most plaintiffs, or crusaders for a cause, Chambers had a national institution, with its own resources, backing him up. "He had what we all referred to as '10 Columbus Circle' behind him," says school board attorney Benjamin Horack, in referring to what was then the Legal Defense

Fund's New York address. "They dang near did us in with paper. But Julius inspired it, coordinated it, and used it effectively," adds Horack, who is now retired. "One of his outstanding qualities is absolutely terrific preparation.

"We used to say he could see discrimination under every possible flat rock," continues Horack when talking about Chambers's thorough research and information-gathering. "Some of the flat rocks he turned over, and found there horrible discrimination salamanders. When I looked, I didn't see them—but he created those salamanders, and then promoted them, and then slayed them."

The school board's lawyers, Horack and William J. Waggoner, "were good lawyers," recalls Chambers without a trace of anger or bitterness in his voice, "but they were not terribly experienced with school desegregation cases. This is true of a lot of lawyers," says Chambers of those who have opposed him. Most of the defense lawyers Chambers faced in court in school desegregation suits had tried only one or two cases that dealt with the school boards they represented, so they knew little about civil rights trials. This inexperience led to errors, such as trying to argue the enormous cost of transporting students. "That was a dead issue because the students were already being transported," says Chambers. The extra busing would not require a substantial amount of money, he notes.

The defense lawyers' basic argument, recalls Chambers, was "that they were taking steps to improve the situation. They recognized the obligation not to discriminate. They did contend that they did not have any affirmative obligation to maximize racial mixing. But they knew that they couldn't maintain an all-black and an all-white school and provide the black schools with inferior facilities. So their basic tactic was that they were making progress because in 1959 they admitted one black student, and in 1965 they closed these black schools in the county, and students could request transfer to whatever school they wanted to attend."

In response, Chambers showed that this kind of progress was

not good enough, that the black children were still receiving an inferior education, detrimental to their well-being and in violation of their rights.

Even if Chambers couldn't accept the school board attorneys' reasoning, he couldn't criticize their courtroom manners. Chambers found the opposing counsel to be polite; they tried to maintain proper decorum during the court proceedings. The same could not be said, however, for the board chairman, a major witness at all the hearings. William Poe "took the firm position that the court was overstepping its bounds" in considering a more aggressive desegregation plan than the board had authorized, and he regularly asserted his views at the school board meetings, to the press, and in court, says the plaintiffs' lawyer. Poe "didn't hesitate at all when given a chance to say something, to tell the court what he thought about the court. And that was true of some other members of the board." As a result, says Chambers, "the board failed to communicate with the court its sincerity in trying to accord equal educational opportunities to minority students." The board's defiant position worked against it.

A minority of the school board members did, however, disagree with their chairman's hardline views and tactics. "That's why the court frequently referred to the board in the plural," explains Chambers. "It recognized that there were differences of opinion" among the members.

After hearing all the evidence from both sides in March 1969, Judge McMillan issued on April twenty-third his first of several orders in the *Swann* case. Judge McMillan "listened to both sides," says Chambers. "He tried to weigh the practical effect of the type of relief we were requesting" and whether the relief the board was suggesting was appropriate. "He wrestled with the 1969 decision of the [U.S. Supreme] Court that said the time for all deliberate speed had run out, and with the practical question of whether the board could really effect desegregation in the middle of the school year. He looked very closely at the extent of transportation that was to be required to effect some desegregation of the students in each of the schools of the system."

Ultimately the judge found that the school board had perpetuated segregation by its practices, and he ordered the board to return by May fifteenth with a desegregation plan that met its constitutional requirements.

The board did so, and the judge held hearings on that plan in June.

Dr. Self, the school superintendent, who reported to the school board, "was a very decent, honest person," says Chambers. At the hearings he "had a real problem in adhering to his principles and at the same time trying to represent the interests of the board as the chairman of the board wanted him to do." Self's subservience to the school board became apparent when the superintendent testified on June 16, 1969, about the desegregation plan the board proposed in response to Judge McMillan's order:

Chambers: In your professional opinion, Dr. Self, would it be feasible for this school system to completely desegregate the staff beginning September 1969?

Self: Yes, but I would qualify it by saying it would be extremely difficult at this point.

Chambers: It would, however, be feasible?

Self: Yes.

Chambers: Dr. Self, in answer to some questions from the Court, you intimated that the staff early stopped consideration of combining any school districts, pairing of any schools, of changing or establishing a feeder system. Did you hear the testimony of one of the board members yesterday—Mr. Poe, I believe it was—that the staff understood from the first board meeting that the board did not want to consider any changing in the student assignment which would require busing?

Self: I heard that testimony.

Chambers: Will you tell the Court, Dr. Self, whether when you began the preparation of your plan you proceeded with this understanding?

Self: Yes.

Chambers: Now, you testified about extensive consideration that the staff gave in the preparation of the plan it presented to the board.

Self: Yes.

Chambers: Despite your extensive study, the board saw fit to modify your plan and in fact water it down considerably.

Self: Acting within their authority, yes.

Chambers: So all the study that you made with respect to teachers was changed by the board.

Self: Again within their authority, yes.

Chambers: Did they spend half as much time as the staff in the staff's preparation of the plan?

Self: I do not know.

On June twenty-ninth, Judge McMillan rejected the plan the board had submitted to him. In late July the board submitted still another desegregation plan; this one closed a few more black schools. Chambers again objected. Following still another hearing, the court temporarily approved the board's most recent plan just so the schools could open in September, but the judge still ordered the board to report back with a more suitable proposal.

The next hearing was in November 1969, when the court

rejected still another board-generated desegregation plan.

Because it became apparent to the judge that the school board could not devise a desegregation proposal acceptable to him, Judge McMillan appointed Dr. John A. Finger, Jr., a consultant from Rhode Island College who had testified as an expert for the plaintiffs, to design a plan for the board.

Chambers had already been criticized for relying on an expert for his case from as far away as Rhode Island, but he maintained that no expert in the Charlotte area was willing to serve. McMillan offered the same reasoning when asked why he chose a plaintiff's witness as his court-appointed consultant—namely that no local expert was willing to design a desegregation plan more stringent than the school board's.

On February 5, 1970, the judge accepted the Finger plan—over any plan submitted by the school board itself—and ordered implementation.

But still Chambers and his clients were not completely satisfied. For example, no traditionally black elementary school ended up with a first grade. Every one of the first grades was placed in the traditionally white schools, so black first-graders had to be bused more than white first-graders. "The average black was involved in transportation for at least nine years or so, and the average white kid for three to six years," recalls Chambers when discussing the court-ordered desegregation plan.

Additionally, Chambers was concerned about "the mixture of black kids with the not-so-wealthy white kids—the type of economic discrimination that was built in the system" so it seemed that classism was replacing racism in the assignment of children to schools.

"I think the court was persuaded by the consultants' feeling that the plan would be more salable if young white kids didn't have to go into black neighborhoods in the early stages; if blacks carried the greater onus of transportation. And the court left closed those black high schools that had been closed earlier by the board. . . . What was finally ordered by the court in 1970 differed in our view in some material respects from what we had been proposing."

The Court of Appeals for the Fourth Circuit upheld Judge McMillan's order in part, but remanded back to the district court that part which required busing of elementary school children. The appellate court thought that the amount of busing required was excessive for young children. The district court then asked the school board to propose an alternative plan, but it did not, so the judge reinstated the consultant plan. And on August 7, 1970, the U.S. Supreme Court upheld all parts of Judge McMillan's order.

Once the Supreme Court issued its decision, says McMillan, "everybody gathered around." Ultimately, in 1975, he dismissed the suit. "Today," says McMillan, "we have the most peaceful school system in the country."

McMillan paid a price for that peace. During and after the trial, he suffered rebukes in his community. "He was ostracized; people wouldn't play golf with him," says Chambers. "He was hanged in effigy. He had to have a guard out at his home. And some of that has continued today," adds Chambers, "although some steps have been taken recently to eliminate much of it." In recent years, for example, Davidson, Johnson C. Smith, and Belmont Abbey Colleges, all in the Charlotte area, have awarded honorary degrees to Judge McMillan. In 1981 he also received the annual silver medallion award from the National Conference of Christians and Jews.

Despite such local mellowing, Chambers is taking nothing for granted in Charlotte. He points out that the final, 1975 Charlotte-Mecklenburg school desegregation plan includes a fall-back provision that should the schools in the future become racially imbalanced, the board would reassign students to eliminate those imbalances. "So periodically the board has made modifications in student assignments in order to eliminate the overconcentration of black kids in certain schools," explains

Chambers. "In several instances white parents have objected to those assignments, and the matter has been back in court—sometimes under *Swann,* sometimes under a different name."

The board has also, because of the increased population in the area, had to build new schools, which necessitated new school zones. The growth has been greater in some areas than in others, which mandates even more new school facilities there. "In order to desegregate those schools, black kids will have to be transported in some instances a longer distance," says Chambers, who worries that that in turn might force the closing of some of the previously black schools because they will become underpopulated.

"Fortunately over the past few years the school system has had an administration and a school board that wanted to maintain a desegregated system. It has acted affirmatively to do that. Whether that continues," concludes Chambers, "is still an open question."

Although the injunction prohibiting discrimination in the operation of the Charlotte-Mecklenburg school system is still outstanding, "I don't know what this board or some later board might try to do," says Chambers, particularly in light of cases such as the recent *Riddick v. School Board of Norfolk* decision in Virginia, which allowed that city to discontinue its desegregation program and return to neighborhood schools. As a result of that decision, forty percent of the black elementary-school students in Norfolk are in schools with a black pupil population of ninety-seven percent or more. The possibility of losing a hard-won goal, of slipping backward in time, "is always there," says Chambers.

Chambers says that he accepted the job as the Legal Defense Fund director-counsel "anticipating a medium-term commitment," but such recent civil rights developments have made him question his original intent. "I have become more concerned about preserving what we have achieved," admits Chambers. "I'm wondering whether I could do more with a longer-term commitment."

Chambers still strongly supports busing as a means for school desegregation and equal opportunity in education. "I think in this environment, it's the most effective remedy," he says. "Residential areas are still very much segregated. There's very little effort [on the part of cities] to promote the integration of housing," and private efforts to integrate communities are hampered by individual families' economic limitations. "As long as that exists," says Chambers, "busing is the only way."

RICHARD "RACEHORSE" HAYNES

Haynes & Fullenweider, Houston

Alexander's/Houston

As a criminal attorney, Richard "Racehorse" Haynes is a Texas legend, no small feat in a state known for its folk heroes, and its love of superlatives. "The reason I use Haynes," a client once told reporters, "is the same reason that I buy a Cadillac. It's simply the best that America has to offer." Nicknamed "Racehorse" by a junior high school football coach, Haynes's practice and clients are typically so colorful they make ample copy for movies, best-selling books, and supermarket tabloids. He represented multimillionaire Fort Worth businessman T. Cullen Davis, acquitted of attempting to murder his estranged wife and of murdering his stepdaughter and wife's boyfriend. Haynes also defended socially prominent Houstonian Dr. John Hill, accused of murdering his wife, but himself murdered before trial. "I've represented a great many men and women in what I call 'the Smith & Wesson divorce,' " says the sixty-one-year-old Haynes, known for his dry sense of humor. "Someone pulls the trigger and then the marriage is over." Once, in a "crucifixion case," Haynes defended a motorcycle gang accused of nailing a woman to a tree. He recently represented a father and son accused of running a slave ranch.

But the Haynes legend embodies more than an array of picturesque cases. It tells the story of a special brand of courtroom lawyering, one that found its genesis in Haynes's blue-collar youth, when he learned not only how to talk to people—how to reach out and persuade them—but also how to hear them, and to understand their thinking and motivation.

Haynes developed his persuasive skills early in life. As a teenager, he and his neighborhood friends liked to head to the downtown movie theaters on Saturday nights. Positioning himself in front of the long lines of people waiting for admission, Haynes would start preaching—and take up a collection. Then he'd give the money away to other people standing at a nearby bus stop.

Haynes knew the people in line—he was one of them—and his humble upbringing as the son of a Houston plasterer serves him well today when building jury rapport. Haynes "has an excellent ability to put forth a case in terms—whether language or demonstrative evidence—that a jury can understand," says his longtime friend Blake Tartt, a commercial civil trial lawyer with Fulbright & Jaworski in Houston and a former president of the State Bar of Texas. "He is able to translate the sometimes difficult and complex matters into terms which the lay person sitting on a jury, and maybe not an extremely well-educated person, can understand, and probably equally important, can relate to." Yet Haynes never talks down to a jury. "Some of that comes from growing up in a place where people talked down to you," explains Tartt.

Nor does Haynes force his opinion. One of his hallmarks is a laid-back demeanor and disarming style. When the five foot nine inch, 160-pound Haynes walks into court, with no armful of books or depositions or files, he doesn't appear to have burned the midnight oil and he can catch a prosecutor off guard. Yet, says Tartt, Haynes is one of the best-prepared lawyers he has ever seen. "It's something lawyers who try civil cases could learn a great deal from," says Tartt. "Instead of coming into court all harried and looking uptight," they should consider better preparation and a more relaxed courtroom manner.

Once Haynes disarms those around him, he begins to win them over with his engaging manner. Anyone who has seen Haynes in court readily agrees that his unusually outgoing personality shines throughout a trial's course. "Haynes was very personable during recesses," even with the prosecution witnesses, recalls one witness who testified against a Haynes client. "He was always chatting and paying attention to what other people had to say."

"He has a very winning personality—jurors like him," adds another Texas lawyer. "He has a good combination of ego and humility."

It's his humility that reminds Haynes he must also listen to what other people are saying in a trial. Listening is a skill at which he excels, and one he thinks young lawyers need to develop. Listening helps Haynes "ferret out the truffles," a phrase referring to the French use of pigs to root in the ground for the gourmet delicacy. He uses the expression in the legal context to describe the discovery of lies by a witness on the stand.

Of course, Haynes learns as much ahead of time about a witness as he can, checking with ex-spouses, fellow employees, acquaintances, and school chums to find out "what kind of person" a witness is. Once in trial, he watches the witness. He listens to what the witness says. And he looks into the witness's eyes. "The eyes are the windows to the soul," says Haynes. By looking into them Haynes tries "mentally to get in sync with the person on the stand or the person who is on the other side of the lawsuit.

You will find that you are almost getting a printout of what that person is thinking," he promises. Particularly during cross-examination, says Haynes, so many lawyers are so preoccupied with their line of questioning that they forget to listen to the witness's answers or to watch the witness responding. The same listening skills apply to jury selection, when with careful listening Haynes can "ferret out" hidden bias against his client.

In 1983, Haynes defended a Britisher, Ian Smalley, accused of international arms smuggling. Despite the heinous nature of the charges, Smalley was a likable defendant. He's a jovial fellow, rotund and bubbly, and you'd think of Santa Claus when you met him, or at least an endearing uncle with an encouraging word and ready pat on the back. In truth, the kindly Englishman is like a Santa Claus bearing presents—but his sack is filled with lethal weapons. Smalley is an unabashed international arms dealer. He readily admits to the line of work that has made him a multimillionaire. But Smalley says he deals only in legitimate arms sales, that he does not court trouble with the law.

In 1981 and 1982, Smalley decided to buy in the United States 100 tanks for Iran and 8,300 antitank missiles for Iraq, even though the purchases were illegal under the U.S. Neutrality Act. Two Texan arms brokers who offered the weapons for sale convinced Smalley that the shipments were covertly authorized by the federal government. The government, the Texan brokers said, was helping Iran ward off threats from its neighbor to the north, the Soviet Union.

Yet in September of 1982, Smalley was arrested and charged with conspiring to smuggle those same tanks and antitank missiles out of the U.S., and into Iran and Iraq. It so happened that the Texas brokers weren't brokers at all. They were government informants working a sting operation. Smalley had been caught in their trap.

Smalley's trial was to be in Dallas, not far from his two-thousand-acre, $1.5 million cattle ranch, where he chose to spend much of his time rather than in his homeland. A devotee of high-style living including travel on the Concorde jet, Smalley put up his ranch as collateral against his bond and maintained from the day of his indictment a cheerful, lighthearted, and very British appearance. On several occasions he even called the U.S. attorney prosecuting his case, James A. Rolfe, a "jolly chap."

But the forty-two-year-old Smalley knew that Rolfe and the U.S. government meant business. If convicted, the Briton faced up to seventy years in prison and $61,000 in fines. So Smalley hired not one but five lawyers, with Haynes leading the pack. Two of those lawyers were Smalley's initial counsel, who referred the litigation to Haynes. Once Haynes accepted leadership in the case they became less involved, except to supply Haynes with support he requested. The other lawyers were two of Haynes's partners who worked directly with him in their law firm.

Not many lawyers get a chance to represent international arms dealers, admits Haynes, who often wears black ostrich-skin boots with his traditional dark pin-striped suits. The press, never hesitant to add its own opinion, labeled the trial the "Dr. Doom case." (Smalley has a doctorate degree in economics and likes to be addressed as "Dr. Smalley.") But despite the case's rarity, Haynes quickly notes that the subject of arms dealing falls in the mainstream of political debate. At the time of Smalley's trial Americans worried about hostages held abroad, and the country nervously watched the Middle East. In the spring and summer of 1987, at the very time Haynes was describing Smalley's trial for this writer, the U.S. Congress and the American public were seeking the truth behind the infamous Iran-contra affair. Representatives of the American government were said to have secretly orchestrated an arms-for-hostages deal with Iran, and with profits from that sale, those same officials allegedly funded Nicaragua's rebel contras. Such actions were contrary to the Reagan administration's public posture of refusing to deal with terrorists and contrary to Congress's ban on aid to the contras. Only months before, Eugene Hasenfus had been pardoned in Nicaragua, after being captured there and found guilty of airlifting arms to the contras.

In Smalley's trial, Haynes convinced the jury to consider his case on its merits, devoid of the emotionalism surrounding any such talk about arms dealing. The jury found that Smalley had been duped and that the story the government witnesses had told the arms dealer was, in large part, a fabricated one. The jurors believed the Englishman when he said he thought the U.S. government wanted the arms deal to go through. To them, Smalley was innocent and, more so, a victim himself.

The Smalley trial highlights Haynes's ability to speak clearly and convincingly to lay persons on a complicated and volatile issue, in this case one that struck at American patriotism and national security. He elevated the jurors beyond their gut emotional reactions to a higher plane of intellectual discussion and decision-making. He led them to think about his client's guilt or innocence based on the facts in the case and on the law as it applied to them.

It was also a trial where Haynes never called a witness himself, but chose rather to make his case strictly with his cross-examination. Through probing questioning of prosecution witnesses, assisted by thorough witness background checks and a computer in the courtroom, Haynes uncovered the truth behind a shaky, misdirected government sting operation.

At the time of the Smalley trial computers in the courtroom were a rarity. But Haynes effectively used this modern-day tool to categorize and organize all the information on the undercover tapes that the prosecution presented in its attempt to prove Smalley's crime. Audiotapes and videotapes have become a popular investigative and prosecutorial tool, but Haynes met the challenge early on by turning this apparently damning evidence to his advantage. With his computer and a high-speed tape recorder, he was quickly able to find, while questioning a witness, relevant portions of the undercover tapes with which to challenge that witness. Haynes played the tapes for the jury to prove his point, that his client had been manipulated and conned into the arms deal.

Law enforcement agents in their zeal to make a case, says Haynes today, too often "take liberties with the law." They don't adhere to proper law enforcement standards and as a result, convict innocent people. In such cases Haynes sees his job—and a job shared by all criminal defense lawyers—as one of defending both his client—and the legal system. And in the Smalley case, Haynes convinced the jury that the system had been poorly served. The system had been abused and so had his client.

Freelance investigators Ronald Ray Tucker and Gary Stephen Howard set up a bogus consulting firm as a front for their government undercover work in arms dealing. They traveled abroad, posing as arms brokers, offering advice and know-how to foreign arms merchants who wanted to buy weapons in the U.S. for South Africa, Iran, Iraq, Libya, and other Middle Eastern governments. Under Tucker and Howard's scenario, U.S. agents would move in and arrest the foreign dealers after they had completed a purchase. In their first sting in Houston in March 1981, Tucker and Howard netted a $600,000 commission, taken out of monies paid the consultants by the dealers for the arms they had hoped to buy. The sting with Smalley was to be Tucker and Howard's second.

Howard first met Smalley in London in 1979. After bringing the Englishman to the attention of the U.S. law enforcement authorities, Howard and Tucker worked for fifteen months with undercover agents from the U.S. Customs Service, the Justice Department, the U.S. Army, and the Texas Department of Public Safety to engage Smalley in an arms deal and to gather enough information to charge him. A U.S. Customs Service agent named Don Winkler posed as a retired Marine Corps colonel in order to participate in meetings with Smalley.

But sometime after the investigation began, Howard and

Tucker started worrying that the U.S. authorities would back off the case, and they secretly told a local television reporter, Charles Duncan of WFAA-TV in Dallas, about the investigation. Apparently the informants thought that a little media attention would help insure Smalley's arrest. With Tucker and Howard's assistance Duncan began following the Smalley investigation and using their undercover tapes and documents, eventually produced a special documentary broadcast about Smalley's arms dealing. Only hours before the broadcast was scheduled to air, in September 1982, the government arrested Smalley.

Initially the Briton was charged only with giving false information when purchasing a hunting gun. But nine days later he was indicted by a grand jury on six counts of firearms violations, plus two counts for conspiring to export munitions to foreign governments illegally. The government later charged Smalley with serving as an unregistered foreign agent and with possessing fraudulent documents.

Court documents filed by the government said that Smalley suggested bribing a government official to help with the Iran-Iraq arms sale. The government also said that Smalley agreed to provide phony papers indicating that the tanks and antitank missiles were for countries other than Iraq and Iran.

The government's evidence consisted of, for the most part, over one hundred hours of secret tape recordings of Smalley's meetings and telephone conversations with the government informants. But the intrigue-laced tapes, recorded in places such as a Washington, D.C., hotel, an Alabama Army depot, and the informants' homes, varied in quality. Some were almost unintelligible.

Smalley pled not guilty. "I drill a little oil, raise a little beef—I'm just a good ol' boy. I'm really not a Bluebeard," he told reporters. The Englishman said that his occupation of arms dealing was both "amoral and apolitical," and that if he didn't deal in arms, someone else would. Smalley's selling point, says Haynes, "is that he is a man of total credibility—he can talk to [Colonel Muammar] Qaddafi [of Libya], he can talk to [the Ayatollah

Ruhollah] Khomeini [of Iran], he can talk to [a variety of] heads of states; and if he says A, they can rely on the fact that it's A, not B." Smalley said that in the U.S. he thought he had been dealing with legitimate government agents who were orchestrating a covertly, but officially, sanctioned sale.

"These guys who made the case for the government are right out of central casting, these 007 guys," says Haynes of the prosecution's chief witnesses.

(Ultimately Tucker and Howard—who later took jobs as deputy sheriffs in Midland County, Texas—sued the federal government. In June 1987 they claimed that the government never reimbursed them for more than $1 million in expenses and lost income from their work on the Smalley investigation. On the other hand, they did spend on their undercover and other businesses some of the $1.2 million Smalley had given them to set up the arms deal.)

Smalley's trial began on January 31, 1983, but because it was in federal district court, not a state court, the judge rather than the lawyers handled the brief jury selection process. Haynes was thus denied a chance to start the trial by exhibiting a major forte: his questioning of jurors during the voir dire.

When Haynes has a chance to handle jury selection, he stresses candor with prospective jurors. "If your case has warts and pimples, tell them." And he adds, lawyers should "be themselves." But most importantly, they should listen to the answers prospective jurors tell them. Hear the nuances in those answers because jurors are trying to tell you about their feelings and biases, says Haynes.

Some have biases or prejudice way deep so they don't even know about it, Haynes continues. So you work with them by asking question after question about their personal feelings and experiences "to get to the point where they intellectually want to tell you" about that bias or prejudice.

"I tell prospective jurors as a preface that they're qualified or they wouldn't be in the courtroom," explains Haynes, "but maybe because of some experience they have a feeling that keeps them from being totally open-minded" in this particular case.

Haynes's ability to work with prospective jurors was especially critical in a 1985 California case involving two prison inmates accused of stabbing to death a third inmate. One of the defendants could not afford a private lawyer and was represented instead by a public defender. But the other defendant was the son of a wealthy banker, and he hired Haynes to represent his son.

During a lengthy, seven-week jury selection, Haynes had to find jurors who would not automatically be biased in favor of police officers and prison guards, and who wouldn't automatically assume they always told the truth. One prospective juror, Joseph M. Paglieroni, gave a suspicious Haynes particular cause for concern. The defense attorney repeatedly questioned Paglieroni about his longtime friendship with a law enforcement officer. Despite this close relationship, Paglieroni insisted over and over again that he could still be a fair juror. "I would listen to all of the evidence and then I would make my decision based on that," said Paglieroni stubbornly.

Finally Haynes was able to bring out what he sensed was the truth about Paglieroni's natural inclinations.

Haynes: . . . Doesn't [a] police officer have a little edge going in, in your own mind?

Paglieroni: Yes. . . .

Haynes: . . . You start off with a feeling that the police officer's going to do—has done the right thing; isn't that the way you feel?

Paglieroni: Yes. . . .

Haynes: Okay. And to that extent you have a slight bias then in favor of the police officer?

Paglieroni: If you say so.

Haynes: Well, if I say so, don't matter. It's what you say.

Paglieroni: I would say yes. I said that before.

Haynes: All right.

Paglieroni: Three times.

Haynes: And to the extent that you have that slight bias, then you're not exactly in dead zero, neutral, are you?

Paglieroni: No.

Haynes: No. Okay. I appreciate your candor on that, Mr. Paglieroni.

Because of his candor, the judge excused Paglieroni as a juror.

It so happened that after only four days of testimony in this trial Haynes proved on cross-examination that the prosecutor did not have evidence to prove that the defendants were the murderers. So, in the midst of the trial, the prosecutor moved to dismiss his own case.

With the jury in place in the Texas trial of the arms merchant, Haynes's overriding task was to diffuse the intense emotion in the courtroom that grew out of talk on international arms dealing. "This was the period of time of the hostage crisis in Iran, and fear of the Libyan government," recalls Richard Anderson, a sole practitioner in Dallas and one of the two original attorneys representing Smalley. Haynes needed to dissipate the anxiety and hostility surrounding the mere idea of selling weapons to countries such as these so he could make the jury concentrate on the government's case.

"In all my conversations with the jurors, with the witnesses, and with the court in the presence of the jurors, I tried to put the case in the proper perspective," says Haynes. Whenever he spoke in the courtroom, Haynes talked strictly about the facts in the case, avoiding any general, emotional discussion of arms sales. His tone was professional, and his presentation intellectual, to ward off any potential "lynch mob" approach to justice. It was as if Haynes were saying to the jurors: "This is America and we resolve these matters by the law, on the basis of the facts, not on the basis of the emotional overlay." Thus in his tone, and in his choice of words, Haynes challenged the jurors to resolve the Smalley case with reason, knowledge, and the law as their guides—rather than their emotional reactions. Slowly, over the course of the trial, this calm, rational approach to the case did have its desired effect. The jurors began to focus on Smalley's situation, rather than on the subject of arms dealing.

But first, the prosecution and Haynes gave their brief opening statements—about fifteen or twenty minutes each. "Opening statements are difficult for the lawyer always," asserts Haynes. "Criminal lawyers are generally trying a case in the dark, and despite the rules that permit discovery, prosecutors can within the rules hide the ball a lot. So [as a trial unfolds] you're really reacting to something that's reasonably new most of the time. You don't want to have any loss of credibility with the jury by saying something" in an opening statement that won't turn out to be true as the trial progresses. "That's the end of the line if you make promises you can't deliver on," warns Haynes.

For his opening, Haynes says he purposely left himself "a little running room. I didn't know how [the witnesses] were going to come down," he explains. "The witnesses that were going to participate had already demonstrated that they had selective memories about facts. With a prosecution based on witnesses whose memories are flexible, you can find that what you thought was going to be the testimony is one hundred eighty [degrees] off. So the opening statement has to be able to deal with that."

Haynes did present his theory to the jury that the informants, posing as arms dealers, had convinced Smalley, himself an avowed international arms dealer, that the White House had wanted him to sell the arms to Iraq and Iran. Haynes said that Smalley thought he was part of a secret U.S. government plan to enhance the U.S. political position in the Middle East. "These people represented that they were spokespersons for the government," Haynes says he told the jury. "As a matter of fact, they were able to get [him] on a military facility and examine one hundred tanks—and [they have] pictures of [the investigators and Smalley] walking around the tanks," adds Haynes to illustrate how convincing the agents were.

But Smalley was tricked, argued Haynes. In many ways the situation was comparable to that of John DeLorean, the infamous automaker accused of cocaine dealing. In both cases undercover government agents, who were working temporarily for the government and who were anxious to prove their worth, set up the sting operations. In both cases they convinced the law enforcement authorities that they had a solid case. And in both cases initial government enthusiasm was based on questionable information. Yet once the government authorities had progressed far enough into the sting, they felt committed to pursue their case, focusing only on the conduct of the accused, rather than reviewing the conduct of the undercover agents.

And both the DeLorean and Smalley trials had sinister and emotion-laden overtones, one involving illicit drug deals, the other, international arms smuggling.

During the course of Smalley's two-week trial, prosecutor Rolfe called surprisingly few witnesses for the government. The first, an officer with the State Department's Office of Munitions Control, said his agency had no records that Smalley had even applied to export the weapons. A U.S. Bureau of Alcohol, Tobacco and Firearms agent subsequently testified that he had posed as a weapons dealer with the informant Howard in a Washington, D.C., meeting with Smalley. There, he said, Smalley talked of arms sales to multiple countries, including Libya. However, when the prosecutor played the tape of that meeting, the jurors found the conversation difficult to understand, and Haynes objected to the juror transcript, saying it was full of inaccuracies.

The third day of the trial, undercover agent Howard took the stand. (Howard's cohort Tucker never testified because, Rolfe says, it would have been repetitious: "He couldn't add anything to what Howard said.") Under questioning by Rolfe, Howard testified that Smalley had talked with him about selling weapons to numerous foreign nations, including South Africa, Libya, Venezuela, and Iran. In all, Howard testified for four days about his meetings and conversations with Smalley and about the arms deal they arranged.

When his turn came to cross-examine Howard, Haynes performed at his best. "We had to flush these people out," says Haynes today. "People like this who do not have the credentials to become members of a law enforcement agency per se—like Customs, DEA, FBI, or the CIA—but then work for them [as contractors] and become the alter ego of the agency, they do things that your basic agent is trained and knows not to do. They don't have the same constraints on them that the badge-carrying federal has.

"We see some of this soldier-of-fortune mentality surface now in the contra affair," continues Haynes, still irate over what he views as the undercover investigators' audacity. In undercover cases, as in drug cases (which Haynes doesn't take on a regular basis), "you are always dealing with confidential informants who are rogues, with criminal histories themselves, who are in deep trouble and who are buying their way out of this trouble by making cases on other people. And they do so without regard for the limits and the parameters the law imposes on law enforcement people. Many times the law enforcement people—because their mindset is that the end justifies the means—just close their eyes to the finagling around," says Haynes.

And in an era of increased street crime, the average juror may also be likely to go along with suspect law enforcement activity, agreeing that the end justifies the means. Public outcry in support of New York subway vigilante Bernhard H. Goetz illustrates a shared fear and citizen belief that crime must be stopped—in any way possible.

"Thirty years ago," says Haynes, "when you asked the traditional question of prospective jurors—how many here have been recent victims of some sort of criminal episode or activity—out of fifty people you might get three or four hands. Today, you ask that question and you get several rows of hands of people who have been recent victims of having their stereos ripped out of their cars or their cars stolen. They've been abused. People in the urban areas have had purses jerked out of their arms and necklaces jerked off their necks." It's no wonder that jurors tend to support any kind of law enforcement official trying to do a job—regardless of how that official carries it out. "It does cause the people who sit on the jury to be less inclined to want to follow the constraints that are imposed on the law to make sure they don't convict somebody" who is innocent, warns Haynes.

Lawyers today must be wary of this juror mindset. "If lawyers think of themselves as I do—as freedom's trustees—they should be more vigorous in predicating their objections and legal positions on the provisions of their own state constitutions, calling them into play, so that their own state reviewing courts on appeal will have to face head-on whether their own state constitutions and provisions mean what they say," suggests Haynes, who stresses reliance on the highest set of law enforcement standards, whether they be federal or state.

Haynes dug into Howard during cross-examination, at times flashing on a screen transparencies of Howard's earlier grand jury and trial testimony so the prosecution witness could not contradict himself. "He talked so much, in so many places, and told so many stories, that he had to admit the truth because he knew I could flash on the wall previous [contradicting] statements," explains Haynes. "We had every statement he had ever made," including those to various government officials and to the press. With these "we could compel him to tell the truth," recalls Haynes.

Under this cross-examination, Howard admitted he at times had misled the government during the Smalley investigation. He also admitted that he had not fully accounted for the $1.2 million Smalley had given him, and said that he had used some of the money for business, to buy land in Florida and a Cadillac. Haynes led Howard to explain in general how government-approved sting operations can be profitable, and how in an earlier sting he and Tucker had made $600,000.

Haynes specifically attacked the way in which the undercover investigators and the U.S. Attorney's Office presented their evidence. For example, one transcript Haynes objected to showed Smalley saying: "I've got to go to the airport and meet the Russians." "That sounds pretty sinister in this context of a meeting to discuss the sale of one hundred tanks to Iran and eighty-four hundred antitank weapons to Iraq," explains Haynes. "We had people look at it—but the transcript kept coming back the same. [So] I listened to the tape on a little Sony Walkman" belonging to one of my kids, Haynes continues. "Sure enough, my guy is not saying 'I'm going to get to the airport *to meet the Russians.*' He is saying 'I have to leave for the airport *to beat the rush hour.*' " Smalley's words were misunderstood because of his heavy British accent, says Haynes. "Once you snap to what he's saying, it's clear as a bell. But before that time, since the printed word was before you, you tended to hear what you saw. I had the benefit of listening to it without the transcript in front of me. And of course once I called it to everybody's attention, everybody else heard it—including the jury.

"All lawyers who try criminal cases today are confronted with the growing use of wire recordings and videotapings of meetings," notes Haynes in discussing how to deal with this prosecution technique. "The government has the equipment and clearly all of the tools you can get to capture evidence that will assist the prosecution and the jury." Many times the same equipment will also help the accused. In Texas, for example, police videotape people stopped in their automobiles under the suspicion of driving while intoxicated. Such videotapes are much more accurate in reflecting a person's physical state and ability to walk a line than just relying on the police officer's personal opinion as to whether a driver is or is not drunk, says Haynes. This benefits the driver. But lawyers also need to understand "how a cooperating individual with an agenda can create a tape that in the sterile atmosphere of the courtroom will seem sinister and will be supportive of the prosecutorial contingents," continues Haynes. He learned this lesson well when he represented Cullen Davis for a second time, when Davis was accused of conspiring to murder the judge in his divorce trial. Davis had been shown, by a confidential police informant, a photograph of the judge. In the photo the judge appeared to have been murdered. Upon seeing it, Davis responded "good," and that response was recorded.

"Probably from a circumstantial-fact point of view, that was as difficult a case and as celebrated a case as I have participated in," says Haynes. "We had a good jury—intelligent. We deliberately selected them that way, the most intelligent we could find" so they could understand an entrapment theory based on the defendant's unawareness that his conversations with a police informant were being taped, explains Haynes, who also says that he relates best to intellectual people. Davis was acquitted.

"Lawyers need to know how to break down a recorded conversation made by a confidential informant with the agenda so it can be fairly and reasonably understood by a jury," instructs the trial attorney. "Who initiates the topic? Who reinitiates the topic? Who interrupts? Who wins the interruptions?" By answering these questions a lawyer can find out and show others who orchestrated, and then manipulated, a recorded conversation, that is, who controlled the conversation to achieve a desired effect.

To begin with, Haynes showed the jury that Tucker and

Howard had not fully recorded their dealings with Smalley. Reviewing for the jury the informants' phone records, Haynes proved that they had taped only a small fraction of the telephone conversations with Smalley. To drive home this point, Haynes showed the jury a large chart indicating in one color the days conversations were held, and in another color the days they were recorded. "It was very telling," says assisting attorney Richard Anderson.

But most importantly, believes Haynes, when dealing with undercover recordings, a defense lawyer needs to know exactly what information is contained on tapes the prosecution has. Jan Fox, a Haynes & Fullenweider partner who assisted with the Smalley case, took charge of computerizing with an Apple II-plus computer and Visidex software all the information on the one-hundred-plus hours of Smalley tapes. "It was a crash program," says Haynes today. "Jan did a ton of work getting the materials together and putting the case on the computer. What gets in that computer is no better than the lawyers" who do the work, adds Haynes while praising his younger partner.

First, Fox "listened to the tapes with the defense in mind, summarizing anything that might play into the defense or prosecution," she explains. She used a high-speed tape recorder to move back and forth on the tapes; it had a calibrator that enabled her to indicate the exact location on a tape of material she found helpful.

Then Fox organized the information on the tapes by "key-wording" them: She assigned a word to represent every theory or topic of interest to the defense and then wrote down exactly where that theory or topic appeared on each tape. For example, every time she heard any conversation that would support a theory of government knowledge—and approval—of the arms shipment, Fox listed that part of the conversation under "GOVT." Using a computer program that worked much like an electronic index-card system, she then compiled a listing of every position on every tape that she had key-worded as GOVT.

The computer could show on a screen any key word Fox

requested with the points on each tape she had listed under that key word. The screen also showed by each point a summary of the conversation on the tape at that location, who the key speakers were, and where that particular tape was on file in Haynes & Fullenweider's office.

"We could also search for summary words," adds Fox. For example, when the government informants took Smalley through the Alabama Army depot, they showed him the tanks that were for sale, indicating that they were all marked with yellow tape. With her computer program Fox was able to type in the search words "government" and "yellow tape" to find out exactly where on the tapes this visit was recorded. Then using her high-speed tape recorder—which could run through a ninety-minute tape in one and one-half minutes—Fox quickly found the conversation she wanted. (The tape recorder actually stopped on the spot she requested on the machine.)

As another example, Fox also used the key word "SNAKE." It stood for any conversation on a tape "that could bite you," or harm the defense. One tape of a meeting in Dallas between Smalley, Howard, and the undercover U.S. Customs Service agent Don Winkler recorded the two other men pressing Smalley about how they would keep the arms sale secret once the arms had arrived by ship in the Middle East. Smalley replied jokingly, "We'll kill the captain and the crew." Fox quickly labeled this a SNAKE.

When the prosecutor asked Winkler, who followed Howard as a witness, whether Smalley was violent, Winkler answered yes and cited as proof Smalley's comment about the crew. Winkler admitted that he had laughed when he heard Smalley say this, but nonetheless, he insisted on the stand that Smalley had been serious.

Jack Zimmerman, a second attorney from Haynes's firm who assisted him with the Smalley case, handled Winkler's cross-examination. Zimmerman again asked Winkler if he was certain Smalley was serious.

Absolutely, responded Winkler once again.

Sitting in the courtroom with her computer and high-speed tape recorder, Fox quickly found the cited conversation on one of the tapes—and with the judge's permission, she played it for the jury. The government had already placed loudspeakers in the courtroom and had provided every juror with headsets for listening to the undercover tapes when the prosecution played them in support of its case.

"Everybody laughed" when they heard Smalley make the remark about killing the crew, says Fox, explaining that it was obvious from the tone of Smalley's voice that he was just kidding. Had only Winkler's testimony and a transcript of the tape been made available to the jurors, they wouldn't have known that Smalley—who came across on the tapes as likable, charming, literate, and funny—was not serious. Winkler also admitted under cross-examination that he had neglected to mention his own laughter when he described this conversation to the grand jury that indicted Smalley—or to the judge who set Smalley's bond. "The key is knowing their material better than they know it," concludes Fox.

The tapes similarly helped out whenever Haynes wanted to show that a prosecution witness wasn't telling the truth. For example, Fox had key-worded as "LIE" all conversations in which the government informant made false representations to Smalley. Under this key word she included the informants' statement that the tanks on the Alabama Army depot marked with yellow tape on their barrels were approved for sale by the government.

"During the trial, apparent government approval of the transaction became an issue," says Fox. "On the witness stand Howard denied that he ever told the accused that the Department of Defense had approved the sale of the tanks." At that point Fox didn't want to call up on her computer every lie the informants ever told Smalley, just the lie relating to the government's approval of the sale. In minutes a search for the key word LIE and the summary words "yellow tape" got her what Haynes needed to discredit the witness. He played that portion of the tape, in the courtroom in front of Howard and the jury, forcing Howard to acknowledge that one of the agents had actually told Smalley that "people in Washington" knew of the sale.

Before long, "all we had to do was to start the computer disk drive whirring—and they would change their testimony on the stand," says Fox.

"The courts have let us" bring computers to trial, says Haynes. "The first time we brought a computer in, the government started worrying and said, 'Golly, Judge, we don't have one' and 'It makes a little noise.' And the jury was intensely interested in it. The judge said, 'Well, get one if you want one.' "

Today, Haynes uses computers in other complex litigation, allowing ready retrieval in court of as many as eight thousand documents for one past case. Fox has developed computer-assisted trial work into an exact science, down to her list of equipment and supplies for the courtroom (a computer, at least one and preferably two disk drives, a monitor, a carrying case if the computer is not self-contained, an extension cord with multiple sockets, a three-prong adapter, a screwdriver to remove socket plates, a computer table, masking tape to hold down the extension cord so it doesn't trip anyone, and a locking file cabinet for the source material). Put the computer "close enough to the counsel table for easy verbal communication and note passing between the operator and trial counsel," advises Fox today. "Ideally it should be on a separate table which forms an L with the counsel table. It should not block the lawyers' view of the jury or the witnesses, and the monitor should be in a position for opposing counsel and the jury to view it during trial."

While Haynes relies on machines and modern technology in the courtroom, he doesn't forget the more intangible human element of lawyering—his own personal approach to understanding and working with witnesses.

To begin with, Haynes strongly believes in learning how to handle witnesses by observing other successful lawyers. As a young attorney, he frequently stole off to court to watch his hero, Percy

Foreman, also of Houston. Haynes similarly favors reading books about great lawyers, and reading in general. "Read the classics, one hour every day, drunk or sober," he advises. "Reading the classics gives a feeling of confidence" when trying a case. "If one reads the classics, one has a better perspective on the vagaries of life. There are really no new plots," says Haynes.

Perhaps it is a vast exposure to "the vagaries of life" that gives Haynes his uncanny ability to detect when a witness is not telling the truth—or is elaborating on the truth. First, Haynes keeps in mind that "words used by the original interrogator can dictate the facts" in an answer. If an individual was asked how fast a car was going at the time of a crash, the response would be higher because of the influence of the words "fast" and "crash" than if the question was phrased differently, perhaps as, "At what *speed* were you going at the time of the *accident?*" the trial attorney suggests.

Then, adds Haynes, when witnesses retell a story, they may modify their version of the facts to make themselves look and sound better. "In the retelling of it they put a little frosting on the corn bread—and they tell it to the point that by the time it's trial time, they believe it. They believe not only the corn bread but the frosting that they put on it themselves in the telling and retelling.

"So the witness himself is unable to separate out what he really saw, and what he really did and really heard, from what he now believes he really saw and really did and really heard.

"The jurors who come on the scene a year or year and a half later to make the resolution on the issues are disadvantaged," says Haynes. "They get the frosting-on-the-corn-bread version." (Haynes admits that his witnesses for the defense also put "frosting on their corn bread by the time it gets to the courthouse.")

Finally, says Haynes, when telling others how to understand witness mentality, "there's something in all of us that causes us to talk to different people differently. So a witness stresses under different circumstances different things from time to time—not necessarily lies, but half-truths. And of course, half-truths are half-lies."

Haynes turns this knowledge about human communication into one of his greatest abilities as a lawyer: determining when a witness is not telling the truth, or as he says, knowing how to "ferret out the truffles." Some people are honest and simply can't accurately remember an event, explains Haynes. But others are dishonest and are so convincing they could pass a polygraph test. Pathological liars believe themselves that they are telling the truth, and those are the witnesses that are the hardest to ferret out. Haynes described this skill in an interview for *Barrister* magazine, published by the Young Lawyers' Division of the American Bar Association. In his description he emphasizes prior research about a witness, followed by careful observation and listening:

"You have to know what you seek and how to seek it. You cannot ferret it out unless you have given some thought to the witness that you are going to be examining. You've got to pay careful attention to the direct examination that is conducted by the other side to see if, in fact, you can detect if a person is taking some liberties with the truth. You've got to really be super observant and listen very carefully to what is said.

"I have seen very competent people have an idea of what questions they want to ask, then mechanically go through asking those questions without really listening carefully to what is being said. If you only listen partially, you do not catch the nuances that suggest to a seasoned practitioner that this witness is not telling the truth, and what the lawyer needs in order to make cross-examination the engine for ferreting out the truth. You've got to be able to smell a truffle, and you've got to be able to know when to let go of the rabbit trail that some lying witnesses put you on because you're taken down the road of irrelevancy."

In one of his cases, illustrates Haynes, "I knew that the witness knew where he bought the gun and from whom he bought it, and he was protecting that person. Obviously the reason for protecting that person was that they were close.

"The reason I knew was that he had been in the penitentiary [where inmates often develop close relationships]. Within a matter of half a dozen or so questions I had caused him to admit to the jury on cross-exam that, yes, indeed, he had lied when he said he didn't know where he had bought it; indeed, that he'd lied when he said he didn't know from whom he bought it because he did not know that person.

"Finally I told him that that person from whom he had bought that weapon was a man who had been his cellmate in the prison. The guy came apart like a six-bit suitcase in the rain."

Even informant Gary Howard—a star prosecution witness in the Smalley trial—admires Haynes's questioning skills. "If it can be deemed fun to sit up there and let him barbecue you, it can be fun just to watch him work," says Howard. "He is a touch of carnival barker and Southern Baptist minister."

Haynes shows a "willingness to engage the other person," says Fox when describing her senior partner's cross-examination technique. "It's very much like a boxing match (Haynes was a Golden Gloves boxer) and it becomes very personal. It's a glove-to-glove, toe-to-toe competition" where Haynes is both fearless and intense. "It's as if," explains Fox, "he's saying 'I'm deadly serious; and I'm deadly sincere.' "

After eight days of trial, U.S. Attorney Rolfe concluded his presentation of witnesses, and the judge announced a one-hour break. When the court reconvened, Haynes made a surprise move. He indicated that he, too, would keep the proceeding brief: He would call no witnesses of his own. Content to stand on the defense he presented with his cross-examinations, Haynes also rested his case.

In many of his cases, as with Smalley, Haynes does not put his client on the stand. It's not required, and it's often risky that a jury will misjudge the defendant. Especially if the other side has not proven its case, it's "silly to put even the most articulate defendant on the stand because it might weaken your case and strengthen theirs," says Haynes. "More people than not are unable to articulate their position" in a courtroom setting because they are nervous and apprehensive and have the most to lose. "If a jury seizes on that testimony as a way to measure credibility," warns Haynes, "you lose." Jurors might have responded particularly negatively to Smalley because of his heavy British accent.

Even without putting Smalley on the stand, Haynes had been prepared to call several dozen witnesses of his own. But he says he decided not to use them when he realized that the government, after it rested, hadn't made its case. "I did not want to make it a swearing match. I wanted to make it stand or fall on the credibility of what the government put on, and I thought that the contradictions that [I had] developed between the various witnesses presented by the government was more than adequate to assist the jury in resolving the issues." The government witnesses had offered differing stories on the Smalley arms deal, confusing rather than helping the jury understand what had transpired. They couldn't be sure.

"Juries are charged with not returning a verdict against the accused *unless* they are personally satisfied beyond a reasonable doubt" that the person is guilty, concludes Haynes. He explains the terms "beyond a reasonable doubt" by asking a listener to imagine that death is the punishment for the crime. "Are you so persuaded by the evidence in this case that if this were a death penalty case, if this were the option facing you, you could vote for the death penalty, the infliction of death?" he queries as illustration of his logic. "If so, then you've satisfied this burden. If no, then your obligation under the law is to find the person not guilty. The prosecution hasn't made its case." And that's exactly how Haynes predicted the jury would respond to the evidence against his client. Putting on additional evidence and witnesses testifying in Smalley's favor might even have harmed rather than helped what Haynes felt was already a strong position. He didn't want to take that unnecessary chance, however small it might have been.

The next day, after Haynes had rested his case, both prosecution and defense attorneys delivered their final plea to the jury—their closing arguments. According to press accounts, Rolfe and assistant prosecutor Shirley Baccus-Lobel attacked what they portrayed as Smalley's opportunism and greed. "If there's a person in this courtroom who believes it's in the best interest of the United States to support the regime of the Ayatollah Khomeini, then we can all hang up our cleats and go home," said Baccus-Lobel.

"How in the world are we ever going to stop wars with people like Ian Smalley running loose to sell weapons to anyone who will buy?" demanded Rolfe.

But Haynes's fiery oratory vastly overshadowed the prosecution's. The defense attorney lambasted the government witnesses, calling them liars with "almost blistered" lips. He said they had duped Smalley, an internationally known and respected businessman, and cheated him out of $1.2 million. The tapes showed that Howard, not Smalley, set up the arms deal, stressed Haynes.

Haynes emphasized in his summation that a jury couldn't convict Smalley without proving his intent to violate the law. He asked the jury to focus on the verbal representations and physical facts presented to Smalley to convince him that the U.S. government sanctioned the arms sale. Haynes talked about the tour of the Alabama Army post, the government-provided name tags and computer printouts of arms, and the other trappings of government authorization provided Smalley. Haynes also asked the jurors to consider the cold transcripts of the tapes in the context of what was being said, not based solely on the actual meanings of the words they contained. The jurors couldn't go straight from the transcript, argued Haynes. They had to listen to the whole conversation in context, including the kidding and horseplay, and the general atmosphere generated by people talking when they're relaxed and off their guard.

As he ended his closing, Haynes walked over to his client. He put his hand on Smalley's shoulder and asked the jury not to be prejudiced against him. "Ian Smalley, you can get justice in the

United States," said Haynes, looking straight at the Englishman, who was quietly crying. "You," said Haynes, "don't have to be afraid."

"I always tell the jurors," explains Haynes today, "that [their decision] is not a mob function. It has to be unanimous and they are obligated by their oath as jurors to fully and fairly exchange ideas and views. But they are *not,* in the final analysis, to do anything in violence to their conscience just to be popular or reach a majority or reach a verdict."

On the second day of their deliberations the jurors asked to hear the entire tape recording of a two-and-a-half-hour meeting between Smalley and the government agents and informants in Washington, D.C., even though only portions of the tape had been played during the trial.

The third day, the jurors told U.S. District Judge Robert M. Hill that they were deadlocked, that they could not agree on a verdict. Haynes moved for a mistrial, but the judge refused. Instead, he told the jurors to keep trying.

Haynes wouldn't have been unhappy to finish with a hung jury. "You have a great deal of success on a second trial," he explains, "because you now have a transcript [from the first trial]. It's the classic discovery. It's easier to ferret out the truffles" knowing the prosecution's strategy behind its case and having time to study in depth their witnesses' testimony. The problem with a second trial, Haynes admits, is the cost to the litigants. "Nobody puts after-tax dollars aside to pay for criminal litigation," notes the trial attorney.

But with the jury again sequestered, Haynes grew increasingly nervous.

Then, on the fourth day, after more than twenty hours of deliberation, and after again listening to almost all the prosecution tapes in the privacy of the jury room, the jurors came back again into the courtroom. The one juror who had been holding out for conviction had changed his mind. The jury acquitted Ian Smalley of all charges.

"We felt to have a conspiracy you had to have criminal intent," jury foreman Thomas Dyer of Dallas told reporters after Smalley's acquittal. "We felt that his mindset was not criminal."

Dyer said the informant Howard's testimony and the misleading government transcripts influenced the jurors to decide in Smalley's favor.

"I think the government owes him an apology," continued Dyer, speaking out on Smalley's behalf as a victim of a misdirected Customs Bureau sting operation. "I was outraged when I heard the evidence."

That was exactly what Richard "Racehorse" Haynes had wanted to hear.

"I believe in justice in my country and now in yours," a jubilant Smalley told reporters who sought him out. Some of the jurors asked Smalley and Haynes to autograph their copies of the transcripts they had used during the trial.

To this day, Rolfe says he does not agree with the verdict because he still thinks Smalley was guilty, that he knew he was working an illegal arms deal. But adds Rolfe, Haynes "won the case fair and square. He did a tremendous job. Dr. Smalley was extremely fortunate to have retained Mr. Haynes."

From the spring of 1982 through the spring of 1983, the U.S. Attorney's Office in Dallas and U.S. Customs officials filed criminal charges against twelve persons for illegally exporting military equipment and technology. In all, Ian Smalley was the only one acquitted.

Thinking back on their case, Haynes and some of the other defense lawyers speculate that in the beginning the government was in fact doing business with Smalley and was looking to make a covert arms deal. "But the political situation changed and somebody got cold feet as far as the prospect of selling one hundred surplus tanks to Iran at a time when our relationship [with that country] was not all that popular," says Haynes. The government backed down from the sale.

"But I think it started off to be a bona fide sale of surplus material—covertly done. And then it got out of hand and the government backed down—but [Tucker and Howard] kept on and turned it into a Customs bust for self-gain." If the sale had been a sting from the very beginning, says Haynes to support his theory, the government could have ended it and could have argued its case much earlier. If it were really a bust, "they could have closed down on him a lot sooner." The government didn't need to string Smalley along for so long, concludes Haynes—unless it actually had hoped the deal would go through.

Or perhaps, suggests cocounsel Jan Fox, the Smalley deal was both an anticipated arms sale and a Customs bust at the same time, and two U.S. agencies were working at cross-purposes, each not fully aware of the other's activities. If that was the case, either outcome—an arms sale or an arms bust—would have been satisfactory for the American government, Fox speculates.

Most importantly, Smalley was acquitted, another victory for Haynes, who still refuses to reveal his total win-loss record. "I don't ever talk about that," insists Haynes, who works eighty hours a week in a building the firm constructed in 1984 just outside downtown Houston. Haynes says that if he publicized his win-loss record, the newspapers would print it before every trial "and make it sound like a sporting event. It's not a sporting event," he says firmly. But he adds when pushed: "I have been very fortunate in the past thirty-one years in terms of being on the right side of lawsuits."

Others would like to have a similar record—or at least to undo Haynes's. Opponents have hired private investigators to put beepers on his car and follow him; others have for espionage purposes bought Haynes's trash from garbage collectors. Today, every Haynes & Fullenweider door is locked, with visitor entrance provided only after identification over an intercom. When leaving his office, Haynes double-locks his own door, even if his secretary is still in. Now every piece of trash he generates is shredded, as is that of all others in the building. "I do not want anything that I'm obligated to maintain confidentiality about to become non-confidential," he explains.

Of course, others also covet Haynes's material success. While he won't discuss his income, when asked whether a report that he earned $3 million during the four years he represented Cullen Davis was correct, Haynes replied: "At least." His standard retainer fee is, he says, "expensive," followed by a $500 hourly rate, plus expenses. "I try, of course, to delegate work to less expensive, younger professionals or paralegals whose rates are less, but even that can run up," says Haynes.

"If a person came in and struck that plaintive note—I would do it [take the case] for nothing," continues the attorney, who tries to give ten percent of his time to pro bono work. It's "sort of a tithe," he explains, "to a discipline that has been good to me."

Edward Bennett Williams

Williams & Connolly, Washington, D.C.

Tadder/Baltimore

Edward Bennett Williams's name has long been synonymous with trial expertise. Having represented clients such as U.S. Senator Joseph R. McCarthy, Teamsters chief Jimmy Hoffa, and Congressman Adam Clayton Powell, Williams has earned a reputation that has firmly positions him well above most other trial attorneys. Williams's magic touch—as both a superior trial lawyer and a great appellate advocate—has not diminished over time. Last year he again made news after successfully defending the *Washington Post* in a highly publicized libel suit brought against that paper by former Mobil Oil Corporation president William P. Tavoulareas. Most recently, Williams and Arthur Liman teamed up to represent high-profile junk bond guru Michael Milken of Drexel Burnham Lambert.

Many attribute Williams's success to his all-consuming drive and the force of his personality, along with prerequisite intelligence and good judgment. But Williams, sixty-eight, cites still another attribute: creativity. "I believe the practice of trial law is perhaps the most creative art extant," more so than making a motion picture, he says.

A trial lawyer stages a production that is designed to create an impression on the jury, and there is no opportunity for retakes, Williams explains. The trial lawyer has no backdrop, no lighting, no effects to create illusions. There is only the bare stage. Furthermore, the trial lawyer's creativity is curtailed, it has boundaries, because a trial deals with truth, not fiction. Trial lawyers have only the facts, and they must always confine themselves within their limits, says Williams. And in criminal trials, the lawyer must be unanimously successful, creating a positive impression on twelve out of twelve jurors. The criminal lawyer "must win everybody to get an acquittal, whereas a playwright, or a movie producer, who gets ten critics out of twelve on his side has done a great job," Williams concludes.

After graduating from Holy Cross College and Georgetown University Law Center, Williams joined the prestigious Washington, D.C., law firm of Hogan & Hartson. But after five years there, he grew weary of trying negligence cases for insurance, streetcar, and cab companies and moved on in search of his own, predominantly criminal trial practice. Today, Williams's 96-lawyer, world-famous firm fills more than the original building where he first founded his practice and spills over into a second building, also near centrally located Farragut Square and also owned by Williams.

With a work load now fifty percent criminal, fifty percent civil, Williams writes and speaks widely on trial techniques. He has taught at Georgetown and Yale law schools, an activity that he says helped train his mind. Frequently when sharing his trial expertise, Williams draws on examples from his own exhaustive experience. But foremost, he emphasizes hard work as both the foundation and the capstone for winning. "There is no substitute for knowing everything," says Williams. "You have to make sure you know all about the narrow, isolated part of the field" your case involves.

Williams also teaches a philosophy for his profession, one that emphasizes the sanctity of our legal system. No matter how guilty the public or prospective jurors might consider some defendants, Williams is willing to defend vigorously their rights under the law. "The requirement that each man be presumed innocent is basic in our whole system of Anglo-Saxon justice," Williams once wrote. "For in that system we regard human liberty as so important that we would rather have twenty guilty men go free than hazard the conviction of one innocent man." Williams also emphasizes in his writing a "fundamental and essential distinction between moral guilt and legal guilt. As we use the term 'guilt' . . . we are concerned with it only as a legal term. It is essential that this fact be understood; that always we are talking of guilt only within the law. The making of moral judgments is beyond us, and should be, for they are within the exclusive jurisdiction of God."

Is Williams, who is Catholic, a religious man? "The last person who asked me a question similar to that was Eunice Kennedy Shriver," responds the attorney. "She's always probing with me about how I can defend what she regards as scoundrels. So she said to me—we were in church—'Would you defend evil?' She's always trying to think of some metaphysical, dramatic way of putting me on the defense.

"I said to her, 'Eunice, I don't defend evil. I defend people who are accused of evil things. That's very, very different.

" 'Some of those people deny that they committed the evil, and they're entitled to have their guilt adjudicated by an impartial tribunal,' " Williams repeats, relating his response to Shriver.

" 'Others do not deny that they committed the evil. It would be wrong to put them on the stand and let them commit perjury, so we do not do that. We do not put on perjured testimony from the defendant or from witnesses supporting the defendant. But under our system—which is probably the best system ever devised by the human mind—we are entitled to force the sovereign power, the government—the prosecution—to prove the guilt of the accused of the evil charged beyond a reasonable doubt.

" 'And if the sovereign power, the government, cannot prove guilt beyond a reasonable doubt, the person under our system of justice, imperfect as it is, is entitled to go free.' And then I sometimes say," continues Williams, " 'and we leave him to the majestic vengeance of God.' "

"So to wrap up my answer to Eunice," concludes Williams, "I say I'm not defending evil, I'm defending people who are accused of evil."

And so, Williams admits, he is a religious man, and he also admits, a philosophical man. "Yes, yes, I think so," he answers. "Yes, I think so. I'm very interested in those subjects."

Despite the personal commitment, the time, and the energy Williams has dedicated to years of trial work, and to writing and teaching about trial technique, he is far more than just a superb courtroom lawyer. Williams is a respected resource of knowledge and good judgment for others fortunate enough to benefit from his views. Powerhouses in business, politics, and the media regularly seek out Williams's personal advice and his negotiating skills both in Washington, D.C.—where the large and powerful-looking attorney presides from behind a massive desk in an equally massive office—and around the country. Outside legal circles, Williams is widely recognized as a former owner of the Washington Redskins football team, and now president and chairman of the board of the Baltimore Orioles baseball team. He was at one time treasurer of the Democratic National Committee and is currently active as counsel to the bipartisan President's Foreign Intelligence Advisory Board. Chairman of the board of Holy

Cross College and president of the Catholic lay organization Knights of Malta, Williams oversees substantial personal real estate holdings in Washington, D.C. He and his longtime wife, Agnes, who was an attorney at Williams's firm before they married, live in Potomac, Maryland, a favored upscale Washington suburb. Of Williams's seven children, three are from his former marriage, which ended when his first wife died at age thirty-four.

More than a decade has passed since the nation witnessed the 1975 trial of former U.S. Treasury Secretary John B. Connally, charged with accepting illegal payoffs from a dairy industry trade association lobbyist for helping to raise federal milk price supports. Connally, the distinguished-looking former Texas governor who rode in the Dallas motorcade with President John F. Kennedy the day of Kennedy's assassination, and who was shot himself, was acquitted of the payoff charges. Later, after failing in his own 1980 bid for the U.S. Presidency, Connally returned to Texas to invest his personal fortune in business ventures. He failed, and last year he declared bankruptcy, a humbled and saddened man. But Williams, who represented Connally in his "milk fund" trial, still rides the crest of his profession. And to this day, Williams still considers the Connally case one of his most successful ever.

It was a classic courtroom trial: a case of one man's word against another's. Jake Jacobsen, a lawyer-lobbyist from Texas who represented the Associated Milk Producers, Inc., said that he gave Connally two $5,000 payments, one on May 14, 1971, and one on September 24, 1971, as a thank-you for helping bring about higher price supports for milk after the Secretary of Agriculture had initially refused to raise them. Connally maintained that no such payoffs, considered illegal gratuities under the law, were ever made. The trial, says Williams, automatically focused on one theme—credibility. There simply was no other way to look at it.

The government's investigation of the Connally case harks back to the infamous White House tape recordings from Richard

Nixon's presidency. The tapes, studied exhaustively by the Watergate Special Prosecutor's Office, included a March 23, 1971, conversation between Connally and Nixon regarding milk supports that the government guarantees to dairy farmers. During their conversation, Connally urged Nixon to back an increase for the farmers. Connally allegedly suggested to Nixon that the political support which an organized group as large as the dairy industry could lend the president would be substantial. Two days later the Secretary of Agriculture raised price supports for milk. Later, when the government studied the White House tapes, it linked Connally's expressed support of the dairy industry that day with the two $5,000 payments Jacobsen allegedly gave Connally.

"The tape was not exactly a model of clarity," says Williams today. "The government had prepared transcripts that were designed to help the jurors understand the tapes, but they were not great tapes." Still, he continues, the prosecutors put that taped conversation in to show that Connally, a longtime supporter of the American farmer, had taken a position on price supports for dairy farmers that was consistent with what Jacobsen asked him to do, and they were saying it was conduct responsive to accepting a[n illegal] gratuity. After Connally denied the accusations before a federal grand jury, he was also charged with perjury and with conspiring to obstruct justice.

Connally, who had rejoined his prestigious Houston law firm of Vinson & Elkins after leaving the government, was at a terrible disadvantage. "He was a white, southern politician who was reputedly very rich, and not the kind of defendant that would endear himself to a [predominantly black] District of Columbia jury," explains Williams. Williams worried that given Connally's financial success and professional stature, the jurors' natural inclination might not be to empathize with him or to feel sorry for him. Many others familiar with the charges were convinced that Connally could simply not get a fair trial from a D.C. jury. Williams asked for a change of venue in the trial because, he argued at the time, publicity about the case had saturated the city to Connally's detriment. But the motion was denied. "Basically, we had a black jury, with one or two white people on it," recalls the attorney.

Generally when selecting a jury, Williams says he tries to get "twelve clean test tubes—with no residue. If I get twelve clean test tubes [jurors], without any prejudice, I'm happy," he explains. But that seldom happens. "So you do the best you can," continues Williams in describing his quest for a fair trial for every client. To counter any juror ill will or enmity as he anticipated in the Connally trial, Williams reminds jurors "throughout the proceedings that they're sworn to decide the case solely on the evidence and the law." He similarly reminds the jury of the burden of proof on the government. Williams says that lawyers should talk with jurors frequently throughout a trial about these courtroom principles, and in fact, "as often as you can." Emphasize, instructs Williams, "that they would want the same."

Connally had to fight not only his worries over potentially nonsympathetic jurors, but also a hostile political environment in the heavily Democratic District of Columbia. "The Watergate atmosphere had polluted the city," recalls Williams. "It was a very, very, very hostile atmosphere to anyone who had been identified with the Nixon Administration, especially to one who was from the South, was politically conservative, and who had left the Democratic Party. He had a lot of strikes against him in that case." Connally, fifty-eight years old at the time of the trial, had been in Nixon's cabinet as the top Treasury official from February 1971 until June 1972. He resigned just prior to the infamous Watergate Democratic headquarters break-in and subsequent cover-up.

"The interesting thing about that trial," recalls University of Texas law professor Michael E. Tigar, who formerly worked at Williams & Connolly and who assisted Williams in the Connally trial, "is that going into it, the press felt it was a foregone conclusion Connally would be convicted." After all, Tigar explains, the case had been brought by the Watergate Special Prosecutor's Office.

But in Connally's case the Special Prosecutor's Office turned out to be wrong. In court, Williams successfully argued that in April 1971 Jacobsen indeed had requested and received $10,000 from Bob Lilly, an executive with Associated Milk Producers, after telling Lilly that Connally had been helpful in the fight for higher price supports. Williams explained to the jury that Jacobsen told Lilly he would give the money to Connally to share with various candidates for congress and their campaign committees. But when Connally refused Jacobsen's first $5,000 offer, Jacobsen kept it—as well as the second $5,000. Later, when Connally left the Nixon administration to serve as chairman of a group called Democrats for Nixon, Jacobsen offered him the full $10,000. Connally again refused, citing adverse publicity about the dairy farmers' association and its extensive political contributions.

To support this version of the story, Williams proved to the jury that Jacobsen had testified on several earlier occasions that Connally had refused the cash. Williams referred to Jacobsen's previous testimony when he appeared before two grand juries, testimony to which Williams was entitled because Jacobsen took the stand against Connally as a chief prosecution witness. Edward Bennett Williams also referred to Jacobsen's testimony when he appeared before the Senate Committee on Presidential Campaign Activities (the Watergate or Ervin Committee, named after Senator Sam Ervin of North Carolina), and when he appeared as a witness in a lawsuit brought by Ralph Nader. During all of that earlier testimony, all under oath, Jacobsen "told a totally different story from what he told at [Connally's] trial," says Williams. On those earlier occasions Jacobsen said that after Connally refused the money, he, Jacobsen, subsequently put it in a safe deposit box "and forgot about it."

Why did Jacobsen contradict his earlier, original testimony when later testifying against Connally? During Connally's trial Williams explained the turnaround. In February 1974 a federal grand jury had indicted Jacobsen for conspiring to defraud a savings and loan association, and two grand juries had indicted him for perjury. The government charged Jacobsen with conspiring to take for his own use funds from the First San Angelo Savings and Loan Association, of which Jacobsen was a controlling shareholder, board member, and chairman of the board.

However—in return for testimony against Connally—the government agreed to drop its charges against Jacobsen and to allow him to plead guilty to one count, that is, giving gratuities to a public official. This deal reduced Jacobsen's possible prison sentence from forty to two years. The prosecutor's bargain also gave Jacobsen reason to believe that he might still be able to keep his license to practice law. Thus it was only when he cut his deal with the government that Jacobsen made a sudden about-face in his story about Connally, maintaining that Connally *had* accepted the two $5,000 offers. Jacobsen also said that his previous lies were part of a cover-up he and Connally had planned. The government then charged Connally with accepting illegal gratuities.

Williams was quick to emphasize for the jurors that what they were witnessing was the result of a plea bargain, and that Jacobsen's arrangement with the government, one designed specifically to save his own future, cast Jacobsen's credibility in doubt. By the end of Connally's three-week trial, with its display of tapes, parade of witnesses, direct examinations, and cross-examinations, the jury decided that Jacobsen—not Connally—was the liar. And the lying version of Jacobsen's story was the new one, the one he told after his plea bargain with the government. Unconvinced that Connally ever took the money, the jury found the defendant innocent of the charges.

Among the strategies and techniques Williams demonstrated in Connally's trial was a decision to narrow the courtroom debate. By focusing on a single issue, the attorney reasoned, he could more easily prove his client's innocence. In this case Williams decided to limit the contest to the charge of accepting illegal gratuities. Even though Connally was charged at the same time with conspiring to obstruct justice and with perjury, Williams convinced the court to sever those counts, providing that they be argued in another, separate trial. Because the arrangement was made before the trial even began, the judge prohibited the prosecutor from telling the jury about the other charges.

Once the trial started, Williams flamboyantly displayed his command of the courtroom, a hallmark of his trial technique. He moved confidently around the room, watching the jurors' reactions to the testimony they heard and to the witnesses they saw. Yet, despite his own considerable presence, Williams was careful not to steal the show: He kept the jury's minds and eyes focused on the witnesses and the defendant, knowing that these key actors would be the ones to convince the jury to vote for acquittal or for conviction. Williams says that in the courtroom he works to keep his own power in check, trying never to appear too harsh or too caustic, and trying never to win too big. "The lawyer is the director," he emphasizes again, "not the leading actor. The leading actor is the defendant." The lawyer is "trying to get an acquittal for the defendant, and how he deports himself, testifies, his demeanor, is important." The jury's attention must stay on that defendant, not on the lawyer, to find in the defendant's favor.

When Williams cross-examined Jacobsen, Williams kept the spotlight on the prosecution's chief witness—but for negative rather than positive reasons. "It was clear that we had to break down Jacobsen as a credible witness," explains Williams, who kept a tight, controlling grip on Jacobsen's testimony as he responded to a barrage of questions. The result was what Williams calls the perfect cross-examination—one in which there are no negative answers. The attorney had so carefully planned his questions, to which he already knew all the answers, that Jacobsen could respond only "yes," "yes," "yes," agreeing with everything the defendant's lawyer asked him. "I don't ask any questions to which I don't know the answers," emphasizes Williams. Thus the information gathered through this lengthy, intricate line of questioning gave Williams all the ammunition he needed for his closing argument. With Jacobsen's own answers, Williams was able to show that the lobbyist was a liar, someone who could not be trusted, someone who desperately wanted to save his own neck by sacrificing another's.

On the other hand, Williams wanted to show that his client was credible. To do so, the defense attorney decided, despite the highly charged political atmosphere at the time, and despite the potentially negative perceptions about Connally, to put his own client on the stand. It's a trial strategy Williams favors. "I don't think you have much of a chance without putting your client on the stand," says Williams. "Of course [Connally] denied so vigorously that he had ever taken any money or anything of value, and he's a pretty powerful, articulate, and convincing person," adds the attorney. "It was clear that he would have to testify himself [to convince the jury], and he did. And he testified very effectively."

Williams knew that Connally, with his confident, forceful demeanor, would make a better impression on the stand than would Jacobsen in this courtroom battle of one man against another. On the stand Connally would be the more credible of the two. "Connally's testimony was consistent. He had testified at the grand jury level and he had testified the same way every time—and Jacobsen hadn't," explains Williams. "In the battle of credibility, we had the decided edge."

Williams also called character witnesses to bolster further his client's credibility. Williams wanted to dispel any negative perceptions the jurors might have about his famous and rich client; he chose carefully the people he would be calling, judging which ones would make the best impression on the jury when they testified that Connally was an honest and honorable person. To make his point, Williams masterfully explained to the jurors why he called the character witnesses, and what their presence meant about Connally's case. And the jury was visibly impressed.

Some say Williams won his case before it began, when he successfully argued to sever the charges against Connally. Originally the government charged Connally with five counts in all: two counts of accepting illegal gratuities (gratuities are differentiated from bribes under the law in that they consist of money proffered as gratitude for a past act, rather than as payment for an anticipated future act), one count of conspiring to obstruct justice, and two counts of perjury before a grand jury. Williams moved that the case against Connally be broken in two: one trial on the charges of accepting the two $5,000 gratuities, and a second trial on the charges of conspiring to obstruct justice and perjury.

"I argued substantially that if the government could indict you for perjury for denying the thing that they were accusing you of, in every case they could call the accused before the grand jury, and when he denied that he committed the offense, they just add perjury counts [one for every denial of the crime]. This would be a totally unfair thing to do. It would be a way of multiplying offenses," concludes Williams, who says that he moves to have a trial severed whenever it includes charges of perjury stemming from his client's denial of the crime with which he is initially charged.

U.S. District Court Chief Judge George L. Hart, Jr., apparently agreed with Williams's logic because he granted the motion.

"The most result-oriented thing Williams did in the Connally case," reflects the chief prosecutor in the case, Frank Tuerkheimer, now a law professor at the University of Wisconsin, "was the pretrial motion to sever the counts. It was a major tactical win with tremendous consequences for the outcome."

Some of Williams's opponents and critics claimed that by granting the severance, the judge showed bias in favor of the defense. Williams instead refers to the development as "a big, big procedural victory. I think the only basis for that kind of suggestion was that Judge Hart had been the Republican state chairman for the District of Columbia for a number of years. I suppose people thought 'Well, Connally's got a Republican judge; this is very helpful to him.' " (Originally a Democrat, Connally had switched over to the Republican party.)

"But there was never any indication that Hart had any bias toward Connally," counters Williams. "Basically he called them pretty much down the middle." In fact, adds Williams, "if anything, he'd be in a normal case a progovernment judge. He was pretty much a hard-liner in criminal matters."

As critical as Williams's pretrial severance motion might have been, that early victory would have been for naught without Williams's traditionally thorough pretrial preparation to back him up once in the courtroom. One reason Williams is at the top of his profession is that he prepares his cases fully—and then continues his preparation throughout the course of a trial. Preceding Connally's trial, Williams prepared with total concentration for weeks. He developed not only his side of the case, but also his opponent's, so his defense arguments would be responsive to any attack or development working in the opposition's favor. Williams made sure he could counter all arguments that might possibly be used against him.

Then, during the three-week trial, Williams worked on the case eighteen hours a day. He was in court daily from nine-thirty to four-thirty, followed by "a quick and very early dinner with the lawyers working with me." After dinner Williams was back in his office at work by seven, where he remained until "the morning hours." "For every hour you're in court," offers Williams as a rule of thumb, "you need an hour of preparation during the trial. In other words, if you're in court seven hours a day, you need seven hours outside court to get ready for the next day. There's no substitute for preparation. There should be no surprises; nothing should ever happen in the courtroom that catches you unprepared or surprised. That's optimum. I'm not saying it always happens, but that's what you should strive for."

Connally himself says that first and foremost he was impressed by Williams's "incredible dedication to preparedness. He basically leaves nothing to chance. He spends the time and energy and intellect necessary to fully understand the case—the facts and the law," says the former governor. With this full understanding Williams is able to make quick decisions in trial and to handle on the spot, as they occur, new challenges and turns of events that might threaten his client's case.

Fully prepared, Williams stepped into the courtroom to argue Connally's case. But with the powerhouse of knowledge and know-how he brought to bear, Williams kept firmly in mind his own particular role in the Connally trial. He reminded himself that he was not the most important person in the room. Williams was the producer and director of the entire scene about to unfold before him, but the principle roles would be played by the defendant and the key witnesses. "Anytime that you forget that, I think you are not doing a service for your client," reiterates the attorney.

Foremost in Williams's mind, as the trial director, was to "elicit [from the jurors] affection for the defendant. If you can get that, you have the maximum," the attorney explains. "If you get respect, trust, and admiration, these are all terrific pluses. And you want to avoid disgust and disbelief and contempt. Because if that happens, you're gone." If a lawyer sees a look of disbelief on a juror's face, says Williams, "you try to engage in damage control. Presumably at a recess you'll have an opportunity to talk with the defendant. If you know what provoked the adverse reaction, you'll have to tell him to avoid that kind of thing. Sometimes it's arrogance, just total arrogance," adds Williams as an example, "or hostility or a pugnacious attitude." A lawyer just has to tell the client to stop exhibiting such behavior, says Williams, because it elicits anger and hostility from the jury.

While he focused on the jury's impending reaction to his client, Williams knew he would assert firmly but subtly his own command over the courtroom, just as a movie director would over a set. "The first thing any lawyer whom Ed trains ever learns is control of the territory," explains Tigar. Williams "moves around to indicate that he feels he's comfortable in any part of the courtroom. And he's a master of every single detail in a case.

When you have that control and show it with how you move your body," says Tigar, "that says to the jury, 'I know what I'm talking about. You can believe me when I suggest something.'

"The first thing a good lawyer wants to do is find some reason to move," continues Tigar when explaining Williams's staging. "It is the exact antithesis of random movement." Williams sometimes stands, as in the Connally trial, at the end of the jury box. The jurors must look first at the witness, and then down at Williams. If a witness talks, he has to look through the jurors to Williams. For those in the jury box it's like being in the front row of a tennis match.

But too much command, too much performance control, can backfire on a lawyer. Like other savvy, successful litigators, Williams knows the dangers of "appearing to win too big. If you're beating on the other poor little advocate, and he looks as though he's being overwhelmed, sometimes the sympathy will go out toward him," says Williams, who emphasizes the importance of being "civil, cordial, and pleasant. I think if you're too severe and too harsh and too caustic, it's costly with the jury," he says. "They don't like that."

"Being a trial lawyer is totally different in degree and kind from any other specialty," observed now-deceased University of Minnesota law school professor Irving Younger, who before he died was one of the country's leading experts on trial advocacy and a former member of Williams & Connolly. "You are before the public and doing all the things actors do, but if the audience for one instance senses this is a theatrical performance, you are lost. The jury needs to say 'That lawyer isn't a great showman—he just has a great case,' " concluded Younger. Williams, he said, is "number one in his generation and, based upon my knowledge of those who went before us, one of the all-time great lawyers."

Williams began his presentation of Connally's case by tackling right off the jury's likely misunderstanding about any ties to Watergate. "This, ladies and gentlemen of the jury," stressed Williams early during his opening statement, "is not a Watergate case. Although the prosecution staff is attached to the Watergate prosecution staff, as His Honor said to you this morning, it is not a Watergate case, and my friends at the other [prosecutor's] table will readily agree with this.

"John Connally was out of government, he had finished as Secretary of the Treasury before the episode known as the Watergate episode took place, and before the so-called cover-up took place. This is not a Watergate case, and I want to lay that to rest right at the outset."

To further dispel potential juror negativism about Connally's situation, and perhaps to help the jury even identify with Connally, Williams talked about his client's humble beginnings and about his dedication to political service, particularly as a Democrat. John Connally "is fifty-eight years old. He was born in Floresville, Texas, on February twenty-seventh, 1917, one of eight children," began Williams. "His father was a bus driver. . . . He, members of the jury, while a student at the University of Texas, entered politics, campaigning in 1937, as far back as 1937, for the late President Johnson when he sought office, and he remained in political life all the rest of his days," proclaimed Williams. Williams further noted that Connally had served under President Kennedy as Secretary of the Navy before becoming Secretary of the Treasury, "the first Democrat in the Nixon Administration."

Then Williams detailed precisely what he would prove regarding the events surrounding the dairy association's $10,000. And finally, Williams accused Jacobsen of lying.

After the opening statements, when the time came for the chief prosecutor, Frank Tuerkheimer, to present his evidence, he began painting a picture far different from Williams's. Tuerkheimer called Jacobsen to the stand for direct examination. First, the prosecutor made it clear to the jury that Connally had been perfectly willing to help the dairy farmers in their quest for higher price supports:

Tuerkheimer: You say you told [Connally that the dairy farmers' political action fund] had made a substantial commitment to the President's reelection—you mentioned an amount?

Jacobsen: Yes, I did—two million dollars.

Tuerkheimer: Did you ask him to do anything?

Jacobsen: Yes, I asked him if he would be helpful in trying to get the agriculture department to set the price support at a reasonable level.

Tuerkheimer: What did he say?

Jacobsen: He said he would try to be helpful.

Tuerkheimer: Did you find you needed to convince him to do this?

Jacobsen: No, he understood the problem very well, being a livestock man himself, and he understood the costs, the squeeze problem. . . .

Under the guidance of Tuerkheimer's questioning, Jacobsen also retold his subsequent conversation with Connally, after the Secretary of Agriculture had reversed his initial decision to hold milk price supports and had raised them instead:

Tuerkheimer: Did there come a time after the March twenty-fifth decision [when the Secretary of Agriculture raised the price support level] when you spoke to Mr. Connally on the subject of dairy problems?

Jacobsen: Yes.

Tuerkheimer: Where was that?

Jacobsen: In his office.

Tuerkheimer: When?

Jacobsen: Oh, about a month after.

Tuerkheimer: A month after what?

Jacobsen: After the decision [of the Secretary of Agriculture to raise price supports].

Tuerkheimer: The second decision [to raise price supports, rather than the first decision to hold them at their current level]?

Jacobsen: Yes.

Tuerkheimer: Was anyone else there?

Jacobsen: No.

Tuerkheimer: What did you say and what did he say?

Jacobsen: I think I was talking to him about the dairy import problem, something to do with the dairy people, and he said, he told me how helpful he had been on the price support matter and said in effect that the dairy people raised a lot of money for a lot of people and why didn't I get them to raise a little money for him?

Tuerkheimer: What did you say?

Jacobsen: I said I would see what I could do.

During the one-hour-and-twenty-minute direct examination, Jacobsen told how on May 14, 1971, he had taken money to Connally at the Treasury Department. "He said thank you very much, and he took the envelope and went into the bathroom which was adjoining his office," testified Jacobsen, "and when he came out I didn't see the money anymore." The scenario was repeated, said Jacobsen, when he visited Connally's Treasury office again on September 24, 1971, with another $5,000.

Jacobsen also testified that originally he and Connally together had planned to cover up the "truth" about the two illegal gratuities by claiming that Jacobsen had never given the money to Connally, but had left it instead untouched in a safe deposit box in Austin, Texas. Jacobsen said that Connally had given him another $10,000 to put back in the safe deposit box in place of the original $10,000 in order to confirm this story: "He left the office and was gone about ten minutes and came back with a cigar box that was filled with money, with either a rubber glove, or rubber gloves, and he took the rubber glove or gloves and threw them in the wastebasket and handed me the box with money in it and said, this money should be all right." But it turned out that some of the bills were signed by Connally's successor in office, Treasury Secretary George Shultz, so they were not old enough to have been those provided by Bob Lilly. Jacobsen said that Connally arranged another meeting, this time in Austin, to give Jacobsen bills that had been in circulation while Connally was in office. Those bills would support a claim that the money had remained with Jacobsen ever since 1971.

When Williams stood up to cross-examine Jacobsen, he knew exactly what he was going to do. In fact, says the assisting attorney Michael Tigar, when preparation for the Connally trial was in its last phase, Williams even "drafted the notes of his summation as a way of making sure we would have a case in which nothing would be left out." Thus Williams knew exactly what questions he would need to ask, and the answers Jacobsen would provide in response, to build support for the defense lawyer's closing argument.

It "was conceived to be a cross-examination to which there would be no negative answers," says Williams, who claims that cross-examination skills can be learned only through practice. "The dream of a perfect cross-examination is to ask the witness questions for several hours to which he always has to answer 'yes,' that he can't ever disagree with you."

To get all the answers he needed, Williams tightly organized his cross-examination. "He moves from subject to subject to subject," explains Tigar. "He is painting a picture. When he is done with a particular subject, he will walk back to the lectern and pick up a piece of paper." Then "he pauses to signal [he's moving on to] something new."

The key, emphasizes Williams, is knowing through preparation and planning where the cross-examination can lead, and how it can support a case. Williams disdains cross-examiners he calls "truth seekers—they just shake the Christmas tree and hope something good falls off. Usually more bad stuff comes off than good. That's because the lawyer doesn't know where he's going, let alone how to get there," says Williams. He believes, rather, in controlling a witness to get the results that he knows ahead of time he must have. "The most effective cross-examination is so tightly reined that the witness never has the chance to go his own way," Williams says. "The bridle is so taut on the witness that all he can do is follow your lead, answering your questions, yes or no," and the lawyer simply continues down the path of questioning carefully planned out before the cross-examination even began. Of course, adds Williams, total concurrence never really happens; but he came pretty close to that goal with Jacobsen.

Williams relishes the orchestration of questions and answers during a trial. He knew in the Connally case that his steady and calm cross-examination could undermine everything that Jacobsen had said about Connally.

"I had a case one time where *two* people testified against one," says Williams while on the subject of the Connally trial and Jacobsen's cross-examination. "It was a classic 'whodunit' case. [During that trial] I pulled out of the Old Testament—a part of the Bible called the Apocrypha—the story of Susanna and the Elders," which Williams calls "the first cross-examination reported in the annals of mankind."

Williams, who also briefly referred to the tale during his closing argument in the Connally trial, relishes telling the story even today: Susanna was the wife of a rich and honored man, Williams begins, "and she used to go out into the garden with her attendants and bathe in the pool. And these two old lecherous elders were peeking from behind the tree and they saw her and they were aroused. So they rushed over to her and said if she didn't have sex with them they would say that she did—that she seduced them—to her husband.

"She was pure of heart and she looked at the Lord and she prayed and she decided to resist to the uttermost, and so she did not submit to them and they then did what they said. They went to her husband and they reported that she had engaged in lascivious conduct.

"They held a trial," continues Williams, "and of course they convicted Susanna. They were about to sentence her to death when along came Daniel. And Daniel said, 'Wait! Wait!' Daniel said he wanted to ask questions of the elders.

"He made the two old men separate," continues Williams, referring to the modern-day courtroom rule on the exclusion of witnesses that prohibits any witness from sitting in court and hearing another witness testify because that might influence what the second person says. "Daniel asked the two old men where Susanna committed this act, this adultery. One said, 'Under the oak tree.' Then Daniel had the other one come, and the other one said, 'Under the mastic tree.' Then the crowd roared, and stoned the elders to death, and freed Susanna.

"And Daniel," says Williams, wrapping up the tale with great personal satisfaction, "had engaged in the most effective cross-examination ever recorded."

When Williams's turn came to question Jacobsen in what was to be one of Williams's most effective cross-examinations ever, the defense lawyer first asked the prosecution witness about his preparation for the trial. Williams showed the jury that inconsistencies in Jacobsen's testimony had been apparent from the very beginning:

Williams: Did you go over your direct testimony with the prosecutors?

Jacobsen: Yes.

Williams: And did they discuss questions on cross-examination?

Jacobsen: Yes.

Williams: Did they ask you questions going to inconsistencies or possible inconsistencies in your testimony?

Jacobsen: Yes.

Williams: And would those sessions last for several hours?

Jacobsen: Yes.

Williams also asked Jacobsen about his financial condition in the early 1970s. He made it clear for the jury that Jacobsen, who at one time had fifteen different bank accounts and who sat on the boards or had substantial interests in numerous banks, had declared personal bankruptcy. Because he needed money, Jacobsen would therefore have had reason, Williams seemed to suggest, to keep the dairy association's $10,000 for himself:

Williams: Now, do you remember when you went before the grand jury in this case on May twenty-third of 1974 that Mr. Tuerkheimer asked you what your net worth was in 1971, and you said three million dollars?

Jacobsen: Yes, sir.

Williams: Then he asked you what your net worth was in 1972, and you said three million dollars at the start or about three million dollars, did you not?

Jacobsen: Yes, sir.

Williams: Now, in June of 1972 you filed a [bankruptcy] statement, did you not, in the United States District Court for the District of Texas, West Texas in Austin, and you said that your net worth was minus eight million dollars, did you not? . . .

Jacobsen: Yes, sir. . . .

But Williams's cross-examination was most effective when he got Jacobsen to admit on the stand all the times he had testified that Connally *never* accepted the $10,000. Williams even read pages and pages of Jacobsen's earlier testimony, identifying the place, the time, and the circumstances for each section of transcript. "These were answers that he had given to questions in his prior testimony, which were totally inconsistent with his answers at the trial," recalls Williams, who during the cross-examination would demand of Jacobsen: "Do you remember making those answers?" "Did you make those answers to those questions?" "And he would have to say in every instance 'yes,' he had given that testimony, 'yes,' he had given that testimony," continues Williams. "So, naturally I didn't argue with him, I just established the fact 'yes,' he said this, and 'yes,' he said that.

"The point was we were building a devastating assault on him for final argument," stresses Williams. Through Williams's persistent cross-examination—reviewing point by point all of Jacobsen's earlier testimony before the grand juries, before the Ervin Committee, and in the Nader lawsuit—Williams elicited prior testimony that was "very, very antithetically different" from what Jacobsen had said on direct examination after he changed his story and accused Connally of accepting the money.

On closing, Williams recited each of the times Jacobsen admitted that he had perjured himself, including exchanges such as these:

Q: Did you appear before the grand jury. . . ?

A: On November second.

Q: Did you testify falsely on that occasion?

A: Yes, I did.

....

Q: Then after your grand jury appearance did you talk to Mr. Weitz [the attorney for the Ervin Committee]?

A: Yes, I did.

Q: Did Mr. Weitz talk to you about the money?

A: Yes.

Q: Did you lie to him?

A: Yes.

Q: Later on in the next week . . . did you testify in depositions in Texas in a lawsuit, *Nader v. Butz*?

A: Yes.

Q: Were you asked about money on that occasion?

A: Yes.

Q: It was under oath?

A: Yes.

Q: Did you tell the truth about it?

A: No, I did not.

"It was very difficult for a jury to say that they were going to convict anybody on the testimony of somebody who had perjured himself so many times," concludes Williams today.

The cross-examination, emphasizes Williams when summarizing the lengthy series of "yes" questions he ran through with Jacobsen, was "very, very dull to the spectator. There's no bombast, no confrontational, dramatic interrogation. It's very quiet and it goes along and he's just saying 'yes,' 'yes,' 'yes,' 'yes,' 'yes.' I remember [journalist] Mary McGrory saying that she went to sleep."

Williams demonstrated in other ways that Jacobsen's testimony against Connally in the trial was both vague and dubious. For example, Williams showed that Jacobsen had altered his description of how he handled the $10,000 once he received it from Lilly:

Williams: And you carried ten thousand dollars in your briefcase to the Secretary's office on the fourteenth [of May 1971]?

Jacobsen: That is correct.

Williams: When did you make the decision that you would only give him five, on the way over there?

Jacobsen: No, when I split the money up into two envelopes.

Williams: When did you split the money up?

Jacobsen: I am not sure, sometime after I took it out of the safety deposit box.

Williams: Did you split it up in Austin or in Washington?

Jacobsen: I am not sure.

Williams: What kind of envelopes did you put it in?

Jacobsen: Brown, manila-colored envelopes.

Williams: Were they envelopes you got in your law office or envelopes you got in the Madison Hotel [where Jacobsen was staying]?

Jacobsen: My office.

Williams: Would it be a fair inference to say you split the money up in Austin then?

Jacobsen: I am not sure.

Williams: Would you carry empty envelopes from your law offices to Washington?

Jacobsen: I may have. . . .

Williams: At some point you put five thousand dollars in one envelope and five thousand in the other?

Jacobsen: Yes, sir.

Williams: That either took place in Austin or in Washington?

Jacobsen: Yes, sir.

Williams: But it took place before you left the Madison Hotel to go the Treasury Department, did it not?

Jacobsen: I believe I left my office across the street from it.

Williams: But in any event it took place before you left your office to go to the Treasury Department?

Jacobsen: Yes.

Williams: But you carried both envelopes over there, is that correct?

Jacobsen: Yes, sir . . .

Williams: Do you remember that you told [one of the prosecutors] that you split the money up, you went over and you purchased a box at the American Security and Trust Company and you put five thousand dollars in the box and then you carried five thousand dollars to the Secretary's office?

Jacobsen: Yes, sir, I remember telling him that.

Williams: You told him that?

Jacobsen: Yes, sir, that was a mistake.

Williams: You made a mistake?

Jacobsen: Yes.

Williams: When did you make that mistake?

Jacobsen: I don't remember.

Williams's questioning about Connally's use of the "rubber glove, or gloves" with the cigar box containing the $10,000 that Connally allegedly gave Jacobsen to place back in his safe deposit box most strikingly illustrates how Williams highlighted the unreliability of any testimony from the government's prime witness. "He said [in testimony before a grand jury before the actual trial that] he had one glove," says Williams. "Well, you can't handle money with one glove. When you're counting out money, you can't do it with one hand." This is, in fact, what Jacobsen said he realized after he first testified before the grand jury that there had only been one glove; this was why he changed his testimony on direct examination during the Connally trial.

Williams: What was the logic of it that changed your mind and caused you to testify on Thursday that it was a "glove" or "gloves"?

Jacobsen: Well, the fact that you couldn't hardly handle money with one glove. . . .

Williams: Well, did this come to you yourself?

Jacobsen: Yes.

Williams: Nobody asked you or suggested this to you?

Jacobsen: No.

Williams: The logic was you couldn't hardly, as you put it, handle money with one glove?

Jacobsen: That's correct.

Williams: And that caused you to testify on Thursday that it was "gloves"?

Jacobsen: It was either a glove or gloves, I am not sure.

To Williams it appeared that Jacobsen was more concerned about being logical and consistent than with simply telling the truth.

Like the gloves, "no detail goes unnoticed or unconsidered," says Tigar of Williams's lawyering. Williams might decide during a trial that he doesn't need a fact—but that doesn't mean it's not at his disposal.

As the time passed and Williams got deeper into his cross-examination, Jacobsen looked increasingly shaken. "If a witness testifies," says Williams when asked about Jacobsen's demeanor on the stand, "there are a number of telltale things. When a witness testifies and he looks at the floor, [that's] not good. When a witness testifies sotto voce—low voice—[that's] not good. Worst of all, if he testifies" with his hand over his mouth—if "he has so little confidence in the veracity of what he's saying that he wants to suppress it"—that's a sure sign of an untruthful witness, stresses Williams. The converse about witness demeanor is true as well. "The important thing," says Williams, "is that the person you're preparing to testify is testifying in a strong, clear, forceful manner. Not equivocal, not hesitant—open, eye-to-eye contact, to register the maximum credibility possible." A witness can deliver the same answer, emphasizes Williams, and just by the way he or she delivers it, register totally different juror reactions. "I try to have my witnesses testify in the most forceful, cogent, clear way they can," he summarizes.

"If I have a witness under cross who is testifying quietly with his hand over his mouth and his eyes dropped, looking uncomfortable," Williams continues, returning to the subject of his cross-examination skills and Jacobsen, "then I'll stay with him and make him more and more uncomfortable, more and more incredible. Pretty soon you hope that people will distrust him.

"You chip away and chip away and chip away at the witness until he's just a pile of little stones, although he started out like the Prudential rock," Williams concludes. "You see, the only place where witnesses collapse and confess is the Perry Mason shows. It is, rather, an art form in which you chip and chip and chip and then collect all the pieces for summation."

"Jacobsen looked frail to start with, but by the time he was done he looked beaten," recalls Tigar. "He was gray—his hair, his eyebrows. He had become monochromatic. He appeared to have sweated a little bit."

On the other hand, when Williams called Connally to the

stand, he stood up well under both direct and cross-examination. The tall, white-haired, and dignified defendant "was a very skilled, well-prepared witness," says Williams. "He testified very helpfully in his own cause. He controlled his emotions. It's difficult for a proud man to do when he is on trial" because he has such a strong sense of injustice, which will whet his anger. "And anger is a luxury that no defendant can afford to show in the courtroom," Williams warns.

To help boost Connally's credibility and his side of the case, Williams brought in a cast of character witnesses to impress even the most inveterate celebrity watcher. "The use of character witnesses could never be more dramatically demonstrated than in the Connally case," says Williams. "I had Billy Graham. I had Dean Rusk, Secretary of State under [President Lyndon] Johnson. I had Bob McNamara, who had been Secretary of Defense under Johnson. I had Barbara Jordan from Texas," says Williams, counting off his battery of support.

Actually Jordan, a black congresswoman, was Connally's archenemy politically, and convincing her to testify for the defense was a major coup. "She is a very honest person," explains Williams, "and I said to her, 'Barbara, I only want you to say one thing. I want you to tell me what your opinion is as to whether or not John Connally would be susceptible to a bribe. I know you don't like his political positions. I know you are diametrically opposed to most of the things for which he stands. I know it's not going to help you politically to testify for him. But supposing you were on trial and somebody had accused you of dishonesty. I hope that those people who may even have differed with you on everything—but who believed in your integrity—would come forward and say so.' She did. She was very courageous. She made a big impact."

Other character witnesses included Democratic kingpin Robert Strauss and Lady Bird Johnson. "I had a bunch of others, but the judge said, 'Enough. I've heard enough. You don't have to go on with this,' " recalls Williams, smiling at the thought. In fact, there were character witnesses in the courtroom at Williams's request, whom he never called to the stand precisely because the judge said "enough." "I always kid [motion picture executive] Jack Valenti," Williams adds. "Jack Valenti said, 'You had me down there and you didn't even call me.' I said, 'But you know, you're bench strength,' " laughingly relates the sports-minded Williams.

At one particular point during his parade of character witnesses appearing for Connally, Williams said he realized just how well his strategy was working. Williams was standing right next to the jury box, with his right side touching it. "I asked Billy Graham to state his name. He stated his name. I asked him what his occupation was. His answer was unforgettable," says Williams. "He said [and here Williams drops into an authoritative, ministerial voice, as if he were Graham speaking], 'I preach the gospel of Jesus Christ across the face of the earth.'

"And," says Williams, "the juror who was right next to me said, 'A-a-men.'

"I thought that was a good omen," concludes the attorney, still chuckling as he tells the story today.

Lady Bird Johnson was also exceptionally effective as a character witness. "She was a very beloved figure then and now, and one of the most beloved first ladies that we've had here in this town in my time. Everybody liked her; she's a very warm, gracious person," Williams says.

In the Connally trial "I had the best assembly of character witnesses I've ever had," emphasizes Williams, reflecting on every case he's tried to present time. "It was powerful. Every time one of them would walk in, the whole courtroom would gasp. It was a very, very impressive collection of people."

But bringing in character witnesses has to be more than just show, adds Williams. "Normally in a criminal trial," he explains, "almost any respected member of the community can get five or six other respected members of the community to come in and vouch for his honesty. So when you put character evidence on, if you want to have it persuasive with the jurors, you have to make some arguments to them." Williams based his argument on the fact that a prosecutor is not allowed to question a defendant about facts unrelated to the charges unless the defense during the trial voluntarily begins a line of inquiry into those unrelated facts.

"The argument I generally make is this," explains Williams. "When you put character evidence on, when the defendant does, [the defendant] lays open his whole life to the prosecutor. The prosecutor can then ask anybody who testifies to the defendant's good character about any past acts that he has performed or any rumors about his past conduct that are inconsistent with the good character that the witness has said he has. If they don't have anything—as they didn't on Connally—it permits me to say: 'Now, you've heard these witnesses come in and testify to Connally's reputation for integrity and honesty. And you may have thought a man of John Connally's prestige and stature could get five or six people to testify to his honesty. But the rule is that when a character witness is offered by the defendant, he lays his whole life open to scrutiny by the prosecution and lays himself open to the introduction of anything that he has done in the past, anything that he is rumored to have done in the past, anything that he is accused of having done in the past. If the prosecution with all the resources at its command—the FBI, and all the investigative agencies of government—has been unable to show you a single adverse fact during [Connally's] sixty years of life, you can infer that he has lived sixty years without a blemish.' This is a powerful, powerful argument against his having committed anything as outrageous as having accepted a bribe," concludes Williams.

The "a-a-men" Williams heard from the jury box was only one positive sign in response to his character witnesses. Williams knew that they had influenced the other jurors as well because Williams routinely watches jurors very closely for facial expressions or other signs of belief or disbelief, of approval or disapproval. "I try to watch the jury for reactions, and I try to read reactions," he says. "Sometimes you can be misled, but most frequently you're correct."

When all the trial testimony was completed, the prosecutor delivered his closing argument. Then Williams—who believes only he and not his assistants should speak in the courtroom—rose to his feet for his summation. Williams began quietly, sincerely, with confidence and conviction ringing through his words:

"May it please the Court and ladies and gentlemen of the jury.

"You have been sitting here for almost three weeks in what has been up to now a silent role as the triers of the facts in this somewhat unique criminal trial.

"Following the argument of counsel and the instructions which His Honor will give to you, you will take this case to your jury room to begin your deliberations, all to the end of arriving at a verdict that is fair and right and just.

"It is my purpose in the time that is alloted to me to review with you the significant parts of the evidence, and to superimpose, as it were, over that evidence the instructions on the law which His Honor will give to you . . . because I believe in that way I can be of maximum help to you in your deliberations."

Then Williams hit hard at Jacobsen. "Can you say that a witness [Jacobsen], branded by the government in those terms [as a fraud and a swindler], who proclaims himself to be a liar under oath, can you say that that evidence meets the burden of satisfying you beyond a reasonable doubt of the guilt of a man who came into this courtroom with an impeccable reputation for honor and integrity after almost three scores of his life?" Williams demanded of the jury. "I don't think you can say that. . . .

"Supposing our coworker," continued Williams, "was caught in criminal conduct and faced with the penitentiary, could be told, oh, you can mitigate this, you can eliminate the consequences of your misdeeds if only you give evidence and lay culpability on another.

"Have we reached that point in our society where scoundrels can escape their punishment if only they inculpate others? If so, we should mark it well, that although today it is John Connally, tomorrow it may be you or me."

Williams next summarized Jacobsen's cascade of financial debts, noting that "during 1971 . . . almost every week he had a note coming due. . . . On the very day that he took ten thousand dollars from Mr. Lilly, allegedly for John Connally, he borrowed one hundred thousand dollars. . . .

"The house was crumbling. His financial empire was gone. The sheriff was practically at the door during 1971. . . .

"I say to you members of the jury, as I said to you on the opening day, he knew perfectly well John Connally wouldn't take ten thousand dollars or ten dollars from him. And so, when he got ten thousand dollars from Mr. Lilly, it was a bonanza at a time when he desperately needed it.

". . . This case is styled United States, United States against John Connally, but I want to tell you something," stressed Williams as he wrapped up his closing argument. "The United States will win this case. The United States will win this case. . . .

"After tramping for thirty years across this country in federal courthouses all over the land, I tell you the United States never loses, because when the liberty and reputation of one of its citizens is preserved against false witness, the United States wins, the United States wins the day.

"I think, members of the jury, the greatest experience, the greatest exhilaration, the greatest fulfillment that a human being in this life can have, is to lift the pain and anguish off another if it can be done in justice.

"I ask you at long last to lift the pain and anguish, the humiliation, the ostracism and the suffering from false accusation and innuendo, vilification, and slander, from John Connally and his family, and if you do, the United States will win the day."

And the jurors complied.

Later, the defeated prosecution moved to dismiss the remaining counts against Connally, the two counts of perjury and one count of conspiring to obstruct justice. Judge Hart agreed.

CONCLUSION

Winning in court depends on good legal counsel. The records of these ten litigators show that when the stakes are high, you get what you pay for when you hire the best. Would the outcomes of those cases have been the same without the champions who won them? Did justice prevail? It's hard to answer, especially if you're a lawyer. Attorneys are often leading advocates of the judicial system itself, the first to proclaim that it is the best in the world. Yet they're obliged to say to clients "hire me. You need me to win."

Is that what justice is about? A contest between lawyers to see who is the better-skilled? The answer probably is that the legal system works for all, but works best when a creative expert pushes it to its limits. The skill comes in knowing where the crevasses in the law are hidden and how to explore them. Justice is a friend of people who know best how to find it; it's attracted to intelligence, experience, perspicacity, ingenuity, and perseverance.

And dedication. Top trial lawyers devote themselves above all else to professional excellence. While they may get to know a client intimately during the course of trial preparation and during a trial itself, lawyer and client usually do not form long-lasting friendships. Nor do lawyers necessarily worry about who is in the wrong or in the right. As Edward Bennett Williams says, "I don't defend evil. I defend people who are accused of evil things." Like doctors, whose professional functioning would be impaired if they invested personally and emotionally in a patient, lawyers retain their distance from their clients. Lawyers see them simply as clients in order to call unencumbered their own abilities and judgment to bear on the case at hand. This distancing is a trait to be endorsed and admired; the willingness to represent any client, a blessing. For those of us who may one day stand accused, or who may one day assert a claim, the ever-open door to a sound defense or reasoned plea is enormous comfort. It is a security that benefits us all.

Of course, under our system some lawyers are forgiven if they do appear to be caught up in the emotion of a client's case, and perhaps in some instances they may well be. When a personal injury lawyer represents a severely injured plaintiff or a civil rights lawyer represents deprived black school children, the passion behind their quest may not come as a surprise. But the passion should never be so great that it blinds or inhibits; the successful advocate never allows this emotion to stand in the way of peak performance.

The Ingredients of Success

Some of the recommended ingredients for success are universal. Perhaps the most obvious is old-fashioned hard work. Trial law is not sorcery. Sound, detailed preparation is the soil on which intelligence, insight, and successful oratory grow.

\\ Conclusion \\

Hard work doesn't stop when the trial starts. Top litigators readily acknowledge that the concentration and intensity of their effort continues in court. They keep their minds running at top speed. The intellectual demands are sometimes overwhelming. For Howard Weitzman it may mean a twenty-four-hour-a-day battle fighting prejudicial publicity. For Williams it means working one hour every night after court adjourns for every hour he spent that day in trial.

These lawyers share other traits. They love the challenge of the courtroom battle, the test of the skills that they constantly hone. And they love to win. Ask any trial lawyers about a courtroom victory and they'll remember—to the person—how they celebrated afterward.

To embrace that challenge, time after time, these lawyers all feel confident in their ability to win, to come out on top. They know how good they are, and they're not shy to put their egos and their reputations on the line. Yet this confidence is tempered by realism; they acknowledge that their success is not guaranteed. Not one of these lawyers feels that trial victory is automatic just because they've taken a case. Overconfidence is an invitation to fail. Too much confidence dulls attention to detail, attentiveness in trial, and the ability to respond quickly to changing circumstances. Because the flip side of winning is losing, love of one is often driven by fear of the other. The ten lawyers in this book are too smart, too experienced, and too successful to think that they are invincible.

It is interesting that this combination of confidence and humility is often what appeals most to juries. The ten lawyers here know that the ultimate verdict is the jury's alone, and that the jury is fully aware of its power. Before them humility, not arrogance, is the most appropriate response. Trial lawyers are most convincing when they themselves believe deeply in their client's case; the strength of their conviction provides added force to their arguments. And juries like best those lawyers who believe in themselves. It's hard to accept as a leader in decision-making someone who is not confident and convinced of his or her own ability to lead. Moreover, through some unspoken law of affiliation, a trial lawyer's virtue often seems to rub off on the lawyer's client. A blustering courtroom lawyer only alienates jurors sitting in judgment. While confidence inspires, self-importance and an overbloated ego simply repulse.

All the lawyers in this book know how to learn from others. Haynes cites Percy Forman as his hero; Corboy, his Chicago mentor, sole practitioner James A. Dooley. These attorneys universally seek out success and model themselves after it. Similarly, all know how to learn from their own mistakes. Whether through postverdict jury interviews or thoughtful self-evaluation, they continually review past strategies and techniques and modify them as they move on. Times change and juries change, says Liman when describing his own transformed philosophy on opening statements. Nor do any of these lawyers hesitate to share knowledge with others who aspire to the same success. For them, trial advocacy is both a science and an art, and in both cases they are disciplines to be taught. Fred Bartlit relishes instructing younger lawyers in his firm about the techniques of courtroom success. David Harney has written a leading text on medical malpractice.

Finally, all ten lawyers here demonstrate an obvious love for, and identification with, humankind. Perhaps it is their one trait that cannot be acquired. From Julius Chambers, who toils against racial discrimination; to James Neal, who reaches out to help the criminally accused; to Linda Fairstein, who refuses to allow sexual abusers to continue victimizing others; all these lawyers like to help. They may be the skilled and knowledgeable courtroom professional, but they also understand how to empathize. In the end, it is this empathetic talent that best enables a trial lawyer to communicate—and as so many say, relate to—a client, a witness, a jury. It's hard for people to talk with others they consider beneath them, or with people they don't like. Perhaps it is the ultimate irony that the top trial lawyers in America excel and rise to the top of their profession precisely because they think of themselves as being of the people.

INDEX

INDEX